The Cultural Roots of Slow Food

ECOCRITICAL THEORY AND PRACTICE

Series Editor: Douglas A. Vakoch, METI

Ecocritical Theory and Practice highlights innovative scholarship at the interface of literary/cultural studies and the environment, seeking to foster an ongoing dialogue between academics and environmental activists.

Recent Titles

The Cultural Roots of Slow Food: Peasants, Partisans, and the Landscape of Italian Resistance, by Ilaria Tabusso-Marcyan

The Nonhuman in American Literary Naturalism, edited by Kenneth K. Brandt and Karin M. Danielsson

Ecodisaster Imaginaries in India: Essays in Critical Perspectives, edited by Scott Slovic, Joyjit Ghosh, and Samit Kumar Maiti

An Ibero-American Perspective on Narratives of Pandemics, edited by Zélia M. Bora, Animesh Roy, and Ricardo Ballesteros de la Fuente

The Animal Other in Narratives of Conquest: Uncanny Encounters, by Stacy Hoult

The *Human-Animal Relationship in Pre-Modern Turkish Literature: A Study of The Book of Dede Korkut and The Masnavi, Book I, II*, by Dilek Bulut Sarikaya

Monstrous Women and Ecofeminism in the Victorian Gothic, 1837–1871, by Nicole C. Dittmer

Thomas Pynchon's Animal Tales: Fables for Ecocriticism, by Keita Hatooka

Ecopoetics of Reenchantment: Liminal Realism and Poetic Echoes of the Earth, by Bénédicte Meillon

Indian Feminist Ecocriticism, edited by Douglas A. Vakoch and Nicole Anae

Interrogating Boundaries of the Nonhuman: Literature, Climate Change, and Environmental Crises, edited by Sune Borkfelt and Matthias Stephan

The Cultural Roots of Slow Food

Peasants, Partisans, and the Landscape of Italian Resistance

Ilaria Tabusso Marcyan

LEXINGTON BOOKS
Lanham • Boulder • New York • London

Published by Lexington Books
An imprint of The Rowman & Littlefield Publishing Group, Inc.
4501 Forbes Boulevard, Suite 200, Lanham, Maryland 20706
www.rowman.com

86-90 Paul Street, London EC2A 4NE

British Library Cataloguing in Publication Information Available

Library of Congress Cataloging-in-Publication Data

ISBN 978-1-7936-3949-3 (cloth : alk. paper)
ISBN 978-1-7936-3950-9 (ebook)

Map of Italy with details of mountain chains and the prominent locations referred in chapters 1, 2, and 3. *Source*: Pankaj Nath Joy and Asif Hasan Zeshan

Contents

Acknowledgments

While my name appears as the single author, this book would have never been possible without the support, encouragement, inspiration, intellectual engagement, and knowledge generously shared from the people, the institutions, and the places I visited to which I express my most sincere gratitude.

A series of seemingly fortuitous events in the last decade contributed to research the stories and bioregions present in this book. I would like to thank the following people for sharing with me their valuable time and knowledge. Carlo Petrini, with whom I had my first conversation at the end of a book fair in Torre Pellice, a small town in Val Pellice, in the Alpine mountains of Piedmont, where I happened to be with my brother Michele during a summer weekend; Marco Revelli, son of Nuto Revelli, whom I met on several occasions, the first being at the inauguration of the mountain refuge of Paraloup, in summer 2013; Antonella Tarpino, who warmly invited me to her office at the Einaudi headquarters for a conversation on our shared passion and love of Italian landscape and mountains; Michele Calandri, director of Istituto Storico della Resistenza of Cuneo, who also opened his office to me engaging me in stimulating conversations that allowed me to tie the cultural connections between the Resistance, Nuto Revelli, Carlo Petrini, and Ermanno Olmi; Gabriella Bonini, scientific director of the Emilio Sereni Archive Library, located in Gattatico, Emilia Romagna, on the farm of the Cervi family; Rossano Pazzagli, director with Gabriella Bonini of the Summer School Emilio Sereni, whose intellectual generosity expanded my understanding of the crucial relationship between peasants and Italian landscape; Morena Vannini and the staff of Museo Cervi, who openheartedly took my husband and me to visit the most significant places related to the history of the Cervi family and who introduced us to the nieces and nephews of the seven Cervi brothers, with whom we had illuminating meetings and conversations. Thanks to Giacomo

Gatti, who collaborated with Ermanno Olmi in directing *Terra Madre*, *Rupi del Vino*, and *Our Host Planet*, for generously sharing a hard-to-find digital copy of the short documentary film *Our Host Planet*.

I am particularly grateful to Pasquale Verdicchio, whose intellectual brilliance, mentorship, and friendship have inspired my interpretation of Antonio Gramsci and his concept of the organic intellectual, a pivotal point of reference in this book. Thanks to my dear and old friend Paolo Grassini, who was one of the first people to do research on Antonio Gramsci in the 1970s and gifted me a first Italian edition of *Prison Notebooks* in which Gramsci's writings appear for the first time in the exact chronological order they were originally written.

Special thanks go to Peggy Shaffer, who believed in the value of my research and helped me to improve the quality of my book with her comments, suggestions, conversations, and finally by editing and beautifying the language of this book.

My gratitude goes to Gian Guido Grassi for his exceptional artistic talent and sensitivity toward nature, and for giving me permission to use his art on the book cover. Thanks to my friends Pankaj Nath Joy and Asif Hasan for their generous time and unique creativity in designing the map of Italy.

My gratitude goes to my new colleagues in the Italian section at Arizona State University who, this last year, supported me in finishing this book by alleviating my teaching responsibilities.

Finally, my profound gratitude goes to my immediate family, friends, and spiritual master. To my husband Sonny with whom I engage in daily conversations about farming, food forests, food products and recipes, and whose encouragement, support, and patience in listening to my stories and ideas about this book have no limits; to my brothers Michele and Gabriele with whom I shared ecological sensitivities and who contributed in shaping my vision of the world and life; to my father, Paolo Tabusso, about whom I learned much later in life was a partisan during the Resistance and that, even if he left his body when I was four, is still influential in many choices I make, including researching the connections between partisans and the mountains; to my mother, Vittoria Vason, whose sense of sacrifice was the true proof of her unlimited love; to my friends who often listen to my ideas and inspire me with what they do; my deepest gratitude goes to my spiritual Master and Mother, Sri Mata Amritanandamayi Ma, who is the source of everything. Without her grace none of this would ever have been possible.

Introduction

One of my favorite meals my mother used to cook in wintertime was fonduta, or fondue. This dish comes from the northern mountain region of Val d'Aosta and the main ingredient is local fontina cheese. As you might imagine it is a rich, fatty, and flavorful dish. I loved to spread this warm creamy cheese on french fries, my second-favorite food (I have a long list of favorite foods) and enjoyed it while the cheese was still warm and stringy. Although we all loved it, my mother was never fully satisfied and used to complain that the variety of the fontina cheese was not right. For my brothers and me it was a bit of heaven for a few minutes, while we enjoyed that amazing dense cheese poured onto crunchy homemade french fries. We didn't really pay much attention to her complaints.

While my mother cooked us fonduta when we lived in Rome, my native city, most of her dishes reflected her family and regional roots of Piedmont, and the nearby regions of Val D'Aosta, Liguria, Lombardy, and Veneto. She did her best to reproduce her native dishes and went to the best deli stores of the neighborhood to find the best ingredients. However, the quality was often not up to her standards. It either lacked flavor, or it was not fresh enough, or simply, as my mother often pointed out, the size, shape or color was different. In Italy every dish reflects the specific cultural traditions of its place of origins and the food products grown in that particular geographical region; it is rooted in the territory, climate and soil of that area. The distance between Rome and Turin is around 670 kilometers, a drive of seven or eight hours. While today it may not seem like a long distance, in the 1960s it was almost like moving to another country, with a different lifestyle, culinary and food habits.

I didn't fully grasp my mother's comments until I ate fontina from a local fromagerie in Brusson, Val d'Ayas, a lateral valley on the orographic left side of the central Dora Baltea Valley in Val d'Aosta. Eating fresh fontina was a revealing experience and an awakening. When eaten fresh, fontina emanates the fragrance of the grass, wildflowers, and plants growing in the fertile soil of the alpine valley where the local dairy breed of Pezzata Rossa graze. While these cows produce less milk, their quality reaches its excellence in the summer when the cows graze along the high alpine pastures. When eaten fresh, and at room temperature from a local fromagerie, the experience is beyond words. Fontina tells its own story, and it tells us that a food product like cheese is the result of an ancient alliance and relationship between nonhumans, humans, and their natural environment. This semisoft, unpasteurized cow's milk cheese showcases the knowledge and experience of traditional farmers' practices and of the unchanged daily routines that follow the rhythms of the seasons of its territory.

I finally understood the value of what lies behind a food product only years later, when I attempted to reproduce my mother's fonduta for a dinner with friends. All I could find was a prepackaged slice of fontina in a supermarket. After my experience of eating local cheese in Val d'Aosta, I couldn't buy that sterile and anonymous slice of fontina wrapped in plastic. I ended up giving up on the idea of cooking fonduta for my friends. My story and memory of fonduta, however, is not simply about recipes or food; it is about food traditions and communities connected to specific places, landscapes, lands, soils, practices, and knowledges. My memories of eating fonduta go back to the 1970s and 1980s, the time when Italy began looking out to the world and opened its doors to more international food products and when, in the 1980s, the first American fast-food chains arrived in the country.

Let's return to cheese for a moment. The world, according to the global grassroots organization Slow Food, is home to over 2,000 kinds of cheese. The divide, as I experienced it, is between artisanal and industrial cheese. The diversity of artisanal cheeses comes from the variations of landscapes and pastures, the use of raw milk, the particular local breeds that produce the milk, and finally from the skill of herders and cheesemakers.[1] The pressure of the industrial food market and food safety regulations have marginalized the production realities, needs and contexts of small-scale producers. Among the projects of Slow Food is the work done to defend fragile food production areas, such as mountains, and give visibility and dignity to important occupations, such as livestock herding, and saving breeds at risk of extinction by promoting farming systems that work in harmony with the environment and animal welfare. Founded in 1989, the mission of Slow Food has been to prevent the disappearance of local food cultures and traditions. Small-scale farmers follow traditional practices that are in harmony with the land. Their products contain the knowledge of those who cultivate them.

Up to the first half of the twentieth century small-scale farmers in Italy were referred to as peasants. Until the years of World War II peasants made up over 50 percent of the Italian population.[2] In examining the period from the Italian Resistance during World War II to the present, this book considers Italian peasant culture, its impact on intellectual activism, and its significance in eventually shaping the Slow Food Movement. Focusing on the work of a variety of intellectual activists and related food justice literature and documentary films, I argue that contemporary forms of environmental activism, as they are rooted in local food and sustainable farming, are built on Italian peasant culture and its contributions to the Resistance movement. The partisan movement, one of the most united and impactful movements of civil resistance in Italy of the last century, can also be said to have succeeded due to the support and participation of local populations and peasants. Thanks to the peasants' knowledge of the territory, and their connections with the local communities, the Resistance was able to thrive and succeed in their mission.

The Resistance was a period of encounter and exchange of experience between two worlds that up to that point had been separate, the urban and intellectual resistance on one side and peasant culture on the other. This unprecedented encounter and experience contributed to the creation after World War II of a new legacy of organic intellectuals. The term is inspired by Antonio Gramsci's original text "The Formation of the Intellectuals." Some examples of the new generation of organic intellectuals I propose in this book are through the analysis of the work of Alcide Cervi, Nuto Revelli, and Ermanno Olmi. Their work, personal experience, and vision of resistance foreground the roots and became a model of the Slow Food grassroots movement. It is important to remember that the Italian Resistance helped finally break with over twenty years of fascism in Italy. The success of this bottom-up, spontaneous, and organic movement revitalized civil society, bringing a renewed sense of awareness, confidence, and action in political and social matters. More importantly, for the purpose of this book, the Resistance connected partisans with the marginalized peasant world and culture. This historical moment explains the Italian roots of the Slow Food movement and illustrates how, from this very Italian historical context, Slow Food has expanded to become a model and a leader in the global environmental movement of food justice.

The interdisciplinary analysis presented here follows the rationale of environmental cultural studies as introduced and presented by Luis I. Prádanos in his recent edited volume *A Companion to Spanish Environmental Cultural Studies*. Compared to literary ecocricitism, environmental cultural studies is more inclusive, embracing scholars working on conservation ecology, environmental history, sustainability, anthropology, ethnography, geography, political ecology, and more. As pointed out by Prádanos, environmental cultural studies enriches the debates in environmental humanities by calling attention to the "cultural processes, practices, and manifestations needed to understand (and respond to) the socio-ecological crisis."[3] "If we recognize that the environmental crisis is a 'crisis of perception,'" continues Prádanos, "then we need to start paying attention to the complex ways in which culture and power determine how we perceive—and relate to—everything that exists."[4] Serenella Iovino, Enrico Cesaretti, and Elena Past stress the essential role of engaging in conversations among diverse disciplines in order to "really know what 'environment' means and what 'ecological crisis' implies."[5] Recognizing that the current ecological and environmental crisis is foremost a cultural crisis in which humans need to acknowledge their role, take responsibility and act accordingly, has been the driving motivation for this book.

In postwar Italy the rise of the new peasantry laid the groundwork for a new environmental politics that sought to reframe the connections between soil, food, and social justice, one in which past peasant traditions are acknowledged for their biocultural, bioregional, and ecological value. In the analysis and reading of the authors and texts presented in the chapters that follow, I reevaluate and reinterpret the concept of the organic intellectual as presented by Antonio Gramsci, to better explain how some peasants and the progressive Italian intellectual figures emerged after World War II became what Gramsci called organic intellectuals. In his famous essays "The Southern Question" and "The Formation of the Intellectuals" Gramsci explains, "Every social group, coming into existence on the original terrain of an essential function in the world of economic production, creates together within itself, organically, one or more strata of intellectuals which give it homogeneity and an awareness of its own function, not only in the economic, but also in the social and political fields."[6] These concepts constitute the fundamental principle of what he calls "the organic intellectual." Gramsci refers to the new professional roles that emerged at the beginning of the twentieth century in Italy, those of entrepreneur or industrial technician. He later specifies that the organic intellectuals "are for the most part 'specializations' of partial aspects of the primitive activity of that new social type which the new class has brought into prominence.[7] The organic intellectuals therefore are leaders generating from the specialization of each profession and have the power to make social changes. Gramsci recognizes not only the continuing transformation and evolution of social classes, but also how they constantly originate their own new intellectual elaboration of their functions within society. However, his analysis focuses on the politics and professional classes of the emerging urban industrial culture.

In contrast to what Gramsci claims in his famous essay, I look to the hinterlands to demonstrate that peasants, by sharing their knowledge of the land and traditional practices, produce their own organic intellectuals. The new and contemporary peasantry are in fact the new organic intellectuals. Gramsci does not acknowledge the peasant classes and their ability to represent themselves. He writes, "Thus it is to be noted that the mass of the peasantry, although it performs an essential function in the world of production, does not elaborate its own 'organic' intellectuals, nor does it 'assimilate' any stratum of 'traditional' intellectuals, although it is from the peasantry that other social groups draw many of their intellectuals and a high proportion of traditional intellectuals are of peasant origin."[8] As other scholars have noted, Gramsci is referring mainly to professionals like lawyers or priests who may have peasant origins but once they become "traditional intellectuals" they no longer recognize their rural roots. On the contrary, according to Gramsci, and in line with Marx's revolutionary interpretation of the working class, the proletarians would be able to create their own intellectuals who represent, belong to, and remain intellectuals of their class. It is, therefore, in the industrial and urban context that organic intellectuals may form and gain social status according to Gramsci.

Gramsci's theory offers valid points. *The Prison Notebooks* and "The Formation of the Intellectuals," written between 1926 and 1937 during his imprisonment, were influenced by the Marxist interpretation of the peasantry, and by the repressive politics of Mussolini during his fascist regime. The Fascists considered the working class as a threat and the peasants as a mass easier to control and manipulate. Gramsci died in 1937, before the outbreak of World War II and the active role peasants played in the Resistance movement. During the Resistance many peasants became partisans, as documented by the famous seven Cervi brothers and the many other testimonies left by many staffette.[9] The collaboration between partisans and peasants, I contend, introduced a more practical function of the intellectual and brought attention to other kinds of knowledge from the land, local territories, and communities. Gramsci's writings analyzed in this book propose concepts key to understanding the renewed attention on the part of the postwar intellectual toward peasants, and provide a new perspective on the impact and legacy of the Italian Resistance and peasant culture in shaping the political culture of the Slow Food movement.

The Resistance represented the breaking point after twenty years of fascist dictatorship in Italy, bringing together individuals coming from disparate social, economic, and cultural strata. Considered as a world apart, isolated, difficult to know, understand and relate to, peasants opened for the first time their homes to the world while supporting the partisans. Many who would emerge in postwar Italy as a new intellectual class, such as Italo Calvino, Cesare Pavese, Elio Vittorini, Primo Levi, Carlo Levi, Beppe Fenoglio, and Mario Rigoni Stern, among others, served in the Resistance and relied on peasant knowledge and assistance to enact their political agenda. By participating in the Resistance, they integrated urban and rural experience, introducing a more socially and politically involved image and role of the intellectual. Many of them enrolled in the Communist Party and became the new generation of leftist authors who, as Italian literary critic Asor Rosa points out, expressed the necessity "to enhance the social function and popular content of the literary and artistic activity."[10]

The experience of the war and the end of fascism motivated the new generation of intellectuals to go beyond the elitist ideal of the man of letters and, instead, to take on a new form of literary and cultural "engagement."[11] The spirit of Resistance was manifested through a moral indignation and rebellion toward the economic and social contradictions present in Italy during the postwar period. As Vittorini explained in *Il Politecnico*, the weekly magazine he founded sponsored by PCI (Italian Communist Party), intellectual engagement had to include the civil aspect and needed to stress the "practical" value of the culture.[12] In other words, the new intellectual needed to address and embrace the people. This intellectual attitude, which I define as an initial exemplification of intellectual activism, emanated from the experience with local people during the Resistance and sowed the seeds for the rise of the new organic intellectuals after World War II.

As Asor Rosa stresses, and according to many intellectuals who participated in the Resistance, "The culture of Resistance lays the foundations of its request of renewal on the general observation that, in Italy, the problem of survival is far from being solved. . . . Poverty, hunger, social and mental oppression are, like fifty, one hundred years before, the enemies to identify and to fight."[13] The authors of the literature of the Resistance and neorealism share an anti-fascist past and a strong desire to create the foundations of a new culture. Their names intertwine, overlap, and often are the same. Writers like Calvino, Vittorini, Pavese, Carlo Levi, and Viganò are considered both neorealist authors and representatives of the literature of the Resistance. Others like Fenoglio, Stern, and Revelli, although their literary production expands into different themes, are mainly related to, and acknowledged for their works on World War II, their partisan experience, and novels on the Resistance. Nevertheless, all these authors were committed to social engagement with a moral and ethical intent; and all of them embraced an urge to reach the people by using a simple and concise language. Between 1947 and 1951, the circulation of several writings by Antonio Gramsci influenced the orientation of the Communist party and the emergence of a new intellectual conscience. Writings like "The Southern Question" and "The Formation of the Intellectuals" became essential points of reference in the left's plans to achieve political power by reaching the working class and the peasants. Gramsci provided a conceptual framework for the new and engaged intellectuals to reach the people.

In his essay "The Southern Question," Gramsci argues that the peasant class could help transform Italian society and empower the proletariat and subaltern classes by forming a coalition with and following the urban workers of the north. Written in 1926 under the fascist regime and published in 1930, "The Southern Question" reflects a traditional Marxist conceptualization of the proletariat, alienated from industrial labor. In this view, peasants were remnants of a feudal past: poor, backward, and powerless. Gramsci writes, "What can a poor peasant achieve by occupying uncultivated or poorly cultivated land? Without machinery, without accommodation at the workplace, without credit to tide him over till harvest, without cooperative institutions to purchase the harvest (if the peasant hasn't hung himself from the strongest bush or the least sickly fig tree on his uncultivated land before harvest time) and save him from the clutches of the usurers, what can a poor peasant achieve by occupation?"[14] Although Fascist propaganda used the image of the working farmer to create and inspire a form of nationalism based on agrarian principles, Mussolini's policies benefited the medium and large landowners and the old aristocratic class. Landowners continued to support, especially in the south, the passive reality of the latifundia, extensive parcels of privately owned land, in which peasants had no ability to introduce better or more efficient methods of cultivation. In terms of economic policy, the increase in the monetary value of the Italian "lira" in the late 1920s resulted in several cuts to public investments in agriculture. In addition, the implementation of the "Battle for Grain," an increase in taxation on the production of grains during fascism, aggravated the already miserable conditions of small landowners and farmworkers, and contributed to the fall in price of the land.[15]

This analysis contributes to Italian cultural scholarship by considering Italian peasant culture beyond its traditional and stereotypical representation as passive and guarded—a social group silenced by their hardships, mistrustful of the state, and disempowered by industrialization. Although I refer to Gramsci's writing and ideas presented in "The Southern Question" to discuss Italian peasant culture, I focus on the peasant realities of northern Italy. This study does not intend to neglect or obliterate the multiple and equally fundamental stories of peasants set in the south of Italy that contributed and still contribute to Italian peasant culture. Rather, I have consciously chosen to map the stories and realities connected to specific territories where the Resistance took place, namely the regions of Emilia Romagna and Piedmont in order to demonstrate how the connections between partisans and peasants in the Resistance sowed the seeds for the modern Slow Food Movement.

While referring mainly to two Italian regions, my study demonstrates, however, that at particular historical moments, Italian peasants made very specific conscious choices and became, both intellectually and in practice, engaged in protecting their land and their people. That legacy has continued and has surfaced today through the new peasantry and new organic intellectuals. The food communities that are connected through Terra Madre, the network of small-scale farmers, breeders, fishers and food artisans launched by Slow Food in 2004, are one of the many examples of new peasantry and new organic intellectuals present today in Italy and around the world. These people, and the communities they form, whether residents of a city tired of a disconnected and isolated life, like urban farmers or members of community gardens, or young educated people who are interested in putting ethical and eco-environmental values into the practice of agriculture, make a conscious choice in which the sacrifice involved is part of the commitment to rebuild a more harmonious relationship with the land. Refusing to engage with a present in which the driving factors are competition and economic profit, the new peasantry and organic intellectuals work toward the revitalization of ancient and traditional agricultural knowledges and practices in harmony with the biological needs of the territory they inhabit. They integrate their work with a renewed awareness that makes it possible to overcome the current ecological and cultural crisis through a radical sociocultural practice, and approach to farming, rejecting the consumeristic logic of the global food system.

Italian peasants during the Resistance embodied a form of bioregional awareness and attitude. Gary Snyder points out, "In the old ways, the flora and fauna and landforms are parts *of the culture*."[16] For the new peasantry, in Italy and elsewhere, the bond with the land is born out of necessity and steeped in history, respect, and gratitude. The land is the center of their life and their epistemologies. While the place where they live is delineated by political borders, their work is defined through its bioregional characteristics such as climate, soil, vegetation, and animal presence. Stories, myths, and legends enrich the local culture and take shape from the interrelation and experiences between humans and the surrounding natural elements such as rivers, lakes, forests, rocks, plants, animals, planes, mountains, or hills. Italian peasant culture is fundamentally based in local realities and influenced by the landscape and natural surroundings. In a few words, as many of the peasant testimonies from Nuto Revelli tell us, the place is experienced and rearticulated through all the elements that help to form that space.

Although the rural environment plays a central role in my interpretation, I am not arguing that peasants had an inherently ecological worldview. As the texts I analyze suggest, the peasant relationship with the land was pragmatic and based on the desire to advantageously transform the soil for material and economic benefit. However, peasants did conceptualize the land as an ally. In this way they understood the land as something to be valued and respected; and they saw their relationship to it in terms of a mutually beneficial alliance. As Alcide Cervi, Nuto Revelli, and Carlo Petrini have often remarked, peasants recognized that the land literally allowed them to live from the fruits of their labor. Peasants understood that their survival depended on the good condition of their land, animals, and plants, and on their care for them.

In the chapters that follow, I argue that traditional intellectuals who participated in the Resistance and collaborated with rural peasants during the war were transformed by their experiences with peasant culture. After the war, they returned to the countryside with a new appreciation for the knowledge and labor of the peasants and a new vision of a leftist political party that linked agricultural laborers and industrial laborers. Writers, historians, and filmmakers, such as A. Cervi, N. Revelli, and E. Olmi became the supporters of the new organic intellectuals and through their documentation of the new peasantry they laid the foundations for what would become the International Slow Food Movement, which embodies a new politics linking social, environmental and food justice.

The authors and texts examined in this book focus on the peasant experience in northern Italy where the Resistance and the partisan movement endured the longest. Although locally based, the stories and representations analyzed in each chapter engage questions common to all Italian peasants, both in the north and the south. The story of the Cervi family presented in chapter 1 reverses the idea of the traditional passive and conservative peasant and presents the story of a peasant family intellectually engaged both in the improvement of agricultural techniques and in the Resistance movement. Although Calvino's intellectual influence is noticeably present, I argue that Alcide Cervi through his memoirs sets the example for what an organic intellectual might be. While Alcide's story of his family offers a critical interpretation of Italian peasant life, his language and metaphors reveal a vision of the world constantly connected to nature and farming tradition. Alcide Cervi's legacy, and his figure as an organic intellectual, is still alive today and lives through the events organized by the Museo Cervi located in the family's original farmhouse, and the Institute and Archive Emilio Sereni, also located on that same land.

My Gramscian reading of the role of the organic intellectual develops further in chapter 2, which focuses on peasant testimonies collected by Nuto Revelli. This chapter analyzes Nuto Revelli's work and peasant testimonies as two examples of organic intellectuals, and introduces the emergence of an environmental consciousness in the 1970s. The testimonies presented in Revelli's volumes are one of the first authentic and original transcriptions of Italian peasant voices. Using Gramsci's words, although peasants do not directly participate in a "critical elaboration" of their reality, they do indirectly contribute to "the foundation of a new and integral conception of the world." Their testimonies not only inform us of their world, but also become important points of reference for the realization of several contemporary projects focused on the repopulation of abandoned areas, of which the mountain village Paraloup, near Cuneo, is an example.

Viganò's novel *L'Agnese va a morire* is the only novel on and of the Resistance that has a woman as protagonist. Agnese is a peasant woman actively engaged in the Resistance. Chapter 3 presents an ecofeminist reading of the protagonist of this novel through a reinterpretation of the concept of backgrounding as discussed by Val Plumwood. "Backgrounding" I demonstrate in my reading of Agnese and the natural environment where the partisans' actions take place, is not invisible and secondary, but on the contrary primary to the success of the missions of the Resistance. Backgrounding is further analyzed by looking at contemporary examples of women engaged in what is traditionally considered a male profession, shepherding.

Chapter 4 analyzes a selection of Ermanno Olmi's documentaries in order to show how they reveal the director's attention to the interrelation between Italian landscape and what Olmi calls "ordinary people." These ordinary people represent a society in transition and, while they are the new postwar labor class working for Edisonvolta, their faces and hands carry all the traits of their peasant origins to which they are still connected. Olmi's late film documentaries such as *Rupi del Vino* and *Terra Madre* align with the new and contemporary organic intellectuals represented by small-scale farmers and the global movement of Slow Food. Lastly *Our Host Planet*, his last short film, is the artist's final ecological testament and a reminder of humans' role and responsibility on this planet.

Finally, the conclusion showcases how, according to Carlo Petrini, Slow Food's global grassroots movement emerges from the cultural horizon left by the Italian Resistance and the partisan movement, and how it is deeply rooted in Italian peasant traditions. Slow Food, the Terra Madre gathering and network, and Carlo Petrini, fully explicate through their activism related to food and agriculture, the social function and practical role played by the new organic intellectual. Slow Food and Terra Madre are only two of the multitude of examples of grassroot movements that are flourishing in Italy and around the planet. These grassroot movements rediscover, revalue and re-center peasant culture and local indigenous practices along with their history as an opportunity to recognize the need to develop an environmental consciousness. Some movements such as the Navdanya organization in India, or the international movement La Via Campesina, have food production and food cultures as their points of departure, and work toward unity among peasants, landless people, women farmers, and indigenous people. Others like the

African Green Belt Movement or the historical Indian Chipko movement, which fights deforestation, seek to promote environmental conservation. They all express different forms of food and social justice and have in common a deep connection to the land, ecological consciousness, and the awareness that humans are not separate from other living beings. We all are, as Olmi elegantly and poetically shows in his last short documentary, *Our Host Planet*, temporary guests on this planet earth.

This book is far from exhaustive or complete. There are multiple impactful realities and stories around Italy and the world that cannot be summarized in a single book. This is simply a first step in situating the global practices and politics of Slow Food in its original cultural, geographical, and historical context. By drawing attention to the partnership between partisans and peasants in the Italian Resistance and recognizing the ensuing role played by the new organic intellectuals in postwar Italy in defining an environmentally rooted leftist politics that sought to link the country and the city, I seek to show how local culture and history can help global society to re-harmonize and reconnect to its surroundings in a socially just, bioculturally focused, environmentally resilient ways. I have found these local traditions and cultures in my community, in my neighborhood, in my region. These usually small pockets of reality happily invited me to dig my hands in the soil, to feel it, smell it, and maybe even taste it. They helped me connect my ancestral nature with the place where I lived. I did it, and it transformed me and my relationship with the bioregion and watershed in which I live, wherever I am.

NOTES

1. https://www.slowfood.com/what-we-do/themes/slow-cheese/ Last accessed on 02/18/2023.
2. Istituto Alcide Cervi, *Le campagne italiane e la Resistenza*, (Bologna: Grafis edizioni, 1995), 11.
3. Luis I. Prádanos, edit., *A Companion to Spanish Cultural Studies*, (Woodbridge: HTamesis, 2023), 3.
4. Ibid.
5. Serenella Iovino, Enrico Cesaretti, and Elena Past, eds., *Italy and the Environmental Humanities*, (Charlottesville: University of Virginia Press, 2018), 3.
6. Antonio Gramsci, "The Intellectuals" in *Selection from the Prison Notebooks*, ed and translated by Quintin Hoare and Geoffrey Nowell Smith, (New York: International Publishers, 1971), 5.
7. Ibid. 6.
8. Ibid.

9. During the Resistance "staffette," or dispatch riders, were women carrying messages and supplies from partisan collaborators or headquarters in the cities to those hiding in the remote hillsides, or vice versa. Many staffette were peasant women.

10. Asor Rosa, *Scrittori e Popolo. Il populismo nella letteratura italiana contemporanea*, (Torino: Einaudi, 1988), 128.

11. Romano Luperini, *Il Novecento: apparati ideologici, ceto intellettuale, sistemi formali nella letteratura italiana contemporanea*, (Torino: Loescher, 1981), 379.

12. Elio Vittorini, "Una nuova cultura," *Il Politecnico*, no. 1, 1945, in *Il Novecento*, 383.

13. Asor Rosa, *Scrittori e Popolo*, 133.

14. Antonio Gramsci, *The Southern Question*, translated by Pasquale Verdicchio, (West Lafayette, IN: Bordighera In. Purdue University, 1995), 18.

15. Oddino Bo, "Considerazioni sulla politica agrarian del post-fascismo," in https://www.israt.it/editoria/asti-contemporanea/8-asti-contemporanea-n-4/11-la-lotta-al-femminile-4.html Last accessed on 12/30/2022. The official website of the Institute for the History of Resistance and Contemporary Society of the Asti province is www.israt.it The Institute for the History of the Resistance is associated with the National Institute for the History of the Movement of National Liberation (istituto nazionale per la storia del movimento di liberazione nazionale) and holds a library of 35,000 volumes, a collection of over seven hundred different newspaper and magazines, an audio library, and a historical archive. It is possible to consult the titles online, and many of them are now also available electronically.

16. Gary Snyder, *The Practice of the Wild*, (San Francisco: North Point Press, 1990), 37. The italics are from the original text.

Chapter One

A Story of Peasant Resistance

*The Cervi Family**

THE HISTORICAL AND SOCIAL CONTEXT

In 1940, Italy entered World War II as part of the Axis powers alongside Germany and Japan. In July 1943, after suffering multiple military losses in several campaigns, and losing its colonies, king Vittorio Emanuele III deposed the fascist prime minister Benito Mussolini. Over this three-year period, during which Italy lost thousands of soldiers, the war had not yet entered Italian territory. Only after signing the armistice with the Allied armed forces on September 8, 1943, did the country experience some of the war's harshest battles. The battles fought in Italian territory during World War II, the Resistance movement, and the struggles for liberation between 1943 and 1945 represent some of the most critical and intense events of twentieth-century Italian history. Within recent historical Italian context, the Resistance Movement, therefore, represents a significant example of civil and political struggle "from below," as described by Marxist theorist Antonio Gramsci. If, in his famous essay "The Southern Question"[1] Gramsci referred to the masses of peasants with this term, then the period of the Resistance can also be considered a powerful and spontaneous movement from below that saw common people, from civilians in the cities to peasants in the countryside, uniting forces and exchanging their services for a common purpose: the liberation of the country from the Germans and from Mussolini's regime. Furthermore, the Resistance also inspired several critical and fundamental democratic principles adopted in the Italian constitution. The increase of political and

---

*This chapter is a revision and expansion of the essay titled "The Cervi Family: A Peasant Story," published in the volume *Ecocritical Approaches to Italian Culture and Literature* by Lexington Books, in 2016.

civil discontent resulting from over twenty years of fascist oppression, Nazi occupation of Italian territory, and the announcement of Italian withdrawal by General Pietro Badoglio on September 8, finally allowed the strong anti-fascist movement to coalesce and operate both visibly and steadily.

The Italian peasantry played a central role in the success of the Resistance Movement. While peasants have historically been acknowledged as supportive of the Resistance, there are still many gaps in the evaluation of peasant-partisan relations. As the historian Anna Bravo highlights in her presentation at the conference on *Contadini e Partigiani,* historiographers initially relegated peasant society mostly to the background of the Resistance and were more interested in emphasizing the political ideology of the movement.[2] Not until the 1970s did historians and researchers start to pay more attention to the active involvement of rural people in the Resistance, realizing that the fragmentation of the territory and the local nature of the peasant culture required more detailed study of the different realities connected to the geographical areas involved. Nonetheless, research has been uneven and has offered notably little interdisciplinary work in developing a cohesive vision of this multifaceted and often stereotyped relationship between peasants and partisans. Up to this time, the partisan experience has prevailed. It is important to acknowledge and stress that the connection between the Resistance and the rural world is based on specific local realities. Each region and each area within those regions, from the valleys to the hills or the mountains, was characterized by local conditions, people, and geography. Within the Resistance Movement, peasant knowledge of the local area provided vital support and a source of networking for continual repositioning of the partisans in the territory.

Peasants have constituted a majority of the Italian population since the Middle Ages. At the end of the nineteenth century, during Italian unification, peasants represented 60 percent of the Italian population. After less than a century, in the first half of the twentieth century and throughout World War II, peasants constituted 52 percent of the population.[3] During this period, although peasants dominated the Italian population, they exerted little to no presence and influence in prevailing social and political decisions. Under the Fascist and the Nazi occupation during the World War II, however, peasant support and presence in the partisan movement proved crucial to the final success of the Resistance. At the end of the war, Italy had to rebuild as a country and nation, redefining its position in the world. In the aftermath, historians, politicians, and intellectuals finally began to acknowledge the critical role of the peasants in the outcome of the Resistance movement.

In an article published in the newspaper *Il Mondo* in 1953, historian Gaetano Salvemini wrote, "the participation of Italian peasants in the partisan fight is the most important fact in the Italian history of our century."[4] The first official acknowledgment of peasant participation in the struggles for liberation dated back three years earlier to 1949. Ferruccio Parri, anti-fascist journalist and later politician, summarized the peasant contribution to the Resistance:

> Their contribution to the war of liberation in general, particularly those in the mountain areas, was noteworthy. The brutality partisans had to endure against the Nazi-fascists forced them to often look for refuge in the countryside, where they were hosted and fraternally assisted by peasant families. They harshly paid for this support through innumerable executions and deportations. Nazi and fascist reprisals were, in fact, more severe and bloody in the countryside and the mountains than in urban areas. [5]

By pointing out the support and solidarity of peasants, and the geographical settings where the Resistance most frequently took place, Parri was one of the first Italian politicians to acknowledge and focus on the formative role peasants played in the Resistance.

Particularly significant within this context is the story of the Cervi family, peasants from the rural area of Gattatico, in the northern region of Emilia Romagna between the cities of Reggio Emilia and Parma. The whole family was actively involved in the anti-fascist movement, and they were among the first farmers in the area to join the partisans in 1943. At the beginning of the war the Cervi house became a hiding place for many prisoners who escaped prison camps. With the fall of fascism in July 1943, the family's fame had reached far beyond the local area of Gattatico, and their barn became a temporary deposit for the weapons to be distributed to the partisans hiding in the hills of the region. The brief yet intense partisan experience of the seven brothers ended in November 1943, when a fascist squad attacked and burned the Cervis' house, capturing the seven brothers and their father, Alcide Cervi. After over a month held in the prison of Reggio Emilia, the seven brothers were executed by the fascists at the shooting range of the city. The only one spared was their father. This tragic story remained in the memory of the region of Emilia Romagna and became an important national symbol of anti-fascist sacrifice.

After the war, the Italian Communist Party (PCI) recognized and indirectly appropriated the anti-fascist wartime activities of the Cervi family in their political agenda. This agenda served as an important model to spread communist values throughout Italy. In those years, the Italian Communist Party (PCI) enjoyed a strong influence and worked toward maintaining and increasing that influence in all social strata. As the former partisan, journalist, and member of the Communist Party Sandro Curzi emphasized, it was during this time that the communist party "rediscovered" and engaged with the writings of the Marxist theoretician Antonio Gramsci with the purpose of reaching the subaltern classes and the population at large.[6]

Gramsci, in his article "Workers and Peasants," published in 1919 in the newspaper *L'Ordine Nuovo*, examined the peasant and worker situation to better understand the economic and social conditions of Italy after World War I, as well as the possibilities for a new proletarian revolution. Some of Gramsci's observations shed light on the actions of Alcide Cervi as a role model for his sons. In the first part of the article, Gramsci analyzes the historical conditions of backwardness and the underdevelopment of peasant society, especially of Southern Italy. Toward the end of the article, he focuses on the potential of including and empowering the peasant masses in the new communist revolution. He writes:

> Thusly organized, the peasants will become an element of order and progress; abandoned to themselves, in the impossibility of taking systematic and disciplined action, they will become a formless commotion, a chaotic disorder of exasperate passions to the point of the most cruel barbarism from the unheard of suffering that are more and more frighteningly looming.[7]

Gramsci acknowledged the fundamental role of peasants in the rise of the new Italian Communist Party. However, while he recognized the importance of peasants' presence and participation in the Italian communist party, he didn't believe in their ability to self-organize. They needed, according to the founder of the Italian communist party, a guide that could give sense and direction to their demands and bring them out of their suffering. Thus, Gramsci added:

> It is absolutely necessary to join the city and the countryside, inspire institutions of poor peasants in the countryside on which the socialist State can be founded and developed, through which it will be possible for the socialist State to promote the introduction of machinery and determine the grand process of transformation of agrarian economy.[8]

The solution, therefore, is in the union of the poor urban labor class with peasants. This coalition will give peasants more power and possibility to be represented and recognized as an essential part of the foundation of the socialist state Gramsci was hoping to establish. While these words do not reflect the contemporary rural reality, through this logic the 1955 publication of Alcide Cervi's biography, *I miei sette figli* (My Seven Sons), edited by the journalist and member of the PCI Renato Nicolai, became part and parcel of an ideologically driven communist propaganda campaign. The PCI saw in this biography the possibility to reach people by using the story of one of their own in which they might recognize themselves.

Although the ideological and political aspect cannot be discounted, it is important to reexamine the story of the Cervi family and their work as farmers to understand their story as a story of the Resistance itself. Before the tragic execution of the seven brothers, the charismatic personality and intellectual curiosity of Aldo, the third born of the seven brothers, for example, contributed to bringing more awareness to the social and political role of peasants.

During his brief imprisonment Aldo learned more about agricultural innovations and anti-fascist movements in Italy and Europe and, once released, he shared his new gained knowledge with his family. During the Resistance the Cervi family organized the partisan movement in their area, becoming an important local point of reference not only because of their anti-fascist efforts, but also for their knowledge of the area, demonstrating the critical role of local peasant support in this historical moment.

Emilia Romagna, a region once characterized by uneven and irregular rural terrain, changed its original landscape configuration thanks to the agricultural improvements made at the beginning of the twentieth century. For example, the Cervi family was the first to flatten the land in that area to improve its fertility and maximize production.[9] Their vanguard and innovative approach to farming transformed the surrounding landscape, influencing and inaugurating a new understanding of the living dynamics that connect land, humans, and non-humans. Peasant family backgrounds and labor, as well as the agricultural history of Emilia Romagna, offer important testimony about the relationship between local peasants and their land, and how humans and surrounding environments are deeply intertwined. These relationships show how the territory of Emilia Romagna framed the story and choices of the Cervi family, and how farmwork and the dedication of this family toward the land they cultivated, helped shape the landscape, leaving visible traces in the contemporary bio-culture of the region.

In his famous essay "The Formation of the Intellectuals," included in the first volume of *Prison Notebooks*, Gramsci states, "Every social group, coming into existence on the original terrain of an essential function in the world of economic production, creates together with itself, organically, one or more strata of intellectuals which give it homogeneity and an awareness of its function not only in the economic but in the social and political fields."[10] According to Gramsci, every social class develops its own organic intellectual that has the potential to change the hegemonic culture by giving political, social and economic awareness to their social group.

The story of the life of Alcide Cervi inspired the linguistic style of the two articles about the Cervi family written and published in 1953 by Italian writer and journalist Italo Calvino. Alcide Cervi's oral narrative style and the two articles previously published by Calvino consequently inspired the linguistic style of editor Renato Nicolai, the journalist of the PCI's newspapers, who transcribed the memoir of the Cervi family in *My Seven Sons.* Given that Renato Nicolai, an urban intellectual, transcribed Alcide Cervi's memoir, how does one determine the role and intent of the organic intellectual vis-à-vis the hegemonic culture? Who is really speaking, and who is using whom?

The memoir presented by Renato Nicolai follows the logic of populism as explained by literary critic Alberto Asor Rosa. According to Asor Rosa the term populism is legitimate in the literary discourse only if people are represented positively. "*For populism to be present*" he argues, "*the people need to be represented as a model.*"[11] In his analysis of the use of populism in modern and contemporary Italian literature Asor Rosa indicates, especially when referring to contemporary writers and writers of the Resistance, a shift from a culture of the elite to a culture of the people as a calculated ideological maneuver supported by the intellectual class to support political and ideological purposes. The memoir resulting from Nicolai's interviews with Alcide Cervi becomes an instrument for the PCI to reach the rural people by showcasing a story in which they can relate to and identify with.

The tragic story of the Cervi sons and the story of Alcide Cervi's survival was known among the new generation of intellectuals. Many who would emerge as pivotal intellectuals of the post–World War II era, such as Cesare Pavese, Elio Vittorini, Renata Viganò, Beppe Fenoglio, Rigoni Stern, and Italo Calvino, to name a few, were directly and indirectly involved with partisan and anti-fascist organizations. They understood that the Resistance was a movement born of the people, whose common objectives were the reestablishment of basic social values and rights. Both the intellectual and political classes understood that to reach the people, culture had to come from the people. Italo Calvino was already a well-known writer and journalist in the 1950s. His articles on the Cervi family, published two years before the release of the memoir *My Seven Sons*, motivated the editor and journalist Renato Nicolai to reuse Calvino's language style as a formula to support the ideological project of the PCI.

The work of Asor Rosa and his concept of "a culture of the people," reveals that the language and the episodes narrated by Alcide Cervi in *My Seven Sons* through the mediator of Nicolai are vehicles of resistance that shift the focus from ideological and theoretical purposes to an opportunity to present the life of a peasant family and the knowledge and wisdom of peasants by way of pragmatic examples and experiences. In other words, Alcide Cervi, while sharing the unique story of his life in his simple language, is sharing and exposing the reality and conditions of Italian peasants in general, and in doing so, he becomes a leader and representative of peasants. As a speaker and as a political and cultural agent, Alcide Cervi is elevated to the position of organic intellectual. Calvino and Nicolai are instrumental in this process. By embracing the simple linguistic style of Alcide Cervi, they not only give voice to the peasants, but they also honor the peasant perspective. This narrative helps to define the language and culture of the new peasantry in the post–World War II era.

Italo Calvino's Influence in *My Seven Sons*

Former partisan and young journalist Italo Calvino had already reached fame as a writer with the publication of his first novel *The Path to the Spiders' Nest* in 1947. His articles on the story of the Cervi family and their role in the Resistance movement appeared in the newspapers, *Patria indipendente* in January 1953, and *L'Unità* in December of the same year. Before writing the article Calvino met several times with the surviving father Alcide Cervi and some other family members.[12] The simplicity of the language adopted by Calvino seems to be inspired by the testimonies of the protagonists, the farm, and the natural environment where the meetings took place. Calvino grounds the story in the land and its protagonists—a peasant family and its sons.

The opening paragraph of the January 1953 article "Through Seven Conscious Faces, Our Strenuous Rebirth,"[13] introduces the seven brothers by describing their land and farm. As if Calvino is describing a photo, or as if a cameraman is shooting a panorama of the farm while a voice-over describes the place and the people who live there, the author constructs a microcosm of reality where the agricultural land is the setting, and the peasants are the agents on this specific slice of land. "Here from this agricultural row starts the seven brothers' land."[14] Calvino does not present the family members and their story as partisans, rather he surveys the space in which they lived, giving visibility to the fruit of their labor. Agricultural work acquires a specific shape—the row—through the presence and hard work of humans. Calvino indirectly connects the Italian landscape with the century-old human presence in the environment as it has evolved from the interactions between the two.

The row serves as an emblem of how peasants used and shaped the natural world in the most economic yet fruitful way possible. "Here from this agricultural row starts the seven brothers' land."[15] The row consisted mainly of elms and maples trees, equally distanced, upon which farmers would grow grapevines. It characterized, and still characterizes, the landscape of the Po Valley in the region of Emilia Romagna. The row is, in fact, part of the "piantata padana," a style of orchards in the Po Valley. This typical arrangement of trees had multiple agricultural advantages. The leaves from the trees were integrated in the bovines' diet, and the vertical trunks of the trees, in addition to providing support for the vines, allowed enough space to cultivate the surrounding land. In fact, bovine milk production furnished the main source of sustenance for the Cervi family, and the leaves from the trees supplemented the family's cultivation of grass in the diet of the stock.

Mountains, hills, plains, gulfs, and natural basins create a variety of soils, climates, botanical and agricultural domains. Italian territory, due to its unique stretched-out boot shape, includes very diverse and rich geographical features along with a range of soil and climate conditions. The famous saying, "the hundred agricultural Italies,"[16] coined by Stefano Jacini after his 1877 study of the agrarian situation of farmers in Italy,[17] celebrates the abundant natural diversity from which humans have adapted and molded different rural cultures across Italy. It is exactly this agricultural and natural landscape that furnishes a strategic setting for the Resistance movement during World War II. Regarding the discourse on Italian Resistance, historian Ernesto Ragionieri rightly affirms:

> The hundred agricultural Italies, heritage of centuries of division of the country, did not suddenly disappear: recent studies demonstrate that also in these situations the small owner from Piedmont did not correspond to the sharecropper from Tuscany: different were the times of actions in the fight, the intensity of participation and also the guides they chose. But common was, somehow, the inclination that the Resistance imposed on their behavior.[18]

While the historical, cultural, and geographical differences among peasants have been acknowledged, scholars continue to reinforce the ideological aspect of the Resistance as a unifying factor, an aspect which the political forces, postwar intellectual strata, and also later generations, appear to maintain. Yet, the essential role of the landscape, combined with peasant knowledge and practices with all its environmental, ecological, and political implications for the success of the Italian Resistance, cannot be underestimated.

Historian Piero Bevilacqua's interesting interpretation of the Italian agricultural landscape of Ferrara and Reggio Emilia compares and connects the organization of these landscapes to those of the ancient Roman agrarian colonies. The geometrical shape of the fields corresponds to a rational order of the territory, whereby small roads connected the different "centuratio," Roman grids. Even today in Emilia Romagna the Via Emilia, along the agricultural fields, reproduces the ancient lines of the Roman "centuratio."[19] The row, therefore, connects ancient practices of organizing and shaping the land in a rational and methodical way with more modern agricultural necessities.

The row, and the mutual beneficial relationship between trees, vines, and grass, can also be read as a symbol of the need for unity in the political ascendancy and success of the PCI soon after World War II. Gramsci in his 1919 article "Workers and Peasants" evokes the sense of discipline and organizational practices needed for the possible advent of a communist revolution. In his call to unite worker and peasant forces, Gramsci states, "Communist revolution is essentially a problem of organization and discipline."[20] Gramsci's article is taking into consideration the unsolved issues created in the first phase of the history of Italian unification by Giuseppe Garibaldi's liberation of Sicily in 1860, in particular the failure "to formulate a program in answer to the needs of the popular masses."[21] As literary critic Pasquale Verdicchio notes, Gramsci is identifying potential alliances that "might set the national project on a more equitable track."[22] In the aftermath of World War II, attempts to create alliances between the working labor class of the northern industry and the peasants, or farmers of the countryside, were still much alive in the plans of the rising PCI. Calvino's choice to use the row in the opening sentence of his article, therefore, fulfills both the need of using a simple visual agricultural example to be seen and understood by peasants, as well as the ideological purpose of attracting peasant masses in the PCI plans.

Calvino knew that the land was a central agent in the economy of rural life. Before presenting us with the family, the author presents us with their land. In this way Calvino is suggesting a relationship between base and superstructure. The agricultural organization of the space offered by the row gives us a specific image of the area that we can easily picture in our minds when thinking of the Emilia Romagna landscape. By using the row as the subject of his first sentence, Calvino immediately creates a vivid image that relates to the region and all its natural and agricultural characteristics. Furthermore, the row is a distinctive mark of human intervention on nature in the region, and an implicit suggestion that the actions, choices, and outcomes of the Cervi family are, directly and indirectly, interwoven with, and influenced by, the territory and landscape, the place where they lived. The land shapes the means of production, which in turn defines the social and political beliefs and practices of the region.

As literary and environmental historian, Lawrence Buell argues, "Place entails spatial location, entails a spatial container of some sort. But space as against place connotes geometrical or topographical abstraction, whereas place is 'space to which meaning has been ascribed."[23] Building on Beull's logic, Cervi's land and farm is the place where all is included: family efforts and labor, as well as ideas on how to improve cultivation, agricultural practices and experimentations. In a few words, Cervi's land comprises the whole story of the Cervi family, economically, intellectually, and ecologically. Calvino, after meeting with the surviving farmer and father Alcide Cervi notices how the story of the Cervi family is inseparable from that place, that geographical structure, that region, and more specifically that farm on which they live and work. The land, the farm, and the labor devoted to working the soil, are all essential co-protagonists in the story.

Calvino continues the article by describing the Cervis' land and the work performed by each of the seven brothers. The simple language and the immediacy of its content reproduce certain characteristics of the spoken language of the peasants. This simplicity is coupled with the pragmatic wisdom distinctive of peasants, underscoring the necessity of their consistent physical presence in the fields. In this way, Calvino emphasizes that a peasants' life and prosperity is directly connected and dependent on the land. "This plain has been worked by the arms of the seven brothers, these canals, this vineyard, everything around here, has been done by the seven brothers."[24] Pointing to the brothers' arms, Calvino stresses the physical strength required to work the land, the fortitude needed to harness and withstand natural elements, and the ability required to adjust to natural obstacles.

Calvino then expands by presenting the farm, identifying the responsibilities of each brother, and giving details of the night of November 1943, the night when the family was attacked in their home and captured by the fascists. Calvino's last sentence in the paragraph returns to the land, once more connecting the people to their roots and their place of origin. "The story of the seven Cervi brothers all unfolded here, on this farm, on this land."[25] The Cervis' farm becomes the symbol and metaphor of Italian peasant life. In simple words, using a language easily comprehended and pervasive among most of the Italian population, Calvino connects two historically separated and distant social and cultural worlds: those of the intellectual and the peasant.

Calvino continues to focus on the farm and its land as the place and space that bonds different generations of the family. The second paragraph returns to the present time, introducing the reader to the children of the seven brothers still engaged in working the farm; he notes the boy repairing the wagon wheels and the girl feeding the chickens. Describing Alcide Cervi, the father of the seven brothers, Calvino refers to him as "that short man, solid and knotty as a tree stump."[26] The juxtaposition between the human figure and the natural element of the knotty tree creates a powerful and interchangeable image suggesting durability, strength, and power of resistance against human and natural obstacles, but also wisdom and knowledge due to age and endurance in life. The sentence also reinforces and confirms this deep and symbiotic relationship between peasants and landscape. Alcide, like a tree stump, has survived all kinds of weather and violence, yet, like the tree he still supports new growth. This analogy between a tree trunk, the old man, and landscape, will be reused in several writings about Alcide Cervi.

Historian Luciano Casali, in the introduction to the 2010 printing of *My Seven Sons,* refers to the language used by Calvino as "almost a people's language . . . drawn directly from the protagonists' testimony, from Alcide's folktale way of recounting . . . the same "people's language" that would distinguish *My Seven Sons* in 1955.[27] The concept of "populismo" as discussed by literary critic Asor Rosa explains Calvino's writing style. Calvino's articles confirm that style acts as a political and ideological instrument to reach and open a dialogue with the peasants. Asor Rosa traces the use of the concept of "*populismo*" in Italian literary production back to the 1800s Italian Risorgimento, with the unification of Italy, and Asor Rosa sees its maximum expression during the Resistance and post-Resistance period.[28] He recognizes, in this last historical time, the moment in which a "culture from the people" is imposing itself, in different artistic, literary and cultural forms, over a culture from the elite.[29] He states, "Resistance and post-Resistance populism is probably the most conscious, the most organized, to an ideological and political level, of all our literary tradition."[30] In his historical analysis of the use of populism in Italian literature, Asor Rosa recognizes in the neorealist literature and literature of the Resistance a renewed awareness of the role of common people as a vehicle for deep social and political transformation.

Nevertheless, Calvino is not new to this writing style. Calvino's *The Path to the Spider's Nest*, published in 1947, is one of the first novels about the Resistance. The story revolves around the experience of a boy with the partisans in the mountains of Liguria. In this novel the author uses very simple, young, and mocking language. In the remarkable preface of the revised edition of the novel in 1964, the author recounts how having just survived the war, the civil war, "established an immediate communication between the writer and his public: you were face to face, equal, loaded with stories to tell."[31] Although the Resistance had already established its ideological, political, and social significance, the literary explosion following World War II was driven by the need to reach out to the people who experienced, lived, and survived the war. It was an existential, physiological, collective manifestation, and above all, a necessity. Calvino continues, "this was my experience, my experience multiplied by the experience of others."[32] The author recognizes the personal and civil aspect of it, adding a more intimate tone to the ideological message of the movement. Likewise, the articles written about the Cervi family carry a similar motive. The story of the seven brothers reflects their sacrifice and commitment, first toward their land and later against fascism. Their story spoke to the hearts of people in a very simple and immediate language with which many could recognize and identify with regardless of their social status.

Furthermore, Calvino's articles paved the way for what several scholars commonly refer to as the myth of the Cervi family. The title of the first article, "Through Seven Conscious Faces, Our Strenuous Rebirth," links the brothers and the postwar period. By pointing to their faces, Calvino establishes an inspiring model while also building the foundation for the myth of the family. The recent tragic and heroic past, and the difficult and nevertheless-full-of-possibilities present, are both included in this short, incisive title and statement. The adjective "conscious," used to describe the faces of seven brothers who died fighting fascism and the German occupation, not only refers to the bravery and strength with which they faced their destiny, but also to the sense of sacrifice understood by the entire social category of peasants and farmers, and the ideals and values they embraced. On the other hand, the adjective "strenuous" used in the second part of the title, refers to the whole country and the surviving members of the Cervi family. The father Alcide Cervi is the one who, once again, is guiding the surviving family and directs the work on the farm. His testimony becomes a symbol of resistance and endurance, both for the family and for the country.

Transitioning from Sharecroppers to Small Landowners: A Peasants' Story

In the first page of *My Seven Sons* editor Renato Nicolai includes a brief note clarifying that the memoir is the result of numerous conversations with Alcide Cervi and that, as editor, he did his best to keep intact the expressions and emotions shared by Alcide Cervi during their meetings. The result is a book written in first person, whose voice is, based on the editor's note, the one of Alcide Cervi. After the first chapter explaining the reasons of writing this biography, the father Cervi begins by remembering the origin of his family as sharecropper farmers and their participation in the fight against the tax on "*macinato*" (milled flour).[33] Although Cervi does not spend much time detailing his family battles at the dawn of the unification of Italy, these actions foreshadow the choices his son will make during the German occupation and, on a larger scale, highlight the crucial role the region of Emilia Romagna already plays within the Italian farming economy and communist ideology.

At the end of 1800, Italy was exclusively a peasant country, and its economy still followed a feudal organization controlled by the agrarian bourgeoisie. New forms of capitalism, however, started to penetrate the Italian rural economy. The tax on "*macinato*" (milling grain), approved in 1868 was created to help restore the State funds depleted from the military expenses of the newborn Italian Kingdom. This tax, called also "tax of desperation,"[34] consisted of a tax levied on grains based on the quantity of the grain milled. The miller would pay the tax calculated by the number of rotations of the mill stone recorded by a mechanical meter installed by the State. The rounds of the mill, according to the statesmen, corresponded to the quantity of cereal milled. The tax would be different based on the variety of the grain or cereal, be it rye, oats, wheat, corn, or chestnut. By 1871 the State had installed 150 thousand mechanical meters.[35] One of the first consequences of this tax was the price increase of cereal and bread. On one hand, this new law helped to restore Italian State finances, however, on the other, it increased discontent among the peasants whose cultivation and income was based on cereal. Emilia Romagna was the first region that reinforced this form of agricultural capitalism and became the epicenter of the peasant insurrection.

Sharecropping, a private contractual system between the landlord and the peasant family, developed in the Middle Ages in the central and northern regions of Emilia Romagna, Tuscany, Umbria, Marche, Lombardy, Piedmont, and Veneto. Depending on the region, and the landlord requests, the contract would usually stipulate an equal share of the products cultivated or animals and the profit gained from it, although often more than the half of the profit and the products would go to the landlord. The landlord usually would provide the tools to cultivate the land. The contract would include different clauses reflecting on the family work, the production in the field to be shared, and the conditions asked by the landlord to end the sharecropping relationship. While the stipulations of the contract could be different based on the agreements made between the landlord and the peasant family, sharecropping had two common characteristics: the land to cultivate, which included a farmhouse for the peasants, and a family-based organization of the work. As historian Luciano Pazzagli stresses, the family, not the single person, was at the center of the sharecropping system. Each member of the family would be included in the farm work, making essential a good distribution and organization of responsibilities.[36]

Sharecropping established and reinforced a negative image of the farming structure because farmers were always bound to, and dependent upon, the land from the landlord and had very few possibilities for improving their living conditions and emerging from poverty. Once the contract ended, or if it was not renewed, the peasant family had to move out with their few things, that usually wouldn't include more than some personal possessions and, if lucky, a few farm animals, and find new land to farm. According to writer, politician, and historian, Emilio Sereni, the subjugation of the sharecropper to the landlord was even "more humiliating, and onerous than the Sicilian "*metatiere*"—harvester—or the Roman colonist."[37] As Sereni explains, there was a static relation between the peasant family, "the colonic family,"[38] and the farm. The landlord controlled and supervised both the work life and the private life of the sharecropper family. Sharecroppers were not allowed, or they needed permission, to perform any kind of work outside the landlord's property.[39]

In addition, most of the time, landlords did not live on the property, yet decided what to cultivate and how to use the land even if their knowledge about agricultural techniques was very limited or nonexistent. This kind of control kept the life of farmers stagnant and discouraged agricultural improvement. When a landlord was not living on the farm the sharecropper dealt with a leaseholder who lived on the farm and imposed a severe contract and form of control. On this matter, Alcide Cervi described the sharecropping agreement as a form of robbery: "you would sign an agreement but then there were so many other clauses asking for more that there was nothing left."[40] The sharecropper was often responsible for the expenses of agricultural improvements, which imposed heavy burdens on their income and made any economic improvement or the possibility of economic independence almost impossible.

The reality of sharecropping in central Italy lasted until the first half of the twentieth century, creating a delay in the development of independent agricultural systems. Scholars note that, although sharecroppers' living conditions were harsh and miserable, they never really organized to rebel against this system. Historian Sergio Anselmi justifies this behavior by referring to the fact that sharecropping guaranteed food, a place to stay for the family, and the possibility of creating sporadic personal income by selling, when possible, handcrafts or surplus crops.[41] Being able to cover the basic human needs contributed, according to the Anselmi, to preserving the semi-slave relationship with the landlord until the end of World War II in central Italy.

Anselmi saw in the plains and square fields demarcated by the roads of Emilia Romagna a convenient geographical rural organization that efficiently connected a range of small cities. This rural landscape helped to develop the grain, meat, and silk market that guaranteed a steady, if small, income for peasant families still living under sharecropping agreements.[42] In this way, sharecropping prevailed because of the enticing possibility of some independent economic income, no matter how small. On the other hand, historian Fabrizio Spaggiari locates the lasting reality of sharecropping in the extreme dependence on the land. To find land to cultivate as a sharecropper was essential for a farmer; one year without land meant the end of the sharecropper because his material goods comprised of livestock, seeds, and agricultural instruments, if they had any, not being productively used in the fields, would be wasted and lost.[43] According to Spaggiari this is the reason sharecroppers often accepted infamously inequitable contracts with the landlord or the lessor.

The Family

The story of the Cervi family is an example of how some peasant families were able to overcome the oppression of the landlord. The hard work and sacrifice spent in the fields, paired with knowledge of the land and harvesting allowed them to produce richer and more profitable crops. The land, in the extensive narration of Alcide's family, has individual and personal implications as well as objective, social and historical purposes. Before arriving at Campi Rossi, in the county of Gattatico, the family worked as shareholders on three different farms. The first was in the area of Caprara, called Tagliavino, where they lived with Alcide's brothers; the second was at Olmo, north of Praticello, and the last one in Valle Re, in the area of Praticello. On the map, these farms are located near each other, between the counties of Gattatico and Campegine, in the area between Parma and Reggio Emilia, and feature similar landscapes and characteristics. In 1934 the Cervi family was able to save enough money and gain economic independence to free themselves from their condition as sharecroppers and rent a small farm with some land. The difference between the two conditions, as will follow, resided not only in economic growth but also in the ability and courage to experiment with new agricultural techniques, and consequently, the opportunity to improve agricultural conditions.

In the conclusion of *My Seven Sons*, Alcide Cervi summarizes the fate of his family with words of peasant wisdom that reflect his personality and his pragmatic attitude toward life. "When they told me about my sons' death I said—after a harvest a new one follows. But the harvest does not come on its own, you must cultivate, and work hard not to spoil it. I raised seven children, now I had to educate eleven grandchildren."[44] The harvest and his grandchildren both belong to the same natural cycle of life—they both follow the same rules and laws. He also suggests that the past cannot be pondered for too long, and whatever the crops and nature offer, whatever life brings must be faced with practical knowledge and wisdom based on experience.

The attack by the Fascists in November 1943, during which the house was burned and Alcide Cervi and his sons were imprisoned, and the consequent murder of his sons in December 1943, on the other hand, does not follow the natural and harmonious cycle of life. This sudden tragedy forever changed the destiny of the family and can be compared to a sudden ecological disruption, like a natural disaster, an earthquake, a storm, or a cyclone. Alcide Cervi was in his seventies during World War II; his death should have eventually preceded that of his children. Yet, the surviving father, spared by the Fascists' murder, acknowledges his farming experience, and uses rural metaphors to describe how forces of nature, "after a harvest, a new one follows,"[45] overpower human life. The image of the harvest illustrates not only his focus on life over death, but also how life in the fields, and natural and seasonal cycles of agriculture, offered a model worldview. The fruits obtained from the harvests are, conversely, the result of farming labor and imply effort, hard work and the mediation of human beings with nature. Alcide Cervi tells us that in this relationship between humans and nature, the harvest and the family will grow again. Land and family, nature, human and nonhumans, are deeply connected and protagonists in the story of the Cervi family. Their story mirrors many aspects of Italian peasant families in the first half of the twentieth century.

As mentioned earlier, only families, not single farmers, were selected as sharecroppers. The larger the family the better, as each family member equated to more labor employed in specific tasks or responsibilities. In peasant culture, the family unity and its organization were essential for survival. Family also provided the potential for economic and social advancement. Alcide Cervi's story is a good example of the importance of family in breaking the landlord's control and achieving economic independence. Mindful of how numbers in the family counted, in his memoir he mentions that he and his brothers doubled the number of children his father had. In addition, before finding a new farm to work, Alcide worked as a sharecropper with his father's family.[46] He married in 1899 and until 1934 he and his family worked as sharecroppers.[47]

Alcide remembers that as sharecroppers, his family was forced to do "San Martino."[48] San Martino refers to Saint Martin, protector of the poor. In the Christian calendar, "San Martino" falls on November 11. Among the peasants of the area, the saint's name indicated the time of the year when they would move from one farm to another. Autumn marks the end of the harvest period. The strain in the field is over and the agricultural tools returned to the barn. This is the moment, just before wintertime, to negotiate new contracts and move to new farms, a common practice in Emilia Romagna. Seasons, climate conditions, and the products of the land structured the work of each family member and the rhythm of life around the farm. As animals and nature go into hibernation, for the farmer the fall was the time to gather provisions and breeding time to prepare for calving season in the spring. Domestic work such as weaving, spinning, and the maintenance of the agricultural equipment dominated the winter months.

The natural cycle of the seasons and the regional geography shaped the organization and division of labor among family members. Alcide Cervi, in fact, associated his sons based on the role they played on the farm. The organization of responsibilities was still very similar to the one of the sharecropper family. Following the patriarchal tradition, the family was governed by the male figure of "vergaro, massaro, capoccia or azdor" and the female figure of "vergara, massaia, capoccia, azdora."[49] The origin of the word "vergaro" from the Latin "ververius," is shepherd. In the countryside of Emilia Romagna, the Tuscan area of Maremma and other regions of central Italy "vergaro" referred to the person who safeguards the herds of several shepherds, helping them to survive through winter. Similarly, "vergara" is the woman, not necessarily the wife, responsible in helping the "vergaro" by attending the activities in the farm and managing the farmhouse.[50] In the sharecropper family, the oldest son worked closely with the "azdor," he oversaw the storehouse and managed the plow, the wagon, or the harrow. The other sons attended to the rest of the duties under the direction of the first son.

The seven Cervi brothers, although united and covering responsibilities based on their personal attitudes, mimicked this established model. Alcide

Cervi remembers how Gelindo, the first son, went with him to look for land to rent. When still sharecroppers, Alcide and his family, passionate about increasing the productivity of the land, went to the landlord with a detailed proposal on how to double the profitability of the land. Upon the refusal of the landlord to agree to the new agricultural changes, the Cervi family decided not to renew the contract as sharecroppers and to look for some land to rent. Alcide Cervi and his son Gelindo found some land in "Campi Rossi," "a land filled with bumps and holes," [51] the area of Gattatico where they ended up living. Being the oldest, he was the one who accompanied the father to the fair to buy the bull used to plow and level the new land.[52] Antenore, the second son, was responsible for the fields. Father Cervi remembers him as very serious about his work: "He had his mind fixed on the production of grain, and how to produce more of it."[53] Agostino and Ovidio, the fifth and sixth brothers, looked after the cattle and the barn.

Historian Renzo Renzi stresses how this division of labor among the farmers of Emilia Romagna and the area of Campegine was particularly important as livestock holdings were the real sign of progress, even more than the land.[54] Alcide Cervi observes, "Those who are familiar with the agriculture in Emilia, know that the most important production of the region is milk, that the real 'capital' are the cows. Nevertheless, everything depends on forage, that needs to be of good quality, and quantity. Only in this way is milk abundant, fat, and rich of flavor."[55]

It is interesting to note that although the Cervi family held a decent number of livestock, and cattle played an important role in the family economy by providing a source of income through the production of milk, butter and cheese, the land and the agricultural work related to it, which is mainly forage, remain the focus of the Alcide's story. Historian Rossano Pazzagli notes, in fact, that by the beginning of 1900 in the Po Valley, agriculture focused mainly on animal husbandry and cereal, producing around 40 percent of Italian wheat. The agricultural landscape is not only characterized by what is cultivated, but also how it is cultivated, what practices and techniques are involved in the cultivation. The landscape and the natural environment are, in fact, included as essential elements of Cervi daily life as if family, farm, and landscape are not separated but constantly directly and indirectly interconnected, and part of the same representation. When mentioning their beginnings as small farmers, Alcide Cervi dedicates an entire chapter in explaining how they thought and ended up leveling the land of Campi Rossi, significantly increasing the production of forage.

Time and effort spent in agricultural improvement therefore play an important role in the Cervi family memoir. However, when talking of his children Alcide adopts an intimate and sentimental tone. The first episodes he cites recounts memories of his sons' childhood, their games and their personalities. Ettore, the youngest brother, is introduced in an affectionate tone remembering when, as a little boy, he would hide in the grass and ask his brother to find him. "Ettore was the youngest, and when we would come to the fields the grass was taller than him. He would hide in the grass and then with his soft voice he would say—I am not here anymore."[56] Later in the memoir, remembering his sons' death, Alcide refers back to this childhood game in the grass: "now the high grass has covered you all, and you are not here any longer."[57] The grass is a symbol of life and death. The grass referred to is the field covered with young wheat and where the young Ettore, guided by his older brothers, learned the use of the sickle. The grass, through the image and memory of Alcide, holds the double purpose of protector and barrier. The grass is used as forage and is a source of sustenance and a playground as experienced by Ettore, carrying out its function of protector and supporter of life. By covering Ettore's body, the grass transforms its function into a link between the father and the son.

Genoeffa, Alcide's wife, holds a special role in the biography. His wife Genoeffa is the only female family member Alcide cites in his memoir. The two daughters of the family, Rina and Diomira, are absent from the story. They were married when the seven brothers were killed and, by cultural tradition, they belonged to a different family and were no longer part of the family of origin.[58] Genoeffa on the other hand is mentioned several times and acquires the visibility necessary to understand and illustrate the role of women and mothers in Italian peasant families in the first half of the twentieth century. She is the "azdora," the female counterpart of the azdor, Alcide. As a mother she is a vital point of reference and supporter of her sons, and before any family member makes a decision, they seek out her opinion. She also plays a decisive supporting role during the time of the Resistance. Nicolai, in his contribution to the twenty-year memorial of Genoeffa's death, offers a more politicized and localized image of the "azdora" of Emilia Romagna. Genoeffa not only manages the family daily life of the farm and offers moral and practical support to the men of the house, notes Nicolai, but she also expects them to engage in the social and political activities of local peasant life with the same commitment they demonstrate in the fields.[59] Nicolai points out that historically peasant women in this area supported the participation of their husbands and sons in social struggles, like the fights against the taxes on "macinato" in 1869 or as protagonists in the rice workers' strikes in the first half of the twentieth century. These women, Renato Nicolai observes, have seen men fight and often "be injured or die."[60] After September 8, 1943, Change "Genoveffa" with "Genoeffa" transforms the Cervis' house as a temporary hotel to help and support the injured drifters, the soldiers who abandoned their military camps after the declaration of change of allies made by General Badoglio on the radio and joined the partisan movement. She made sure there was always enough food for everyone, including chicken. "Genoveffa would order to purchase more chicken, when we couldn't kill our owns."[61]

It is important to consider, however, the relevance of the daily routine performed by the *azdora*. Genoeffa took care of all the responsibilities that were not connected to work in the field: those activities considered as domestic work. As *azdora*, she knew the schedule and routine of each family member, and she decided the work and responsibilities of the other women of the house. Genoeffa was responsible for the courtyard animals, an essential component of the farm economy, and the cultivation of herbs and vegetables around the house used for the family's consumption. She also performed spinning and weaving jobs. Alcide remembers, "She did all the blouses, and the handkerchiefs, and the shirts and the socks we wore, for all eight men."[62] Although not mentioned, it is understood that her daughters assisted her. The labors performed by the *azdora* matched and often exceeded the work and responsibilities of the *azdor*. The azdora accounted for a tremendous portion of the family economy and had a great deal of knowledge about farming, making her much more complex than the contemporary housewife to which she might be compared to.

Finally, Genoeffa was responsible for the education of her children. According to Alcide, Genoeffa was a sweet and shy woman who had the gift of making prophesies and she knew how to tell stories that offered a moral message.[63] Reading literary texts was not a common routine in peasant families. Nevertheless, Genoeffa regularly read popular stories or literary texts like *The Brothered*, *The Divine Comedy* and *The Bible*. Through these readings, Alcide comments, she taught the children to have respect and good principles, including a sense of justice.[64] Listening to Genoeffa reading books or telling stories was part of the daily routine of the family, "In the winter in the cowshed, surrounded by the strong heat from the animal, in the summer in the courtyard, in front of the star-spangled sky."[65] To the intimate connection with the seasons and the natural environment, Alcide's words add the family's intellectual experience through Genoeffa's readings. It is interesting to note that the family's moment of reading does not happen in the kitchen, the place of the house usually designated for family gatherings. It could be argued that poor economic conditions of peasants forced humans and nonhumans to share the same space and places. Ironically, however, Alcide Cervi stresses this overlooked proximity with the natural elements, the open sky in the courtyard or the cowshed, as a key factors to bring up the balanced relationship, common in peasants' families, of interdependence between humans and the natural environment. These two apparently separate worlds were, in Alcide's memoir, constantly connected both as integral part of his past and present life. When the land of Campi Rossi is finally leveled, Alcide Cervi invites the neighbor families for a toast and says, "I toast to progress, to the future, to the happiness of people, that from poor and strained, like my land, can become rich and advanced, like tomorrow will be my land."[66]

The Land and Campi Rossi

Alcide concludes the description of his sons with these words, "This is the story of my sons' marriages; the land we cultivated, on the other hand, has a different story, always of growth but much more strenuous."[67] For the farmer Alcide, the land serves human purposes, and its growth is perceived and appreciated in terms of human benefits. When Alcide talks about growth, he is referring to the fertility of the soil. Nevertheless, although he is interested in increasing the productivity of the land, his intervention on the land and landscape is not pure exploitation of this natural resource, and results in creating a beneficial relationship with his land. While humans receive the benefits directly from the fruits of the land mixed with their labor, this land, which was arid and uncultivated, became richer and more fertile thanks to human intervention and labor. Alcide's practical farming knowledge grew out of the interconnection and interdependence between humans, nonhumans, and the land. Human intervention, the Cervi family's work, transformed the configuration of the land and the structure of the soil.

During Fascism the real proof of agricultural progress in the area of Reggiano, was animal farming. Animals, not the land, were the real "capital."[68] The land of the Po Valley, especially the areas around the river Po and Adda, are characterized by sandy, graveled, or clayish soils.[69] Located in the Po Valley the land of Campi Rossi was, during this time, mainly used for grazing with very little rotation for agricultural purposes. While potentially a rich soil, due to over pasture the area ended up becoming semiarid and eroded. The transformation of the agricultural landscape was, therefore, directly connected with the story of the Cervi family and the personal and economic investments they put into improving the quality of the soil.

Alcide created parallels between his children and the land as if, in his experience, the two were related and progressed together. Alcide and his sons were always interested in the improvement of agricultural techniques. This was the main reason the Cervi family ended up moving to so many different farms when they were sharecroppers, as Alcide mentions in the biography. The Cervi family was interested in new forms of cultivating and improving the production of the agricultural land. When referring to his landlords Alcide summarized, "[they] liked things that were not risky."[70] Increasing the productivity of the land implies investing the farmer's personal knowledge, time, energy, and economic funds toward new ideas and experimentations, a risk the semifeudal system of sharecropping was not prepared for, nor interested in supporting. Among the difficulties of being subservient to the demands and expectations of the landlord, Alcide included his frustration as a farmer in not having the freedom to cultivate different crops or use better techniques. While sharecropping, Alcide's sons came up with the idea to level the soil. They realized that the uneven terrain made it difficult to create an efficient irrigation system and, consequently, prevented the growth of forage. According to Alcide, when they tried to persuade the landlord to invest in their project, the landlord replied, "Better an egg today than a chicken tomorrow, I do not want risks, this is it."[71]

The animal world is often a source of inspiration for Italian proverbs, and domestic animals such as chickens stand as testimony to the peasant roots of Italian culture and tradition. Although peasant life, culture, and tradition may vary according to the region, historical background, landscape, and soil, courtyard animals like chickens were and are essential in the rural community and individual economy of the farmer. Representations in art show the iconography of the egg as a symbol of perfection, as for example, seen in the architectural shape of domes or in religious paintings. In the mentality of the pragmatic peasant, the egg loses its sacredness and becomes a secure source of sustenance. In the long term, a flourishing chicken carries the potential of prosperity. Within the stagnant reality of sharecropping, the landlord preferred to assure a small short-term profit, rather than investing in a project for the future that would incur possible risks in the present. In this context, the Cervi family represents, in central and northern Italy, the passage from the old idea of peasant whose main concern was subsistence, shelter, and food, to the new figure of the farmer.

Between the end of the nineteenth century and the first half of the twentieth century, the reclaiming of the land transformed the landscape and geographical course of the Po Valley, paving the way for changes to the agricultural economy in the region, and establishing a more progressive attitude among the peasants. The use of mechanical plowing introduced new forms of technology during the first decades of 1900 and allowed for the transformation of swampland into ample cultivated areas that were interrupted, here and there, by strips of vineyards. The trees along the riverbanks were cut and the land, now cleared, created space to cultivate grains and forage for cattle. Farming techniques and the introduction of agricultural machinery ultimately served human purposes, consequently the land and farm animals could be considered mere instruments to achieve human interests.

Until the economic boom of the 1960s, however, Italy was not yet fully invested in industrial agriculture, and the small improvements farmers made to increase productivity of the land were based on methods that were also beneficial for the soil. Moreover, the farmer established a relationship of mutual exchange with the land. Alcide remembers they were among the first families to build canals to bring water in the fields, and they were the first in the area to buy a tractor. Although it was an anthropocentric vision of the environment and nature, there was an awareness that humans were not a species isolated from nature, but rather part of it. Land was not seen and experienced as a commodity, but as the essential living element that contributed to human prosperity. Seen as a source of sustenance and wealth, there was the desire to continually improve the yield while making sure the land received the proper nutrition and care to sustain those yields into the future.

The implementation of technology in Italian agriculture at the beginning of the twentieth century was slow and gradual. The initial phase of mistrust toward innovation reflected the attitude that diffident peasants, who had been shaped by the traditions of feudalism and sharecropping, harbored toward change. To break this barrier, the first step was to introduce, give access to, and create acceptance of these new concepts. The attention the Cervi family gave to new agricultural techniques makes them, once again, atypical compared to the average peasant family and, at the same time, a model for a new post–World War II peasant social strata. Both the Cervi family story and the attention to farming technology in Emilia Romagna were foundational for the political goals of the left to demonstrate Gramsci's wish in the 1920s for a peasant-led revolution. His desire, in articles regarding a possible alliance between workers and peasants, which he later explained further in "The Southern Question," was becoming a reality.

The region of Emilia Romagna was the first to offer technical demonstrations, classes on agriculture, and literacy courses at the end of the ninetieth century. For example, evening professional courses for the people opened the doors for peasants who were engaged in the fields during the day.[72] Soon the region opened courses on livestock, fruit farming, herbaceous farming, and grafts. Founded in 1894, "Regia Scuola di Zootecnia e Caseificio A. Zanelli" was among the first institutes to offer courses of specialization for cheese factories.[73] This form of education, a practical and applied knowledge in agriculture, allowed Emilia Romagna to develop a more progressive agricultural system and become a vanguard region.

As Calvino mentions in his second article on the family titled "The Seven Brothers," the Cervi family members were considered "new minds,"[74] people who would embrace and implement new ideas at any moment. He remembers how the neighboring farmers were always reticent toward the Cervis' ideas but, pushed by their curiosity, would often stop by their farm, ready to learn from the good outcomes of their innovative practices. Calvino cites the barn and the drinking fountain of the farm as examples of how the family would find technological farming innovations reading books unknown in the area and later put them into practice. The drinking fountain, for instance, allowed the Cervi family to control the quantity of water used for the cattle. Calvino illustrates in this way how their work with cattle became so fruitful that in a few years all the neighbor farmers started to regard them as models.

The family worked with the breeds called "*pezzata nera*," native to the Alps of Val d'Aosta, and Holstein Friesian cattle, bred in Northern Germany, both known for their outstanding milk production.[75] These cows, living on the mountains where the soil is humid and the grass is rich, rely on fertile and abundant forage. By using non-autochthone breeds, the family understood that they had to provide a similar natural environment. Alcide and his sons knew that to be successful they had to begin by changing the configuration of the land and its landscape.

Good forage depends on a generous quantity and even distribution of water. The irregular arid landscape of Campegine did not support an extensive water system, as water would tend to stagnate in holes. Aldo, who used to read magazines on new agricultural technology, found inspiration on how to level the land from an article published in *La Riforma Sociale,* an international magazine on social sciences and politics founded in 1894 and directed from 1922 to 1939 by Luigi Einaudi. As environmental historian Marco Armiero observes, the transformation of landscape through land reclamation has always been an important component in Italian history. During Mussolini's regime, however, agricultural practices became a key element of fascist politics. Land reclamation, for the first time, emerged as a State-sponsored practice.[76] Fascism promoted land recovery through the State entity "*Ente Bonifica*," which supported farmers who committed to participate in the program by financing their project.

The refusal of the landlord to allow the Cervi family to level his land marked the end of their story as sharecroppers and their beginnings as small farmers. Alcide Cervi and his son Aldo asked and received the support of "Ente Bonifica" to level the land of Campi Rossi. Despite the general skepticism of the local office toward their project, the family received the requested fifteen wagons asked to move the soil that was needed to level the land.[77] It was custom in the family to always make important decisions together. Leveling the land required, for the first years, hard work and sacrifices from all the family members. Alcide remembers, "Everybody, also the women, agreed, as long as sharecropping ended, since it did not bring any enthusiasm in the job."[78] The Cervi family did not passively accept the decision made by the landlord. On the contrary, it gave them the courage to step out of this semi-slave relationship and system of agriculture. The word "enthusiasm" indicates how lively and dynamic the Cervi family interpreted and experienced their work as farmers.

The land surface of Campi Rossi was particularly rough and hard to cultivate and once again the family demonstrated strength and determination to persevere at their task, regardless of the obstacles. Aldo, the most charismatic of the seven brothers, comments, "What can you do, Italy is like that, plains and hills, an unusual land. They say we are poor because Italy is badly shaped and needs help. Yet, take this land and transform it. Make an exemplary allotment of it and you will see that it will give more than the other ones. It is a question of intelligence and will."[79] Aldo's proactive approach toward life, nature, and landscape is very distinctive of his family, but also reflects the beginning of a change in mentality on farming in the region of Emilia Romagna. His words denote the practical attitude of the peasant in his environment and characterize the historic passage from sharecropper to small farmer. Through this process, Aldo emerged as an organic intellectual, one who serves as an example of empowerment for peasants, introducing more innovative techniques acquired through education and determination.

The changes of the land in Campi Rossi, the consequent transformation of the agrarian landscape, and the work done by the Cervi family can be seen as an exemplification of the relationship between nature and culture. Ecocritics Kate Rigby and Axel Goodbody in *Ecocritical Theory: New European Approaches* point out how European thinkers are more open to conceive "nature as a cultural responsibility and project."[80] The authors discuss possible differences between the European and American ecocritical approaches by pointing out the geographical distinctions and how European thinkers are concerned with cultural landscapes, with the pastoral rather than wilderness. From their perspective, the variations between the two ecocritical styles might have been geographically influenced by the impact of dense population on European land, its domestication, and eventually by creating an "artificial" nature, dependent for its survival on human agency."[81] The transformations and improvements made by the Cervi family and the influence they had on the surrounding region, from the flattening of the land to improving the water system, are, from this perspective, an example of cultural landscape in which the natural landscape is shaped by human labor and intellect.

At the time of its publication, *My Seven Sons* might have been designed as an instrument of the leftist party to receive more consensus among the middle and lower classes, and to show and reinforce leftist political beliefs and ideological ties to the Italian Resistance. Alcide's words, however, deliver and retain another essential and more powerful message. His family memoir, the brothers' involvement in the Italian Resistance and their murder, and finally the Cervis' connection to their land demonstrate how human intellect, peasant labor, and knowledge of the land have the capability of creating powerful bonds and alliances. Their story, their inquisitive minds and deep knowledge of the local territory, coupled with their anti-fascist beliefs, was already a story of Resistance. Joining the partisan movement and fighting the fascists was, for them, a logical consequence of fighting for their political and intellectual independence. Nature, in this case seen through the eyes, practice, knowledge, and understanding of Italian peasant work and culture of the first half of the twentieth century, had already been perceived and experienced as a "cultural responsibility."

The Legacy

The story of the Cervi family has become a symbol beyond the Resistance and the political purposes of the left party, and Alcide Cervi left much more than a memoir. His story and example have been of great inspiration and are very alive today. While the murder of the seven brothers is a tragedy that speaks to the brutality and inhumanity of fascism as an ideology and practice, their story as farmers is a testimony to the possible and necessary balance between agricultural tradition, innovation, peasant culture and values that maintain a fruitful and respectful relationship between humans and the land they inhabit.

Alcide Cervi died in 1970 at the age of ninety-five. He has left an important legacy in the exact place and space where the family moved in 1934, where they changed their destiny from sharecroppers to farmers. In 1974 the Italian National Alliance of Farmers, today known as Italian Farmers Confederation (CIA, Federazione Italiana Contadini), the National Partisans Association of Italy (ANPI), the province of the city of Reggio Emilia, and the Municipality of Gattatico, established the Alcide Cervi Institute. The Institute focuses on training, teaching, historical research, and dissemination of history establishing relationships with local and national cultural and academic institutions. In 2002, the Cervi house became a permanent museum, Museum Cervi, a "Museum for the history of peasant movements, anti-fascism and resistance in the countryside."[82] In line with the Alcide Cervi Institute mission, the museum hosts initiatives of historic, ethnographic, and environmental interest. The surrounding land, in fact, has become in recent years an agri-environmental park offering educational courses and showcasing the traditional agricultural landscape of the region of Emilia Romagna, with the vine married to the elm. Together with the Department of Science of the University of Modena and the University of Reggio Emilia, a portion of the land has been allocated for the construction of a germplasm bank for soft wheat varieties.[83]

Finally, on the Cervi property, next to the family house, resides the recently constructed Emilio Sereni Archive and Library on Italian rural history. The two constructions, the Cervi family house and now museum, and the archive and library, often collaborate on events and workshops related to peasant culture, history, and agricultural landscape. Former partisan, politician, and historian Emilio Sereni wrote important publications on the history of the

Italian rural landscape in its economic, social, and ecological context such as *The Agrarian Question in Italian National Rebirth* (1946), *Capitalism in the Countryside* (1947), *Old and New in Italian Countryside* (1956), *History of Italian Agricultural Landscape* (1961), and *Agriculture and Rural World* (1976). Emilio Sereni was also one of the founders of the Alcide Cervi Institute and in 1972 donated all his book collection, notes, and publications to the Alcide Cervi Institute. Besides the Emilio Sereni collection and bibliographic files, which alone include over 300,000 bibliographic records, the archive also hosts the National Historic Archive of Peasants Movements, which includes publications related to the history of Italian peasants' movements from their origins to today.[84] An essential point of reference for scholars who work on Italian rural landscape, today the Emilio Sereni Archive and the Alcide Cervi Institute projects cover a vast spectrum of cultural, educational, and civic events. These include the Emilio Sereni Summer School and the School of Government of the Territory, which have made the Alcide Cervi Institute an accredited institution for professional training by the Italian Ministry of Education, University, and Research.[85]

Today the Cervi family farm is a place of intellectual and practical collaboration and transformation, a place that continues to rethink and reevaluate the relationship between humans, the territory, and the politics involved in empowering the beliefs, choices, and practices of farmers. The spirit of freedom and democracy that inspired the seven brothers to join the Italian Resistance continues to be represented in the twenty-first century through the commitment of those who work and attend the events at the Cervi Museum and the Emilio Sereni Archive and Library. One of the goals is to continue to focus on and have as protagonists those who have contributed through their labor to shape Italian landscape—the peasants.

NOTES

1. Antonio Gramsci, *The Southern Question*. Trans. by Pasquale Verdicchio, (West Lafayette, IN: Purdue University, 1995), 39.

2. Anna Bravo, "I partigiani e la popolazione contadina nell'astigiano," in *Contadini e Partigiani*, records of the conference in Asti-Nizza and Monferrato in December 1984, (Alessandria: Edizioni dell'Orso, 1984), 15. This conference was organized for the forty-year anniversary of the Italian Republic and the liberation during World War II in the area of Asti, in Piedmont.

3. Istituto Alcide Cervi, *Le campagne italiane e la Resistenza*, (Bologna: Grafis Edizioni, 1995), 11.

4. *Le campagne italiane e la Resistenza*, 10. The original text is in Italian, the English translation is mine.

5. Ferruccio Parri, "Una dichiarazione di Ferruccio Parri. La Resistenza fu anche contadina" published in the weekly magazine *Lavoro*, Rome, no. 21, 22–28 May,

1949. This article is also present in *Le campagne italiane e la Resistenza,* 55. The English translation is mine.

6. Eva Lucenti, *I fratelli Cervi nascita di un mito*, Istituto Alcide Cervi. Annali 27–28, 2005–2006, (Reggio Emilia: Tecnograf S.p.A.), 236. Eva Lucenti interviewed Sandro Curzi in 2004.

7. Antonio Gramsci. "Workers and Peasants" (from *L'Ordine nuovo*, Aug. 2, 1919) in *The Southern Question*. Translated by Pasquale Verdicchio. Ms in progress.

8. Ibid.

9. This important detail has been stressed both by Italiano Calvino in his article "Nei sette volti consapevoli la nostra faticosa rinascita," as well as in *I miei sette figli*.

10. Antonio Gramsci, "The Formation of the Intellectuals" in *Selections from Prison Notebooks*, edited and translated by Quintin Hoare and Geoffrey Nowell Smith. New York: International Publishers, 1971, 5.

11. Alberto Asor Rosa, *Scrittori e popolo. Il populismo nella letteratura italiana contemporanea*. Roma: Savelli, 1976, 14. The italics are from the author. The first edition was published in 1965. This volume constituted one of the main points of reference of Italian literary criticism of the last fifty years. In 2015 Asor Rosa published with Einaudi a revised version, *Scrittori e oppolo 1965. Scrittori e massa 2015*, in which he reexamines the absence of the concept of populism in light of a changed society, culture, and cultural production.

12. In these pages, I am focusing mainly on the first article published in the newspaper *Patria Indipendente*, as the second presents very similar contents and messages.

13. The original title is "Nei sette volti consapevoli la nostra faticosa rinascita," and the English translation is mine. Both Calvino's articles appear in the collection of writing on the Cervi brothers edited by the Cervi Museum, *Raccolta di scritti e poesie sui fratelli Cervi*.

14. Italo Calvino, "Nei sette volti consapevoli la nostra faticosa rinascita," published in the newspaper *Patria Indipendente* in January 1953. The article I quote is part of the volume *Raccolta di scritti e poesie sui Fratelli Cervi*, edited by Sezione Didattica del Museo Cervi, 3.

15. Ibid.

16. Original, "Le cento Italie agricole."

17. The study Jacini conducted is titled "L'inchiesta agraria e sulle condizioni della classe agricola in Italia."

18. Ernesto Ragionieri, "Dall'unità ad oggi. La storia politica e sociale," in *Storia d'Italia*, vol. IV. Torino: Einaudi, 1976, 2380. English translation is mine.

19. Piero Bevilacqua, *Storia dell'Agricoltura Italiana in Età Contemporanea*, Vol. I, (Venezia: Marsilio, 1989), 12.

20. Antonio Gramsci. "Workers and Peasants" (from *L'Ordine nuovo*, Aug. 2, 1919) in the updated edition of *The Southern Question*. Translated by Pasquale Verdicchio. Manuscript in progress, personal communication.

21. Antonio Gramsci, *The Southern Question,* trans. by Pasquale Verdicchio, (West Lafayette, IN: Bordighera Inc., 1995), 5.

22. Ibid., 4.

23. Lawrence Buell, *The Future of Environmental Criticism. Environmental Crisis and Literary Imagination* (Malden, MA: Blackwell Publishing, 2005), 63.

24. Italo Calvino, "Nei sette volti consapevoli la nostra faticosa rinascita," 3.

25. Ibid.

26. Ibid.

27. Alcide Cervi, *I miei sette figli,* ed. Renato Nicolai, (Torino: Einaudi, 2010), xviii. English translation is authors.

28. Alberto Asor Rosa, *Scrittori e popolo. Il populismo nella letteratura italiana contemporanea*, (Roma: Savelli, 1976), 153. The first edition of this volume is 1965.

29. Ibid.

30. Ibid. English translation is mine.

31. Italo Calvino. *Il sentiero dei nidi di ragno.* 6th ed, (Cles: Oscar Mondadori, 2012), vi. English translation is mine.

32. Ibid., xx.

33. Alcide Cervi, *I miei sette figli*, 10.

34. https://massimedalpassato.it/la-tassa-sul-macinato-e-le-rivolte-del-1868/ Last accessed on 01/15/2023

35. https://www.finanze.gov.it/it/il-dipartimento/fisco-e-storia/i-tributi-nella-storia-ditalia/1868-1884-tassa-sul-macinato/ Last accessed on 01/15/2023.

36. Rossano Pazzagli, "Il paesaggio della mezzadria," in Quaderni n.8 *La Costruzione del Paesaggio Agrario nell'Età Moderna.* Summer School Emilio Sereni, III edizione, (Gattatico (RE): Istituto Alcide Cervi, 2012), 67.

37. Emilio Sereni, *Il capitalismo nelle campagne (1860–1900)*, (Torino: Einaudi, 1947 and 1968), 180. English translation is author's.

38. Ibid.

39. Ibid.

40. Alcide Cervi, *I miei sette figli*, 49.

41. "Mezzadri e mezzadrie nell'Italia centrale" in *Storia dell'Agricoltura Italiana in Età Contemporanea,* ed. Piero Bevilacqua, 224.

42. Ibid., 225.

43. Fabrizio Spaggiari. "Dalla Restaurazione all'Unità d'Italia fra Campeggine e Santa Vittoria" in *La Terra dei Cervi prima dei Cervi. L'agricoltura a Campeggine dal Settecento al fascismo*, (Reggio Emilia: Amministrazione Provinciale di Reggio Emilia, 1982), 76.

44. Alcide Cervi, *I miei sette figli*, 107.

45. Ibid.

46. Ibid., 10.

47. Ibid., 46.

48. Ibid., 18.

49. Daniela Calanca, et all, *Identikit del Novecento. Conflitti, Trasformazioni Sociali, Stili di Vita.* Roma: Donzelli editore, 2004, 102.

50. The definition of the word and its origin is found in https://www.treccani.it/vocabolario/vergaio/ (last checked in 11/12/2022).

51. Alcide Cervi, *I miei sette figli*, 48.

52. Ibid., 53.

53. Ibid., 63.

54. Renzo Renzi, ed. *La Terra dei Cervi prima dei Cervi. L'Agricoltura a Campeggine dal Settecento al Fascismo*, (Reggio Emilia: Amministrazione provinciale di Reggio Emilia, 1982), 117.

55. Alcide Cervi, *I miei sette figli*, 46.
56. Cervi, *I miei sette figli*, 19.
57. Cervi, *I miei sette figli*, 101.
58. https://www.istitutocervi.it/2014/09/29/le-donne-dei-cervi/ (last consulted on 11/12/2022).
59. *Genoeffa Cocconi. Donna, madre, Contadina* in Quaderni del Museo Cervi, Number 2, November 2004 (Reggio Emilia: Tecnograph, 2004), 69.
60. Ibid.
61. Cervi, *I miei sette figli*, 83.
62. Cervi, *I miei sette figli*, 24.
63. Ibid., 21.
64. Ibid., 22.
65. Ibid.
66. Cervi, *I miei sette figli*, 55.
67. Ibid., 46.
68. *La Terra dei Cervi prima dei Cervi*, 117.
69. https://feder.bio/wp-content/uploads/2017/07/PASCOLO-Final-Web.pdf Last accessed on 01/20/2023.
70. *La Terra dei Cervi prima dei Cervi*, 7.
71. Ibid., 48.
72. Spaggiari. "Dalla Restaurazione all'Unità d'Italia fra Campeggine e Santa Vittoria," 121.
73. Ibid.
74. Italo Calvino, "I sette fratelli" in *Raccolta di scritti e poesie sui fratelli Cervi*, 12. The English translation is authors.
75. Eva Lucenti, *I fratelli Cervi nascita di un mito*, 29.
76. Marco Armiero, Roberta Biasillo, Wilko Graf von Hardenberg, *La Natura del Duce*, (Torino: Einaudi Editore, 2022), 30.
77. Cervi, *I miei sette figli*, 51.
78. Ibid., 49.
79. Ibid., 50. "Che volete fare, anche l'Italia è così, pianura e monti, terra strana. E dicono che siamo poveri perché l'Italia è conformata male e per forza ha bisogno di aiuti. Eppure prendete questa terra e la trasformate. Fatene un appezzamento modello e vedrete che darà più degli altri. Il problema è di cervello e di volontà."
80. Axel Goodbody, Kate Rigby, *Ecocritical Theory: New European Approaches*, (Charlottesville: University of Virginia Press, 2011), 3.
81. Ibid.
82. https://www.istitutocervi.it/museo-cervi/ (last visited 11/12/2022).
83. https://www.istitutocervi.it/parco-agroambientale/ (last visited 11/12/2022).
84. https://www.istitutocervi.it/bibliotecasereni/ (last visited 11/13/2022).
85. https://www.istitutocervi.it/bibliotecasereni/ (last visited in 11/13/2022).

Chapter Two

Nuto Revelli and the Disappearing Voices of Peasant Resistance

LISTENING TO PEASANTS' VOICES

World War II is still very present in Italian memory. Many Italian families have members who were directly or indirectly involved with the war and have stories to share about that period. Every year across Italy communities celebrate and remember the anniversary of the beginning of Resistance in 1943 and the liberation of Italy from the German occupation and the fascists in 1945. Some commemorations are official and institutionalized; others are more spontaneous and organic. The latter includes organizers of the "Partisan Bicycling Tourist," a project "of stories and travels bringing together bicycles, history and memory, [and] above all, . . . the Resistance."[1] In 2015, the Partisan Bicycling Tourist commemorated the seventieth anniversary of Italian Liberation by cycling through the mountains and the hills of the northern regions of Piedmont and Liguria. They retraced the pathways and memories of the partisans and writers in these areas: Beppe Fenoglio, Nuto Revelli, and Italo Calvino.[2] The Alps of the Piedmont and Ligurian regions hold scars and historical memories marked by World War II battles. By cycling these areas, this group reconnected and kept alive the history, the stories, the people, their traditions and cultures, and their relationship with the landscapes of these mountains.

In the Ligurian Alpine landscape of northern Italy inhabited by vegetation, rocks, trees, streams and animals, humans represent only one element among many others. Activities such as bicycling, walking, trekking, or simply traveling beyond the city limits into the mountains, hills, woods, and narrow unpaved paths of the region invite and demand a more intimate connection to the surrounding landscape. Writers and former partisans, like Fenoglio and Calvino, must have had this kind of experience when they wrote their novels on the Resistance in the 1950s and 1960s, or like Nuto Revelli, when he collected the testimonies of the disappearing world of the peasants during the 1970s and 1980s.

In the introduction to *The Path to the Spiders' Nests* Italo Calvino writes, "the Resistance represented the fusion between landscape and characters."[3] "Landscape," in Calvino's sentence, comes first. Because of his experience as a partisan, he knows that the surrounding environment plays a foundational role in the success of the Resistance but, as he admits, "in order to represent it, I had given it second place to something else: to people, to stories."[4] Calvino positioned the landscape in a secondary role for strategic purposes, but that did not take away from the important role it played in the Resistance. Like the background of a painting, landscapes—the geography, climate, and ecology of a region—contextualize and often determine the destiny and choices of those who inhabit them. In this environment, to survive and flourish, humans learn to relate to their natural surroundings by interacting and intra-acting in a relationship of respect, understanding, and sometimes fear.

The writings of these former partisans helped draw attention to rural life and the surrounding countryside, bringing a new awareness to what are now understood as environmental issues. Like Calvino, Nuto Revelli was also interested in the connections between the landscape, the people, and their stories. Alpinist first and former army officer, partisan during the Resistance period, and historian later, Revelli was stationed with his partisan brigade, "Italia libera"—"Free Italy," in the small mountain village of Paraloup, 1,361 meters above sea level. Paraloup is the last village in Valle Stura, a valley situated in the rural and marginal area of the Piedmont Alps in the province of Cuneo, near the southeast French border. Its strategic position allowed and still allows, for those who visit it on sunny and clear days, to have a flawless view of the plain of Cuneo up to the more inland Asti area and the Langhe, internationally recognized today for their wine such as Barolo, Barbaresco, or Nebbiolo. During World War II, Paraloup was already semi-abandoned and, in the years following the war the village was fully abandoned. Revelli's partisan experience in the mountains and his direct contact with peasants during the war not only shaped his research and work after the war, but also gave him a renewed sense of justice.

Born in Cuneo, Revelli witnessed the establishment of new factories in the valleys and the consequent depopulation and abandonment of the mountain areas, which resulted in the gradual and consistent degradation of the countryside of the Piedmont region during the 1970s. In this period, he published *The World of the Defeated*, his first collection of peasant testimonies from the Piedmont region.[5] These peasant testimonies became the first collection of rural voices to speak openly and gain a public audience. Revelli's peasant testimonies can be considered, in Gramscian terms, as exemplifications of organic intellectuals. The peasant stories recovered by Revelli express the relationship between Italian peasant culture and the territory and landscape in which they lived. These stories also reflect what has survived and still lives from that culture and those places.

Undoubtedly, Revelli's work presented in *The World of the Defeated*, and in the later publication, *The Strong Link*[6] offer important historical, ethnographical, and anthropological documentation of peasant life. From an ecocritical and bioregional perspective, these testimonies tell the story of how peasants from Piedmont interacted with their environments, and what significance the mountains, plains, hills, and valleys of the region held in their life and culture. These testimonies also tell us what has been lost. Most importantly, Revelli's patient and thorough methodological work offers an opportunity to reevaluate these places and stories from the perspective of bioregionalism.

Bioregionalism transcends the political boundaries of a region, be it a state, nation, or a county, and considers the territory from a "biotically determined framework, primarily based on natural communities and watersheds."[7]After the war Revelli returned to the countryside, the mountains, and the hilly area of The Langhe and saw that the industrial development was squeezing both the peasant world and its environment. Revelli was disturbed by the alarming view of polluted rivers, plastic floating in streams, and mountain valleys covered by waste. Confronted by this environmental degradation and pushed by the desire to learn more about the Piedmontese countryside, Revelli went back to these lands for a sincere and honest encounter with their inhabitants. The stories narrated in Revelli's collections help us to reimagine and remap these areas, deciphering the complex relationship between traditional cultures expressed and practiced by the local peasants and the surrounding bioregions.

These stories and testimonies also offer valuable insights and serve as starting points to present an analysis of histories from below. Revelli's approach can be understood as that of a historical materialist, to use a term coined by the German philosopher Walter Benjamin. Revelli's writing offers a way, as Benjamin defines it, "to brush history against the grain."[8] In his brief treatises on what historical materialism is and does, Benjamin highlights the idea that historians empathize with the victor, and "hence, empathy with the victor invariably benefits the rulers."[9] To celebrate their victory, Benjamin continues, the new rulers march in a procession carrying the spoils, which represent the cultural treasures of the defeated. These spoils "owe their existence not only to the efforts of the great minds and talents who have created them, but also to the anonymous toil of their contemporaries."[10] In contrast, the historical materialist dissociates from the victors as much as possible. The protagonists in Revelli's books on World War II, the Resistance, and the peasants of

Piedmont, are not the generals, the captains, the big landlords, or the industrialists that drove the economic boom in Italy during the 1970s. Rather, the protagonists are the "humbles,"[11] the regular soldiers, the peasant-soldiers, and the peasants themselves. His books talk about the history of Italians with "h" in the lower case, denoting the small-scale, invisible historical actors often obscured or overlooked in the established historical narrative. Revelli, indeed, is interested in the stories of the common people, of those people belonging to the so-called subaltern classes whose names rarely appear in official history textbooks.

Revelli's role and work is not that of the traditional intellectual but is closer to Gramsci's concept of the organic intellectual. According to Gramsci, traditional intellectuals are strictly tied to a profession and hold special qualifications in society, such as scholars, theorists, scientists, etc. Organic intellectuals, in contrast, are less distinguished by their profession, and can manifest, organically, in each social strata. More specifically, Gramsci states, "Every social group, . . . creates together with itself, organically, one or more strata of intellectuals which give it homogeneity and an awareness of its own function, not only in the economic but also in the social and political fields."[12] After the war, Revelli's decision to write did not come from an inner inspiration or a literary calling, but from his own experience as a soldier, and, as he described it, from some sense of "moral duty."[13] It emerged from a new sense of awareness that urged him to tell his story and stories of the war in the first person as a testimony, and from the perspective of the often-forgotten soldiers, a less investigated perspective. Revelli uses a very intimate literary style. His modes of expression appear in the form of a diary, as in *Never Late: Diary of an Alpine in Russia*, (1946) or in *The Last Front*, (1971) a collection of letters of dead soldiers, or even as testimonies from war survivors in *The Road of Davai* (1966). He offers stories from below and gives names, details, and a voice to the soldiers by letting them speak through their own writings rather than simply chronicling their numbers. A soldier himself, he knows that wars are fought by those who combat directly in the fields. In these publications, Revelli favors listening to those who have not been given a voice, and in doing so he is able to present the material gathered in his research with authenticity and without idealizing or exalting these people, the territories, or these times. He narrates the time of war in a simple and immediate way by going straight to the core of these realities.

Revelli's Encounter with Peasants

Revelli connects with the peasants for the first time during the war, before becoming a writer and historian.[14] He first engaged with peasants in 1941, when he was still an "alpino," an Alpine soldier registered in the expert army unit with special training and equipment for mountain service. Although he was a proud member of the Italian army he noticed, without understanding, that the experience of peasant-soldiers was different. They lived the military life as an imposition, "a disease,"[15] and in the army they constantly dreamed of returning to their land.

After the disastrous experience of the retreat from Russia, Revelli fully understood the peasants' position of being neglected and forgotten, and he began to question the actions of the fascists and the role of fascism. Belonging to the generation of "Littorio,"[16] Revelli was used to believing in the party line without question. Only after experiencing the horrors and insanity of the war and fascism during the Russian campaign retreat did Revelli undergo a deep existential, and later political, transformation. This personal crisis led him to join the Resistance as a partisan after the amnesty of September 8, 1943.

Revelli's partisan experience was anchored in the mountains surrounding Cuneo and in the valleys of Gesso, Stura, Grana, and Vermegagna-Roia. These are the valleys where the first partisans' groups of Piedmont named "Justice and Freedom" organized and operated. The surrounding Alpine mountains were wild and untamable, and often reflected the character of the inhabitants: people at the edges, able to orient themselves in wild spaces. Environmental historian Marco Armiero highlights the ways in which fascism transformed the traditional rhetoric of "alpine," Alpine soldiers. Historically, these mountain troops were composed of courageous mountain men trained to protect the valleys from the enemy at any cost, and they were renowned for their fortitude and commitment to the region. Mussolini changed this image by adopting a more aggressive tone portraying Alpine soldiers as fearless men engaged in the name of fascism to build a new empire in distant lands. Under Mussolini Alpine soldiers were not simply valued for their ability and strength to move in high altitude but because, as Armiero stresses, the mountains produced warriors that would preserve the Italian race. Wild nature under fascism was promoted as something to be dominated and domesticated. In this context, mountain people, strengthened by nature, became the prototype of the purest Italian race, embodying Mussolini's dreams of conquest.[17]

Revelli was a mountain man and, although he served as an Alpine soldier under the fascists, his actions and beliefs reflected the traditional ideal of protecting and defending the mountains. During the Resistance the mountains and its inhabitants, these traditionally marginalized wild spaces and people, became the center of action and the source of renewed awareness. Revelli acknowledges that his own survival, and that of the other partisans, depended upon the support from the mountains people along with their knowledge of the territory. It was during the Russian campaign that Revelli learned to appreciate the practical knowledge of the peasant-soldiers. Describing his experience as a partisan, he wrote, "culture means to be able to let a mule walk at one-hundred-and four-degrees Fahrenheit below zero."[18] Mules are hybrid animals, the result of crossbreeding between a male donkey and a female horse. They are known for being hard workers, capable of enduring harsh conditions, and are commonly used to assist with farmwork, carrying heavy loads and plowing fields. Since the end of the 1800s, mules had been adopted by the alpinists to carry weapons and munitions.

Partisans during this period also learned that the accomplishment of simple tasks depended on the collaboration and successful relationships between humans and nonhumans. Mules are known for being intelligent and very stubborn. Taming them requires patience and the ability to direct them without the use of strong coercion that might increase their instinctive resistance. Leandro Scamuzzi, a partisan who joined "Free Italy" and later a political commissary of the section "Justice and Freedom," recalls the transfer from their first headquarters in Madonna del Colletto to Paraloup. During the four-hour march the former partisan describes a skirmish with a mule while trying to load some bags. He comments, "no education degree or school teaches you how to saddle and load a mule."[19] The only one who was able to help was an alpinist and mountain lover who used to hike in the region. Scamuzzi explains that, although it may be simple for those who know how to do it, without experience it can be a very difficult task. If you tighten the girth too hard, the mule slows down because it impedes his breathing. But if the load is too loose, then it falls off the side. Often mules, extremely intelligent animals, inflate their bellies to minimize the cinching; once they exhale, the girth loosens, and the saddle slips sideways.

In Revelli's observation regarding the connection with the local community, culture results from the interaction between humans and nonhumans, acknowledging the natural and ecological context where the peasants live. Cold temperatures and brutal weather in the Alps of northern Italy could not be ignored. The icy cold snow and wind Italian soldiers endured in Russia were relived in the mountains of northern Italy. Experiencing the natural landscape of the peasants as a partisan gave Revelli another opportunity to develop a deeper understanding and appreciation of the local people and their surroundings. Revelli remembers, "The lodges of Paraloup were poorer than the [Russian] izbas, four dry stone walls, a door so short that forced us to bend to enter, a crust of ice as a roof. The wind, passing through, left in the lodges the smell of snow. . . . This was the environment from where my alpinists in Russia were coming from, these were the lodges that [during the Resistance] the alpinists were seeking [to hide] during the days of desperation."[20] The natural landscape of the mountains, the hidden lodges of Paraloup, and the small surrounding mountain villages, coupled with the knowledge of the area by the local people were essential factors for survival, and also supported the partisans' counter attacks against the Germans and the fascists.

After the war, Revelli was drawn to know and understand these people who, during the war, were seen merely as numbers. His experience as a partisan in the Resistance gave him the opportunity to meet them and appreciate their role in the territory. Once again, during the postwar economic boom, Italian peasants, who were historically suspicious of the state, politics, and government, were forgotten and marginalized. In the 1970s, Revelli's attempt to enter the peasant world of Piedmont comes, therefore, from his desire to document a disappearing culture and to collect and preserve honest and genuine testimonies of their knowledge, histories, stories, and traditions grounded in the region. As American author, Kirkpatrick Sale states, "the crucial and perhaps only and all-encompassing task is to understand place, the immediate specific place where we live. . . . And the cultures of the people, of the populations native to the land and of those who have grown up with it, the human social economic arrangements shaped by and adapted to the geomorphic ones, in both urban and rural settings— these are the things that must be appreciated."[21] Revelli embraced this understanding of place. In the 1970s, he went door-to-door among the peasants' homes of the region. He sought to understand and preserve the culture and the place of Piedmont through direct experience.

Revelli's published The *World of the Defeated* and *The Strong Link* respectively in 1977 and 1985. These volumes contain a selection of eighty-five accounts chosen from over 270 audio-recorded testimonies of peasants from Piedmont. They represent a powerful archive of peasant voices, offering valuable and unique stories of life during the period between the end of the 1800s and the first half of the 1900s. Revelli's testimonies do not idealize a disappearing world. He knows that "the ancient seasons of fireflies and songbirds were happy only in the pages written by the 'others,' the literates, the educated."[22] His testimonies speak of migrations, hard work, the war, the condition of peasant women, the material and symbolic meaning of "la roba,"[23] poverty, and hunger. Revelli understood and documented the strong peasant connection to the land, the spirit of survival, the closed communities and typical mistrust of the state—characteristics common to all Italian peasants. He writes, "the history of the poor countryside of the Cuneo area is not a marginal episode, it is not separate. It is the history of half of Italy, of the north as well as the south, of the regions of Veneto as well as Calabria."[24]

The goal is to let the poor country speak through the audio recordings, using peasants voices, so that they can finally "write [their] story."[25] Gramsci's concepts of the organic intellectual and subaltern classes are practiced here through the humble, patient, slow, and thorough task of Revelli's encounters and collection of testimonies. In differentiating between intellectuals of the urban and rural type, Gramsci notes,

> The peasant's attitude towards the intellectual is double and appears contradictory. He respects the social position of the intellectuals and in general that of state employees, but sometimes affects contempt for it, which means that his admiration is mingled with instinctive elements of envy and impassioned anger. One can understand nothing of the collective life of the peasantry and of the germs and ferments of development which exist within it if one does not take into consideration and examine concretely and in depth this effective subordination to the intellectuals. Every organic development of the peasant masses, up to a certain point, is linked to and depends on movements among the intellectuals.[26]

According to Gramsci the respect of peasants for intellectuals is often distant and suspicious. It is the duty of the intellectuals, therefore, to approach peasants and have a direct experience of their reality if they want to truly understand them as, Gramsci believes, the political development of the peasant begins with their guide. Revelli's research method for the book was surely inspired by his wartime collaboration with peasants. He was aware and understood that his role and position could be both a vehicle to enter the peasant world and a possible obstacle. Revelli comments, "It is easy to enter the house of a peasant, where hospitality is part of the tradition. More challenging is to realize a testimony that is the result of an open discussion, of a dialogue in harmony, of a reciprocal commitment, authentic, and constructive."[27] Cautious, skeptical, proud, and suspicious not by nature but by imposition, mistrusting toward the "other" and the State, peasant culture has always been, as Carlo Levi defines it, "a closed world," a world apart. To be able to access their world, Revelli sought the support and collaboration of a mediator, a local person who had gained the trust of the peasants and helped him to overcome Levi's definition of peasants as a separate world. Dalmasin, Revelli's mediator, was a lumberjack who lived in the hill town of San Costanzo, nine kilometers from Cuneo. He organized the meetings and most of the time he personally knew the peasants of the area. Revelli mentions that Dalmasin usually familiarized him in advance with the people he would meet. Revelli notes, "Dalmasin can warm also the most difficult environments. . . . As soon as the interviews begin, Dalmasin helps me with a discretion made of sensitivity, wisdom, and intelligence."[28] Dalmasin was the key figure who helped Revelli enter the peasant world.

As a conscious attitude of respect toward peasants, and as a form of refusal to follow the pace imposed by the new wave of industrial capitalism of the postwar, Revelli admits that "only by imposing on myself a slow rhythm can

I avoid having my research work converted into a mechanical work, into a forced deadline, into a list of testimonies that I have to go through no matter the result."[29] Historically, the process of industrialization has focused on the city, seen as a dynamic process of modernization associated with urban areas as opposed to the rhythmic traditions of rural agriculture. The concentration of population in the cities also contributed to the isolation of the countryside and accentuated the opposition between country and city life. As Emilio Sereni points out, before World War I, Italy's economy was mainly based in agriculture.[30] During World War I, Italy transitioned to agricultural-industrial production, and only after the interwar period did Italy move to a more industrial-agricultural economy.[31] Despite these economic changes across Italy, the peasant population continued to be disregarded, isolated, and forgotten. World War II and the Resistance movement forced, and ironically contributed to, a temporary connection between the two disparate cultures of the city and the country. It is this lost connection between country and city, along with the urge to preserve the stories of a disappearing world, that Revelli was trying to resuscitate. "I run away from Cuneo, a deaf and hypocritical city, and look for the world of the defeated, where a dialogue is still possible, where through dialogue I breath life."[32] While Revelli does not idealize or romanticize rural life, he still finds in peasant people the authentic communication and lifestyle that he cannot recognize in the new wave of capitalism and consumerism.

For Revelli the only way to enter this world was by following their rhythm, their slow pace, patterns, and practices more in line with natural rhythms. Timing, in fact, was essential to entering the peasant world, and winter was the most suitable season because "during the other seasons even the ninety-year-old peasants work."[33] Winter is the time for hibernation for nature and animals. Similarly, even today for peasants and farmers it is the time to retreat from the fields and work inside, at home, or in cowsheds. However, Revelli's perseverance was tested several times when, for example, he went to visit the eighty-two-year-old Maria Isoardi. She turned him away: "I don't have time to waste. . . . Why should I open my heart to you and tell you about my miseries?"[34] When Revelli went to visit her it was the time of milking, and the house was not hospitable. Revelli was aware of the need to overcome the barrier of diffidence built among peasants over centuries of suffering, injustice, and exploitation. Patiently and without expectations, the next day the former partisan went back only to find a spotless kitchen with the coffee machine on the stove and a tray full of food. Most of the peasants knew what hunger was. Offering food, wine, or coffee was the most natural and humble gesture of hospitality. Once peasants let down their guard, Revelli noticed that this atavistic hunger transformed into "hunger to talk"[35] and food became the vehicle to enter, through peasants' words, their hidden world.

The encounter between Revelli and the peasants is a crucial moment of exchange of knowledge in which both the interviewer—Revelli—and the interviewee—the peasant—function as organic intellectuals, although from different perspectives. Gramsci explains, "Each man, finally, outside his professional activity, carries on some form of intellectual activity, . . . he participates in a particular conception of the world, has a conscious line of moral conduct, and therefore contributes to sustain a conception of the world or to modify it, that is, to bring into being new modes of thought."[36] Revelli does not have a traditional academic background, and although his research was often based on original and historical written documents and facts, the best way he knew to reach the peasants was by patiently listening to their stories. He was not looking for direct answers. By being quiet and only sporadically, if necessary, asking a question, Revelli allowed the space and time needed to gain trust and become at ease. He did not take notes during his interviews, because he considered this method and its tools, pen and notebook, an indirect expression of the hierarchical relationships between a literate and most likely an illiterate person. Peasants, on the other hand, open up only if they trust the interlocutor. This trust, as Revelli understood, had to be gained through actions. By returning to Maria Isoardi's house the following day, Revelli demonstrated his sincere and honest intentions.

The use of technology helped to create a more horizontal and objective relationship between Revelli and the peasants he interviewed. "The tape recorder does not disturb, does not distract, and does not intimidate the witness. Sometimes it holds him/her responsible. For the oldest witnesses the tape recorder is just a box, for most of the witnesses it is 'the box that listens and writes everything.'[37] During the interviews Revelli was the witness and the receiver of the stories. Only through the process of writing the books does his role as intellectual and author, organizer and interpreter come to the surface. As historian Lajolo highlights, through his books, Revelli became an intellectual mediator, bridging the gap between two different worlds: the educated world based in print media and the peasant world based in oral culture.[38] Through this process, peasants acquired subjectivity and agency, contributing "new modes of thought"[39] through their testimonies and memories. Thanks to the use of the tape recorder the peasants interviewed did not need to filter their experiences or modify their language, expressions, or their memories. They were able to freely share their world and, using Gramsci's words, by doing so they functioned as organic intellectuals, presenting and defining a particular conception of the world. Finally, if Revelli's work helps to preserve the memory of a vanishing culture, the memories presented by the peasants bring to surface stories that help retrace an Italian history rooted in its peasant culture. Sharing experience, practical knowledge, and traditional practices is how the peasants interviewed have been able to disclose their world and offer essential information to the next generations.

Both *The World of the Defeated* and *The Strong Link* include a long introduction and re-elaboration of the experience and the stories heard by the author. The peasant testimonies presented in the book, on the other hand, do not involve any personal interpretation. In the introduction Revelli discloses that during the transcription he had to adapt the spoken language of the peasants, often dialect or Occitan, and he listened to the recordings at least three times before finalizing the written text.[40] Although Revelli offered a more linear narrative through written language, in the book he never alters or manipulates the style or the content of narration. In the first pages of *The World of the Defeated* Revelli points out that when peasants spoke in dialect, he respected their sentence structure as much as possible, keeping in the written form the most significative dialectal expressions. Gramsci writes, "The problem of creating a new stratum of intellectuals consists therefore in the critical elaboration of the intellectual activity that exists in everyone at a certain degree of development, . . . [which] becomes the foundation of a new and integral conception of the world."[41] Revelli presents a "critical elaboration" of the peasant world and the places where peasants lived. However, the voices of these people offer the other side of the story and contribute, together with Revelli's narrative, a "new and integral conception of the world." Filled with daily struggles and toils and a long legacy of poverty, these stories testify to a rural world that in the 1970s was losing terrain as well as a growing industrial society that was losing its roots. [42] Revelli's peasant voices become the point of reference to understand the social, economic, and environmental changes of the rural society of that time from the perspective and experience of the subaltern classes. In Revelli's testimonies we finally witness the fruitful encounter of two kinds of organic intellectuals, the more educated and the rural. These peasant voices constitute the foundation for the creation of a future generation of organic intellectuals.

Paraloup, a Forgotten Village Filled of Peasants' Memories

No less important than peasant voices are the places where these peasants live. The mountains, valleys, woods, rivers, and plains of the Cuneo area define and influence the life of its inhabitants, just as the inhabitants contribute to shaping the landscape of these areas. Cheryll Glotfelty, Karla Armbruster, and Tom Lynch, expand the definition of bioregionalism beyond the concept of geographical spaces marked by physical and environmental features such as watershed boundaries, soil, and terrain characteristics. In their volume *The Bioregional Imagination,* the editors invite readers to consider bioregionalism as a form of human identity "constituted by a larger community of natural beings—our local bioregion" in which literature helps "people reimagine the places where they lived and their relationship to those places."[43] This bioregional approach offers key elements to understand Paraloup, the Piedmontese mountain village where Revelli's partisan band had its headquarters. Through the lens of bioregionalism, this mountain village, its history and identity, is intimately connected with the surrounding valley and its nonhuman inhabitants, such as wolves, the village's namesake. Paraloup, reinterpreted through the authors' redefinition of bioregion, is a place of Resistance where memories survived and were relived by helping to keep connections with the land, its nonhuman inhabitants, and the surrounding landscape.

Paraloup belongs to the district of Rittana, a small city located at the bottom of the Stura valley, around twenty-four kilometers from the city of Cuneo. In the sixteenth century the surrounding territory was covered with chestnut and oak woods interspersed by pastures and cultivated lands. Peasants mainly grew rye, barley, and fodder and lived in small communities comprising a maximum of twelve homes spread throughout the valley. Cultural historian Walter Cesana notes that the way the local population was organized encouraged the development of small settlements that, according to the size, were referred as "small villages, roofs, or farmhouses."[44] From the end of 1700 through the 1800s, Borgata Paraloup was inhabited by five or six families, totaling approximately thirty people, all belonging to the same family—the Coletto family.[45] The wild nature of the mountains did not facilitate the circulation of people in the valleys and often mountain peasants lived most of their lives in a single place. This was the case of Paraloup where, until the beginning of the twentieth century, intermarriage was still common practice. By the middle of September 1943, when the first partisans arrived on the top of Valle Stura, the small village was already depopulated.

The name Paraloup stems from the Occitan language and literally means "defended from the wolves," formed by the Occitan verb "paràa," to distance from, and the noun "louf," wolf.[46] Local people used to call the village either "Paraluf" — "Paralouf," or "Paralup — "Paraloup," which denotes the influence of the Occitan among the local people, but also emphasizes the common practice of blending the Occitan and Italian in the spoken language, reflecting the French cultural influence in the territory. The locals, when writing, often use the French vowel "ou," pronounced in Italian with the simple vowel "u." Today the official name registered for the village is, in fact, a combination of the two languages. Paraloup, ending with a "p," blending of the French "louf" and the Italian noun "lupo."

The origin of the name Paraloup brings into question not only two different languages and cultures, but also the ancient and conflicted coexistence between humans and nonhumans, specifically wolves. As documented by Walter Cesana, in the first half of 1800, the Alps hosted large numbers of wolves.[47] To control the presence of wolf packs, in 1815 the Kingdom of Savoy supported wolf hunts in the area by offering rewards for killing the predators. After two centuries the wolf population in Italy has drastically changed concentrating mainly in central Apennines. A 2015 study spotted less than a hundred wolves in the Alps.[48] Today, as in the past, the territory continues to be conceived and managed mainly as an extension of human purposes and activities. A recent *National Geographic* article addresses, in fact, that the presence of wolves creates conflicts between local Italian farm communities revealing the myopic anthropocentric vision that fails to consider the function of wolves as a keystone species whose presence contributes to the local ecosystem and sustains the bioregion by helping manage the population of other animals. Italy has been working toward a new management plan for the species since 2015. Yet, the trend of illegal killing persists and the illogical fear of this animal paradoxically has increased in the territories where wolves are less present.[49] Despite this practice of poaching, in 2017–2018 the wolf population in the Italian Western Alps grew, bringing back a total of fifty-one stable wolf packs.[50] The name of the small Alpine village of Paraloup manifests how humans and nonhumans in these mountains share histories, stories, and territories.

The village of Paraloup was popular for its water. Cesana documents that in the first half of 1800, Paraloup provided an important source of water for the surrounding community.[51] Water from the fountain of Paraloup was used regularly by the population of the valley until 1935. While the small village of Paraloup was not populated all year round, its water was used by the local community for water supply and pasture. Until the 1960s it was, in fact, common practice from April to September to graze the cattle on the open meadows above Paraloup. Thanks to the mild temperature of the spring and summer seasons, the abandoned houses and stone huts in disrepair functioned as shelters for the shepherds.

Revelli in his volumes of peasant testimonies reminds us that often the stories of mountain people are stories of hunger. Even today peasant life in the mountains is strenuous and communities are usually poorer than those in the valleys or the plains. Uneven surfaces and slopes prevent inhabitants from cultivating large amounts of land, and severe climate conditions limit the choice and cultivation of crops. The territory, in high elevations, is often public property and shepherds use the land for transit or pay small fees to graze cattle. Before getting married, the family of Maria Goletto, native of the small village of Bicocca, near Rittana, did not have a cart to carry the hay. "My father later bought one," Maria Goletto remembers, "and we had a meadow in the mountains, on the top, two hours [walking] after Gorré, beyond Paraloup, at Taiaré. Eh, my poor mother would carry the two wheels on her head, and my father the ladder[52] on his back, and we would climb the mountain to gather the hay. Once there, we would load the hay bales on the cart and pull the cart through the mountains, pull, pull, and the belly was empty."[53] In Maria Goletto's experience, life in the mountains was hemmed in by work and hardship. Women in the mountains needed to be strong and able to work, because, as she stresses, living in the mountains with no strength to work brings only death.[54] The story of Maria Goletto shared by Revelli invites us to consider that in the most remote areas of Italy rural poverty had similar characteristics, be it in Northern or Southern Italy.

Paolo Riberi, a shepherd from Gorrè, a small village below Paraloup, remembered that as a child while working as a shepherd, he went to Paraloup during the summer.[55] Recalling the pureness of the water, Riberi mentioned a common saying among locals that only the water from Paraloup would produce the best polenta, a simple and staple food common in the diet of peasants of northern Italy. With a nostalgic tone, the old shepherd identified the water as the essential ingredient necessary to make the tastiest polenta. Water indeed has a taste.[56] Its chemical and physical characteristics can affect the flavor of culinary dishes or drinks derived from it. Furthermore, water is the primary source of life for all living beings and, when human impact on the environment is minimized, mountain water is renowned to be among the purest waters.[57] Mountain people knew that nature at that altitude was more powerful than humans and learned to respect and coexist with natural elements. Paraloup, being the last village of the valley, sporadically populated and yet a familiar stop among the local peasant community, became during the Resistance the chosen refuge for the band directed by Nuto Revelli.

The Partisans of Paraloup

In 1943, when "Free Italy," the first partisan group of Piedmont, moved to Paraloup, wolves had already abandoned the valley. The village was only populated during spring and summer seasons. Mario Giovana, former partisan of "Free Italy" and later historian, described Paraloup as a place "sunk in the snow and its solitude."[58] In altitude, snowfalls could last entire days, covering and giving a uniform shape to rocks, shrubs, and trees. Residences, streets, or small trails were concealed by this natural element that temporarily erased any human presence and impact on the natural landscape, returning the mountain to its wild nature. Even today Italian mountains are not very populated, especially in winter, and those who inhabit or choose to live at high altitude need to learn to deal with extreme climate conditions and isolation.

The solitude Giovana referred to can partially explain the intrinsic character of mountain life and the state of abandon of Paraloup.

The original members of "Free Italy" consisted of twelve young professionals, three lawyers, two teachers, two students and five artisans and merchants. They were militant anti-fascists, most of them belonging to the political and ideological movement of "Justice and Freedom"[59] and did not have military experience or any specific knowledge about how to survive in the mountains. They decided to leave the city suddenly after hearing about the Armistice of September 8, 1943, and they carried with them only small bags with some supplies and few weapons. On September 12, "Free Italy" first arrived at Madonna del Colletto, an abandoned church located on top of a hill within an hour's walking distance from Val Gesso and Valle Stura. However, the group realized the location of the church was too dangerous because of its proximity to the more populated centers. The small group began to scout out a more strategic, harder-to-reach location, until they finally decided to move to Paraloup.

The partisans stationed in Paraloup knew that if they wanted to establish a permanent base in the abandoned village, they needed to prepare for the harsh climate conditions and find a way to coexist with the locals of the surrounding villages. As Leandro Scamuzzi, a partisan belonging to "Free Italy," stressed, "we did not want to burden the peasants because of a question of principle, and because we did not want them to become our enemies in a moment of danger. We knew danger would have soon arrived, and they could betray us for fear of losing their belongings."[60] In 1925 Mussolini had introduced the propaganda campaign known as the Battle for Grain with the aim of making Italy self-sufficient in wheat production. As part of this program peasants had to clear their land for grain cultivation. Initially this policy increased wheat production, however in the long run it created serious food shortages and financial difficulty, especially in the mountains among peasants. The Battle for Grain was one of the reasons why some peasants resented Fascism, and partisans knew that they shared a common hatred with peasants for fascists. To gain the support of the peasants, partisans needed to create a relationship based on trust and cooperation. Scamuzzi recalled a meeting with a farmer who was attending his cattle while the band was walking the path from Madonna del Colletto to Paraloup. When the man learned that the young group was going to fight the Germans he offered some of his potatoes saying that he would have given all his belongings to help fight the Nazis and the fascists.[61] The band interpreted this episode as a sign of possible support from locals. While local people often suffered the ravages of war and thus opposed it, it was not always clear which side they might take: the fascists and Germans or the partisans. Historian Chiara Colombini, in fact, stresses that partisan relationships with the local peasants, which ranged from receiving some food supplies to finding a local doctor in times of need, had to be built with careful attention, nothing could be taken for granted.[62] When Revelli moved to Paraloup with his group in February 1944, one of his rules was not to be a burden on the local population and to respect those who were hosting them. He was aware that the partisans would only survive if they befriended the locals.[63]

From September 1943 to spring 1944, during the twenty months of Resistance in the mountains, the support of the local peasants was therefore essential for the survival of the group. Lucia Goletto, one of the last residents of the nearby small village of Gorré and a seasonal inhabitant of Paraloup, was a girl during World War II, and her family was in contact with the partisans of the valley. In her testimony she confirms that local people respected the young group of Paraloup, but she also recalls the impossibility of such a situation wondering if they would have ever survived without the help of local people.[64] She continues by recollecting how her mother would bring the partisans milk and cheese "for free." Lucia Goletto's memory of her mother not asking for compensation reflects peasants' attachment to their land and sense of belonging. However, it also uncovers the attitude of deep solidarity expressed through sharing what they cherish the most, the fruits of their labor.

Peasants manifested solidarity and a spirit of sacrifice toward the partisans often at the risk to their own lives. Local peasants hosted and transported Duccio Galimberti, cofounder with Livio Bianco of the group "Free Italy," to the doctor when the need arose. Caterina Brunetto's family briefly hosted Galimberti when he was wounded in January 1944. She remembers that her husband gave their mattress to Galimberti and said, "When I was an injured soldier in Greece I would have died if nobody helped me. They helped me and now I help others."[65] The neighbor then transported the young commander to Borgo San Dalmazzo the nearest village down the valley, hiding him in a bundle of hay in a small cart pulled by a horse.[66]

Breindl Halpern known as Sara, the "doctor of the partisans," remembers this episode.[67] Sara was a refugee from Poland who, in 1943, was able to leave the Jewish camp of Saint-Martin Vésubie in France and arrived in Valle Stura where she hid until the end of the war.[68] The refugees, like the partisans, were temporary guests in the valley and aware of the dangers the locals were risking by having them around. Sara worked as a nurse to minimize her inconvenient presence. Several times in her testimony she recalled the hospitality of the locals toward her and the partisans. Some details from Sara's memories are useful to understand the tacit support and the solidarity and cooperation between the mountain people and the temporary residents. During those years, Sara helped partisans and locals who, in turn, offered her shelter and food for her services. She remembered that Galimberti, when he arrived injured at Brunetto's family stable, did not dare to request anything more than a temporarily hiding place. It was Sara who asked Caterina Brunetto to bring some rice with milk for the injured partisan.[69] Not only, as Sara recounts, did "that poor lady . . .gladly [do] anything that was asked of her,"[70] but also Caterina risked her life several times to carry messages from the partisans in Paraloup to the base in Cuneo.[71]

Some locals eventually decided to join the partisan group. This was the case for Giovanni Monaco, battle name "Nino," who lived on the eastside of the mountain and joined the group on October 15, 1943. His knowledge of the local territory and people helped the group to effectively use the resources of the land and, for example, how to recognize which wood to use for fire, or whom to contact for their daily food supply. A peasant and a partisan, Nino Monaco in his biography uses metaphors linked to nature to explain the role of Paraloup and the band. Evoking his time in the mountains during the winter of 1944, he writes, "Some groups already detached themselves from us and we lived an autonomous life, others will detach, like *a swarm from a big hive*. The group Free Italy, created by the twelve of Madonna del Colletto, like *a sapling planted in a deserted moor*, grew luxuriant, *plunging its roots* solidly in the ground, and now *it was extending its branches* on a larger ray. The "rebels" of Paraloup became known as the partisans of the mountain."[72]

Nino Monaco uses the metaphor of the hive to talk about Paraloup, and the metaphor of the tree to address the group of the first twelve partisans. He joined the group during the first phase of Free Italy and the group was already large. During his partisan experience he was always stationed in Paraloup. Wild bees usually construct their hives in preexisting structures like rock cavities or trees, usually located above the ground. Similarly, Paraloup was a preexisting structure and not easily reachable. The metaphor of the tree is also used by Alcide Cervi when talking about his family, and Cervi compared the tree branches to his seven children. While Cervi uses the oak as a symbol of longevity and resistance against weather conditions, Nino Monaco uses the sapling to refer to the newly created group and to the young rebels. However, the sapling contains all the potential to grow strong and fertile, as indicated in the second part of the metaphor. It is also interesting to note that the term "rebel" indirectly implies the typical wild and untamable characteristics of the mountains, as Marco Armiero often indicates when addressing the rough personality of the mountain people.[73]

Aldo Quaranta, who joined Free Italy soon after Nino Monaco, refers to the group and their headquarter with another metaphor. "The group of Madonna del Colletto, . . . after few days transferred in Valle Stura, in the farmhouses of Paraloup, will soon represent *the fountain of life* of the whole Justice and

Freedom movement of the Cuneo area."[74] In the mountains public fountains were built by the community to provide water, the natural element and source of life for which Paraloup is famous. The parallel between the benefits of water and the partisan group is clear. Just as water by penetrating the soil nourishes all living beings, and by flowing in streams and rivers reaches distant places, the group through its activities and networking was reawakening a sense of justice and activism against the fascists and the German occupation, nourishing perspectives for a different future and a new life.

These testimonies present the experiences of unrepresented peoples and areas, providing significant historical, cultural, and intellectual insights and disclosing new information about the strategies and daily struggles of peasants and partisans. Also, by using new images and details to reinterpret the events of the past, these people serve as a new stratum of organic intellectuals. Though many peasant testimonies are not spontaneous recollections but answers to some direct or indirect questions, their stories refer to specific and unique personal experiences and memories. Their exposition, oral or written, is the synthesis of a specific way of thinking, of a unique way of conceiving the world that reflects a local culture. Gramsci explains, "the mode of being of the new intellectual can no longer consist in eloquence, . . . but in active participation in practical life, as constructor, organizer, . . . and not just as a simple orator."[75] Although peasants have not always been considered active participants in history, their practical knowledge, cultivated through centuries of experience and constant engagement in the fields, interacting and intra-acting with soils, weather conditions, natural elements, and nonhumans, when shared, contribute to the understanding of peasant culture and a formulation of new epistemologies. The encounter and collaboration between partisans and peasants during the Resistance created the opportunity for peasants to share and make known some of their traditional knowledge. The testimonies of Aldo Quaranta and Nino Monaco are just two examples of this encounter.

September 8, 1943, represented the opportunity to make a different choice than simply blindly or quietly following government orders. In the state of general confusion that day, as historian Claudio Pavone stresses, represented the opportunity to take action. The motivations to join the Resistance were multiple, from disgust from witnessing such terror and death, to rebellion against recent or past injustice, to desire to vindicate the death of a dear one, to antifascism, to love for one own country.[76] Marco Revelli, historian, sociologist, political scientist and son of Nuto Revelli, points out that joining the movement was an individual choice and above all a *personal* choice.[77] The choice to adhere to the Resistance was made in solitude, under an unprecedented historical pressure, but without a sense of hierarchy. It is this historical moment that gave the space and freedom also to the common people, and peasants, to choose a side. The peasants who sided with the partisans became essential assets for the Resistance as their local knowledge and support allowed partisans to survive and succeed.

Nuto Revelli's experience as a partisan in Paraloup confirmed how dependent they were on the local population and their knowledge. He remembers how Sebastiano Vera, after his family was attacked by the Germans and their house was burned, became even more partisan.[78] The stories of peasant Resistance were often even more personal and tied to their local territories. Peasant epistemology, therefore, was based on practical knowledge, tradition, and experience and was intimately tied to the territory. It is this knowledge that Revelli rediscovered in his interviews in the 1970s and 1980s and that he sought to be acknowledged. This is the intellectual legacy left by peasants, the foundation of the new organic intellectuals, including the present trend among young Italians to return to the land.

From a Disappearing World to a Slow Repopulation

In 1984, after almost forty years, Nuto Revelli returned to Paraloup. The Documentary *Le prime bande*, produced by the National Film Archive of the Resistance, filmed and directed by former partisan, journalist and film director Paolo Gobetti chronicles Revelli's return.[79] The film came out after the publication of *The World of the Defeated*. We see images of Revelli and Sandro Galante Garrone, a militant anti-fascist during the war, and Italian magistrate and historian in the postwar era, hiking a mountain trail. While Revelli is walking an old narrow and steep mule path that leads to Paraloup, he says, "dangerous." This single word uttered by a man in his sixties suggests a cautiousness matured with age and experience, but also, and foremost, evokes memories of the Resistance. It evokes the constant risks taken by these young men and how, in dire and threatening times, prudence and safety gave way to a more primordial instinct for survival.

In the scene, the mountaintop looks like an archaeological site. However, the remnants of stone houses evidenced by crumbling walls and collapsing roofs do not convey any traces of the glorious times of the Resistance in the village of Paraloup. They hold a different historical value. They are the remains of a history defined by dignified misery. These ruins are testimony to a past of the centuries-old peasant resistance to the adversity dictated by a wretched life and the more recent resistance of the group Free Italy.

Walking through the ruins, Revelli retraces the different spaces he inhabited during his partisan experience: the dormitory, the kitchen, and the armory. Soon after his attention is caught by the desperate conditions of the small houses. While Galante Garrone and Revelli comment on the state of the ruins, Revelli adds, "These houses were well done, and well maintained. The secret is to fix them immediately as soon as they start collapsing." He then points to a group of ruins, remnants of a house. His comment not only denotes the state of abandonment of the site, but also the lack of will, from the local authorities, to support the survival of the local mountain communities. In the 1980s, Revelli had already published *The World of the Defeated* and had almost finished writing *The Strong Link*. He also had published several books on his experience as a World War II soldier and, although the horrors of the war could never be forgotten, his focus in this phase of his life shifted toward the visible and fast disappearing presence of peasants in the valley. He was aware that peasant depopulation in the small rural villages of the region also signified the disappearance of a culture, and eventually a long-established form of economy and local knowledge.

In the documentary, the houses are inhabited by plants and young trees and are a reminder of the power of nature, of the gradual return to wilderness, but also suggest new forms of coexistence among humans and the surrounding natural environments. Walking among the remains, Revelli adds that the fate of Paraloup is not an exception, mountain valleys are full of semi-abandoned villages where a few people live among the rubble. In Pra Fioretto, a small village reachable only via mule trail, Revelli meets Ghitinota, an old lady who lives alone. She gladly starts a conversation with the former partisan and comments that in wintertime, when snow reaches three or four meters, the next bigger village of San Maurizio is too far.[80] Natural elements paradoxically have contributed indirectly to keep the structures standing suggesting the continuous, dynamic, and porous coexistence and relationship between humans and nature. Ghitinota's small stone house is in fact protected and supported on one side by an old elm, without which, she comments, the structure would be unprotected from wind.

Although most of the old peasants moved to bigger and more organized areas, Ghitinota's recount is an example of those who chose to stay in their native homes and unfortunately, instead of being supported, are isolated.[81] The condition of seclusion and depopulation of Pra Fioretto is, as mentioned by Revelli, a common destiny in many other small villages. According to Mario Cordero, in the area around Rittana there are more than thirty small, abandoned villages.[82] The main wish of those who inhabit Pra Fioretto was not to move but to have a trail big enough for a cart to travel on. Depopulation was not a choice; it was often forced upon the residents who didn't receive the necessary support. Small and simple interventions from the local administration might have helped to prevent a mass emigration of mountain people in the valleys.

Born in Cuneo, Revelli is familiar with the surrounding hills and the landscape of Piedmont and aware of how the natural landscape shapes local cultures. The story of the state of decline of Paraloup mirrors the state of decline of local cultures. The testimonies in *The World of the Defeated* and *The Strong Link* are divided and organized by the geographical areas in which peasants live: countryside, hills, mountains, and the Langhe area, today a UNESCO site and internationally known for its red wines like Barolo, Barbaresco and Nebbiolo. Organizing peasant testimonies by geographical areas is Revelli's way to establish that the landscape and natural settings, up to that time, influenced and shaped human actions, choices, and beliefs in these areas and not vice versa. Revelli comments, "The differences between a small landowner of the mountain and the high Langhe, and a small landowner of the countryside and a low Langhe is often enormous. Not distinguishing, even only verbally, the various forms of agricultures, means to confuse the bone with the meat, melting in the same pot the most disparate and contrasting realities."[83]

Today, in the twenty-first century, when pondering the landscape of the Cuneo area from a train window, or driving by car toward the Stura Valley, it is still possible to admire the green valleys and mountains. Yet, one cannot help but notice the marks left by the industrial investments that began soon after World War II and flourished in the 1960s and 1970s in the countryside. Warehouses, small and bigger factories, some active and some abandoned, often obstruct the view of the surrounding landscape and their foul smell coupled with those emanating from chemical fertilizers in the fields, distract our senses and thoughts away from the agricultural past that has been erased.

The short excerpt from Paolo Gobetti's documentary offers a view of Paraloup in the 1980s and presents a glimpse of Revelli's personality. In a reverse shot, we hear the voice of Galante Garrone commenting to Revelli how the reality of Paraloup is replicated in the many stories narrated in *The World of the Defetead.* The camera slowly focuses on Revelli who, with a tone in between indignation and rebellion, comments, "There are realities that almost push you again . . ." Revelli pauses and while he is looking at Galante Garrone, he smiles slightly. That silence has a stronger message than words and carries the same passion that guided Revelli in his partisan times: a silence reminiscent of the anger he felt when he was working on *The World of the Defeated.* He comments, "to come back to these areas, . . . these realities do not make sense, at 25 kilometers from Cuneo you find realities that . . . scream vendetta." The last word is pronounced softly, as if a part of the author doesn't want to think about war, death, or violence. In the 1980s Revelli witnessed what seemed to be an irreversible process of depopulation and abandonment of these rural areas. As a historian and organic intellectual whose ideas are, as Gramsci stresses, grounded in experience, writing and listening to peasant testimonies provided a new weapon to defend these valleys and mountains.

From the 1960s to the 1980s, the Cuneo valley became one of the most important centers of new industrialization in northern Italy. Many young peasants left their land to go to work in the new factories. Land lost its economic and cultural value. For much of the period, elders continued to work on the farms, sustaining practices and principles of small local agriculture. In these times of social and economic transition from the traditional, family-oriented peasant culture to the newer phase of modern industrialization, younger generations straddled a life in between. Often young people worked in the factories during the week and went back to the fields over the weekend. Revelli understands that it was not possible for peasants to continue such a miserable life. If the big industry did not develop, Revelli comments, most of the young people would have emigrated to foreign countries, as they did in the past.[84] Yet, witnessing the local administration doing nothing to offer alternatives to such a wrecked life, or to avoid the disappearance of peasant culture, did not create a feeling of resignation but, on the contrary, it urged Revelli to continue his research and documentation.

Revelli's attitude anticipates the anger and disgust of present-day environmentalists about the ecological and social damages caused by industry. Witnessing this very dramatic moment in postwar Italy, Revelli saw that the price was visibly paid by peasants and the natural landscape. In the 1970s Revelli recounted the politics of Michelin industry, "The area of Cuneo interests us [Michelin] because it is rich in water. But the "richness" Michelin is referring to is not the water of the Stura river. Michelin aims to recruit thousands of workers, and it would like them all to be peasants."[85] The new industry obliterates Gramsci's hoped-for collaboration between peasants and workers in "The Southern Question." Revelli cannot help but notice that "there isn't any attempt to save at least a minimum equilibrium between the city and the country"[86] or, as he states more optimistically in *The Strong Link*, "my obsession was that we had to save an equilibrium between agriculture and industry before it was too late."[87] The abyss provoked by industry and capitalism permanently scarred Italian soil.

Yet, something has survived, and has resisted. Like heirloom seeds left under the soil, the testimonies gathered by Revelli, have been and are slowly germinating, giving their fruits in different forms and new ways. In 1999, Revelli received the Laurea Honoris from the University of Turin. A young soldier during fascism, and a young partisan during the Resistance and finally, although never an academic, one of the first founders of Italian cultural history, in the last century, Revelli witnessed drastic and significant social, economic, and cultural changes. In his acceptance speech for the award he foreshadowed a revitalization of Paraloup and the emergence of a new peasantry by addressing the younger generation: "I wanted the young to know, to understand, to open their eyes."[88] A few years after Revelli's passing in 2004, documentary film directors Andrea Fenoglio and Diego Mometti returned to the places where Revelli conducted his interviews. After five years of filming and editing, they produced the documentary, *The People Who Are Missing,*[89] which links past generations and realities by comparing them with the current state of the same places. According to Marco Revelli, president of Fondazione Nuto Revelli, by offering images of the places where these communities lived for centuries, this documentary has contextualized and positioned the testimonies gathered by Nuto Revelli. The documentary reveals the emptiness left by the people who are missing by overlapping the voices recorded by Revelli in the 1970s with the contemporary landscape, the abandoned villages, and the suggestive mountains tops once inhabited by those voices. On the other hand, it also explores realities of a new peasantry and farmers who live in the same areas and work the same land once cultivated and inhabited.

In 2006, two years after Revelli's passing, Fondazione Nuto Revelli Onlus was founded. The mission of this nonprofit organization is to "cultivate the memory" by sowing projects that are directly connected to the territory, that can "sprout through young generations and produce culture."[90] Toady Fondazione Nuto Revelli holds the most important archive of oral history in Italy. The small mountain peasant village of Paraloup in 2013 has officially returned to life. Through a patient, methodical and attentive work of balancing history, culture, and environment, Fondazione Nuto Revelli acquired the remaining ruined homes and worked with passion and determination to restore and give a new purpose to the small village. Today Paraloup is a place of living memory (both partisan and peasant), an example of eco-sustainable development, and a mountain refuge, a place connecting humans and nonhumans.

Paraloup today connects past, present and future. The seven surviving houses have been restored, making the signs of the past architectonically visible, combining the old structures of stone with a new wooden infrastructure. Paraloup offers two small restaurants with a beautiful view of the valley, two refuges to host overnight educational groups from schools or simply mountain hikers, a space to organize exhibitions, a hut dedicated to conferences, a hut hosting a permanent video and audio exhibition on the Resistance, and a hut hosting the Museum of Stories. The rocks and the stones of this area are, indeed, filled with stories to share and tell. "The stories come out from the ruins . . . almost naturally undamaged. They are unleashing a new sustainable era. These stories vibrate in the air and transform an inhabited site into a place,"[91] comments historian Antonella Tarpino. It is in those hybrid mountains huts, Tarpino gracefully points out, "that the many narratives of Paraloup will find shelter, walking through the ruins."[92]

In 2023, ten years after its inauguration, and as in *The Strong Link* written in the 1980s, women are the protagonists of a renewed vision and interpretation of rural life in Paraloup. Three young women have managed the refuge at its opening, guaranteeing its availability to the public all year around. They recognized that it was not an easy beginning and that winters are long in the mountains and say that "life in the mountains creates conflict: you desperately love them, but sometimes you also hate them."[93] The memories left by peasants have inspired, and continue to inspire, new generations of farmers to return to the land and their family's original places, contributing to a slow but steady process of re-inhabitation and reevaluation of rural and mountain areas.

More importantly, Fondazione Nuto Revelli and Paraloup demonstrate that something else resists and endures in the collective recounting: a deep respect for the land, for the work put into it and the livelihoods dependent upon it. In 2018 Chef Valeria Morichi arrived in Paraloup. Her work in Paraloup champions local food producers who are in line with conscious ways of production, from their flour to their vegetables and meat. She is working to develop and expand a vegetable garden next to the refuge's restaurant with the aim of becoming self-sufficient.[94] Local peasant culture, traditions, food culture, landscape, the history and traces of Italian Resistance, and the natural resources offered by the surrounding mountains are all giving the space to new organic intellectuals to represent themselves and support the community. Their work, and Paraloup, contribute to put into practice renewed bioregional imaginations. Marco Revelli has understood an essential lesson from the local peasant population and the valleys around Cuneo, "A vocation to slowness and depth—orat least a deeply rooted mistrust for shallow speed—a lesson learned from the mountain landscape, that does not admit shortcuts, and punishes those who run."[95]

NOTES

1. The original name is "Cicloturistapartigiano." This is their Facebook page with their blog history: https://www.facebook.com/cicloturistapartigiano/, last visited on 11/17/2022.

2. https://www.festivalitaca.net/2015/05/cicloturistapartigiano-di-bici-e-di-storie/?fbclid=IwAR0Otv7EYpabTXPOORAuzLiAfHj9EGbi9deKcokZO5f3AODdsxaM5uko6wQ, last visited on 11/17/2022.

3. Italo Calvino, *The Path to the Spiders' Nests*, translated by Archibald Colquhoun (London: Jonathan Cape, 1998), 11. In this quote I refer to the original Italian presentation written by Calvino in *Il sentiero dei nidi di ragno* (Milano: Oscar Mondadori, 2012), ix. Einaudi published the first edition of the novel in 1947, and the introduction I refer to was included in a new reprint in 1964.

4. Ibid.

5. The book does not have an English translation, and the original title is *Il mondo dei vinti*. I will use the English translation *The World of the Defeated* in my chapter, but in the notes and work cited, the page will appear with its original title.

6. The original title is *L'anello forte* and also this book, like all the books of Revelli, has not been translated into English. As for all the books of Revelli that I cite in this chapter, I will use the English title in my writing, but it will appear in the original Italian title in the notes and work cited page.

7. Tom Lynch, Cheryll Glotfelty, and Karla Armbruster. *The Bioregional Imagination: Literature, Ecology, and Place*, (Athens: University of Georgia Press, 2012), Kindle Edition, 2–3.

8. Walter Benjamin, *Illuminations* (New York: Schocken Books, 1968), 257.

9. Ibid., 256.

10. Ibid.

11. Nuto Revelli, *Le due guerre. Guerra fascista e guerra partigiana*, (Torino: Einaudi, 2003), xiii.

12. Antonio Gramsci, *Selections from the Prison Notebooks*. New York: International Publishers, 1977, 4.

13. Marco Revelli, "Non solo un padre" in *Nuto Revelli. Uno storico tra le montagne*, (Torino: Accademia delle Scienze di Torino, 2015), 18.

14. On October 29, 1999, Nuto Revelli received the Laurea Honoris Causa in Educational Science from the University of Turin, as an acknowledgment of his pedagogical talent in making known the history of World War II and after war of Piedmont.

15. Nuto Revelli, *Il mondo dei vinti*. (Torino: Einaudi, 1997), xix.

16. La Gioventù Italiana del Littorio (GIL), the Italian Youth of the Lictor, was a movement of the Italian fascist party established in 1937 as a paramilitary organization to educate young people to fascist ideology.

17. Marco Armiero, *A Rugged Nation: Mountains and the Making of the Modern Italy*, (Cambridge, UK: The White Horse Press, 2011), p. 138–139.

18. Marco Revelli, "Non solo un padre," cit, 28.

19. *Resistenze, quelli di Paraloup.* Edited by Beatrice Verri and Lucio Monaco, (Torino: Gruppo Abele, 2013), 83.

20. Nuto Revelli, *Il mondo dei vinti*, xix.

21. Kirkpatrick Sale, *The Dwellers in the Land: the Bioregional Vision*, (San Francisco: Sierra Club Books, 1985), 42.

22. Nuto Revelli, *L'anello forte*, (Torino: Einaudi, 19), xvii.

23. This word literally means "stuff," and it appears several times in both books. It refers both to the dowry as well as material property in general.

24. Revelli, *Il mondo dei vinti*, VIII.

25. Ibid., xix.

26. Antonio Gramsci, *Selections from the Prison Notebooks*, edited and translated by Quintin Hoare and Geoffrey Nowell Smith. New York: International Publishers, 1971, 14–15.

27. Nuto Revelli, *L'anello forte*, (Torino: Einaudi, 1984), x.

28. Nuto Revelli, *Il mondo dei vinti*, xlii.

29. Nuto Revelli, *L'anello forte*, xix.

30. Emilio Sereni, *La questione agraria nella nascita nazionale italiana*, 31.

31. Ibid.

32. Nuto Revelli, *Il mondo dei vinti*, xxvi.

33. Nuto Revelli, *Il mondo dei vinti*, xxxi.

34. Ibid., xxxi.
35. Ibid., xxix.
36. Antonio Gramsci, *Selections from the Prison Notebooks*, 9.
37. Nuto Revelli, *Il mondo dei vinti*, xxxiii.
38. Laurana Lajolo, "L'interprete del mondo contadino" in *Nuto Revelli, Percorsi di memoria*, a special number edited by Michele Calandri and Mario Cordero of the journal *Il Presente e la Storia,* n. 55, 1st semester, June 1999.
39. Antonio Gramsci, *Selections from the Prison Notebooks*, 9.
40. Nuto Revelli, *Il mondo dei vinti*, vii. Occitan is a Romance language spoken in the southern regions of France, northern areas of Piedmont, and some regions of Spain.
41. Antonio Gramsci, *Selections from the Prison Notebooks*, 9.
42. Serenella Iovino offers an important reading of the peasants of Piedmont and Revelli's work through the lenses of slow violence in her chapter "Slow," in her monograph *Ecocriticism and Italy: Ecology, Resistance, and Liberation* (2016).
43. *The Bioregional Imagination: Literature, Ecology, and Place*, 4.
44. *Resistenze, quelli di Paraloup,* 138.
45. Ibid., 139.
46. Ibid., 9.
47. *Resistenze, quelli di Paraloup*, 137.
48. Lisa Signorile, "Uno, Nessuno e Centomila: quanti lupi ci sono in Italia?" in *National Geographic Italia*, article published on 10/26/2015. http://www.nationalgeographic.it/natura/animali/2015/10/25/news/uno_nessuno_centomila_quanti_lupi_ci_sono_in_italia_-2817615/.
49. https://www.ansa.it/canale_ambiente/notizie/animali/2022/11/23/enpa-i-lupi-in-italia-sono-solo-3.400-non-ce-emergenza_4e76cfc0-c921-4672-81de-11ab3b1fbc65.html#:~:text=La%20popolazione%20di%20lupi%20che,presente%20(Alpi%20e%20Appennini). Last accessed on 02/03/2023.
50. https://www.lifewolfalps.eu/en/the-wolf-in-the-alps/the-wolf-in-the-italian-alps/ Last accessed on 11/25/2022.
51. *Resistenze, quelli di Paraloup*, 139.
52. By ladder, Maria Goletto means the framework of the cart.
53. Nuto Revelli, *L'anello forte*, 121.
54. Ibid., 123.
55. *Resistenze, quelli di Paralaoup*, DVD. The DVD is included with the text and contains recent interviews to peasants or ex-peasants of the area and former partisans stationed in Paraloup during the Resistance.
56. https://www.sciencedirect.com/science/article/pii/S2666821122001697, last accessed on 11/26/2022.
57. https://link.springer.com/article/10.1007/s13201-019-1043-4, last accessed on 11/26/2022.
58. *Resistenze, quelli di Paraloup*, 71.
59. The "Justice and Freedom, "Giustizia e Libertà," I am referring to here is the ideological and political anti-fascist movement originally created in Paris, France, in

1929. The movement conducted an important function of informing and sensitizing international public opinion on Italian fascism. During the time of Italian Resistance, it formed also a partisan brigade called "Justice and Freedom," and was connected with the "Partito d'Azione," "Party of Action," a political party born in 1942 with a radical, republican, liberal socialist, and democratic socialist ideological orientation.

60. *Resistenze, quelli di Paraloup,* 89.

61. Ibid., 84.

62. *Italia Libera. Storia di una formazione partigiana.* Documentary film, RAI, 2019 https://www.raiplay.it/video/2019/04/La-Grande-Storia-Anniversari-La-Liberazione-ad255a77-3d34-4829-94dd-7dd5d2663c27.html, last accessed on 11/27/2022.

63. Revelli, *Le due guerre. Guerra fascista e guerra partigiana.* Torino: Einaudi, 2003, 144–48.

64. *Resistenze, quelli di Paraloup,* DVD.

65. Nuto Revelli, *L'anello forte*, (Torino: Einaudi, 1985), 154.

66. Ibid.

67. *Resistenze, quelli di Paraloup,* 107.

68. *Resistenze, quelli di Paraloup*, 108. Selected passages from Sara's memoir are also present in the volume of Antonella Tarpino, *Spaesati* (Torino: Einaudi, 2013).

69. *Resistenze, quelli di Paraloup,* 113.

70. Ibid.

71. Antonella Tarpino, *Spaesati* (Torino: Einaudi, 2013), p. 55.

72. *Resistenze, quelli di Paraloup*, 122. Lucio Monaco here is quoting the original text from Giovanni Monaco, *Pietà l'è morta* (Milano: edizioni Avanti!, 1955), 69–70. The italic is from Lucio Monaco.

73. Marco Armiero, *A Rugged Nation*, 87.

74. *Resistenze, quelli di Paraloup,* 123. The italic is from Lucio Monaco.

75. Antonio Gramsci. *Prison Notebooks*, 10.

76. Claudio Pavone, *Una Guerra civile. Saggio storico sulla moralità della Resistenza.* Torino: Bollati Boringhieri editore, 2006 (third edition), 31.

77. *Resistenze, quelli di Paraloup,* 14. The italic is from Marco Revelli.

78. Nuto Revelli, *Il mondo dei vinti*, xx.

79. The images of Paolo Gobetti's documentary I refer to are included by Teo de Luigi in his documentary *Resistenze, quelli di Paraloup*. This DVD is included in the book that has the same title.

80. Nuto Revelli, *Il mondo dei vinti*, lxi.

81. For a deeper understanding of the phenomenon of depopulation and of those who choose to stay, read the publications of cultural anthropologist Vito Teti, including *Il senso della memoria. Memoria e storia dei paesi abbandonati* (2014), *Quel che resta. L'italia dei paesi tra abbandoni e ritorni* (2017), *La Restanza* (2022).

82. Antonella Tarpino, *Spaesati*, 52.

83. Nuto Revelli, *L'anello forte*, xx.

84. Nuto Revelli, *Il mondo dei vinti*, l.

85. Nuto Revelli, *Il mondo dei vinti*, xxiii.

86. Ibid., xxiv.

87. Ibid., xviii.

88. Nuto Revelli in *L'Ateneo*, Newsletter of the University of Turin, Italy, vol. 16, no. 6, December–November 1999, 70.

89. Andrea Fenoglio and Diego Mometti, *Il Popolo che manca*, DVD, 2009.

90. "Chi Siamo. Coltivatori di memoria." https://nutorevelli.org/chi-siamo/.

91. Antonella Tarpino, *Spaesati*, 83.

92. Antonella Tarpino, *Spaesati*, 88.

93. http://www.iodonna.it/attualita/in-primo-piano/2016/03/16/le-donne-resistenti-di-fa-la-cosa-giusta/?refresh_ce-cp.

94. https://www.giannellachannel.info/fondazione-nuto-revelli-paraloup-villaggio-alpino-storie-resistenza-innovazione/ last accessed on 11/27/2022.

95. Marco Revelli, booklet included in the DVD *Il Popolo che manca*.

Chapter Three

The Silenced Resistance

L'Agnese va a morire

A WOMAN'S STORY

The first historical books acknowledging the role of women in the Italian Resistance began appearing in the 1970s. More than two decades after World War II, in 1976 Anna Maria Bulzone and Rachele Farina wrote in *The Silenced Resistance* that the Italian Resistance "would not have been developed without the support of women."[1] *The Silenced Resistance* is considered an essential, if not the first, volume to examine the Resistance through the oral testimonies of twelve women partisans. If, as Anna Bravo stresses, the participation of women in Italian Resistance was silent up to this time, the protagonists of this book are finally talking about it.[2] By sharing their roles, experiences, choices, and their memories, they offer a version of the partisan war "outside of the myth."[3] These stories are simple, direct, powerful, and honest. Although the oral histories presented in this volume are narrated by women of Piedmont, one of the regions most involved during the Resistance, their stories speak to the general lack of recognition of all Italian women engaged in the partisan movement.

The testimonies offer new detailed perspectives of the Italian Resistance that go beyond a movement fought with weapons or supported by political ideals. Historians have begun to recognize oral testimonies for their historical and cultural value, and they have inspired researchers to define other categories of the Resistance such as, for example, the civil resistance. This work reveals that the Italian Resistance was, indeed, a resistance of common people exhausted from the war, from fascism, from being occupied by the Germans or simply of being occupied. It was a resistance of people tired of living in fear of death, of being bombed, of seeing their homes and lives destroyed, and it was a resistance of people who refused to go to war. The civilians who joined the

Italian Resistance were women, men, young boys and girls, Italian and foreign soldiers that after September 8, 1943, fled the army and went to the woods, "la macchia."[4] Acknowledging the participation of women in the partisan movement, therefore, offers a broader vision and deeper understanding of the Resistance, including the limitations of established historical interpretations.

In the immediate postwar era, the history of the Italian Resistance focused on the activities of men and sought to legitimize its value in support of political ideologies, most notably those of the left party. The concept of Italian Resistance was directly related to the idea of armed conflict against the enemy, of "armed men defending their country, first serving as soldiers and then by receiving the honors."[5] The first historical publications were therefore dedicated to the military and political resistance, to soldiers who fought the Germans and anti-fascist and communists who organized as partisans. These men gave shape to the political morality in the period between 1943–1945 and inspired the victory of the Italian Republic over the Monarchy in the elections of 1945. Many of the former partisans also guided the writing of the Italian Constitution. Even if the Resistance was in many aspects innovative, it did not change the traditional ideas, hierarchical practices, and patriarchal beliefs of those who participated in the movement.[6] However, the rise and growth of the Italian feminist movement during the 1970s began to challenge this male-centered historical analysis. The women's voices recounted in *The Silenced Resistance*, and the other women's testimonies that appeared in the following years, helped to balance these myopic histories by presenting the actions of strong and determined women. These female voices reveal that during the tragic years of World War II, women abandoned their traditional roles as wives and mothers and learned "to make decisions for themselves, without the help or protection of fathers, husbands, fiancés."[7] They became more independent and took charge of their choices. Journalist and writer Miriam Mafai notes that "coming out from under this role was not always done consciously."[8] It took many years, "at least one generation, for women en masse to be tempted once again to embrace the pleasure of transgression and autonomy."[9]

Why Reread *L'Agnese va a morire*

The first publication that showcased a female partisan protagonist was a neorealist novel released a few years after the war.[10] Published in 1949, Renata Viganò's *L'Agnese va a morire*[11] won the prestigious Italian Viareggio Prize for that year. Feminist author, Renata Viganò, was involved in the partisan movement. In a newspaper article she wrote right after the book was released, Viganò explained that Agnese, the main character, was not fully a fictional character but a woman she encountered during her time in the Resistance.[12]

Viganò stressed that not only was Agnese inspired by a woman the author met during her time in the Resistance, but also that all the details of the novel actually "exist[ed]: actions and men, horizons and villages, colors and temperature."[13] *L'Agnese va a morire* does not focus only on the tragic story of humans during World War II. Landscape, water, climate, and atmospheric conditions also play a central role together with Agnese and the actions of the partisans. Through Agnese's story, the novel emphasizes how during the war humans were connected to and dependent on their natural surroundings. Often the natural elements supported the partisans' actions; yet at other times nature was an obstacle to their success. In this way, the novel brings to light how knowledge of the local area was often essential in the outcome of their actions.

In reading the Resistance as a fundamental Italian civil movement that left a social and cultural legacy for the decades that followed, Viganò's novel provides realistic information about the role of women, more specifically women peasants, both in the Resistance and in their relationship to the natural environment. Read through the lenses of ecofeminism, this essential intimate relationship between women and their natural world, and the elements they have in common, presents a more complex understanding of the Resistance. Thus, Agnese is not only the ideal feminine partisan, as several scholars have noted, but she also represents the caring and supporting characteristics of Mother Earth.[14] Like Mother Earth, Agnese is calm, caring, supportive, and quiet, but also "terrible towards those who attempt to attack [her] laws."[15]

Val Plumwood, in her foundational publication *Feminism and the Mastery of Nature*, discusses how many feminists suspect ecofeminist approaches that foreground the connection between women and nature. They consider this approach "to be regressive and insulting, summoning up images of women as earth mothers, as passive, reproductive animals, contented cows immersed in the body and in the unreflective experiencing of life."[16] While some justification for this criticism has been connected to patriarchal subjugation, oppression and marginalization of women over the centuries, the women-nature connection has been considered only in its negative aspects and consequences. Passivity, on many occasions, can turn into an act of force and often is a characteristic necessary for success.

Plumwood argues that women and nature can create an alliance in which "women *consciously* position themselves *with* nature."[17] She points to the subordination of both women and nature by using the term backgrounding. Backgrounding, according to Plumwood, indicates the way in which both nature and women are treated as inferior to provide the background necessary to a dominant and recognized series of realities. According to Plumwood, backgrounding of women is not a thing of the past and is recognizable in the organization of the economic system and society. Backgrounding of nature, for example, is clearly identifiable in the humans' denial of dependence on the biosphere. Women also are often backgrounded in the public and private spheres by playing traditional, or according to society, secondary roles such as housewives, nurses, secretaries, or in a work environment with hierarchically inferior or less remunerated positions. As Plumwood noted, it cannot be denied that even in current times there are many situations in which women and nature are relegated to subaltern positions, supporting, and perpetuating the dominant patriarchal model.[18]

In the 1970s, cultural anthropologist Sherry B. Ortner in her essay "Is Female to Male as Nature is to Culture?" stirred up debate in feminist and anthropological discourse by critiquing the man/woman and culture/nature dichotomies. Ortner explains the devaluation of women relative to men as a cultural universal, and further stresses that "women are seen 'merely' as being closer to nature than men. That is, culture. . . recognizes that woman is an active participant in its special processes, but sees her as being, at the same time, more rooted in, or having more direct connection *with*, nature."[19] However, being recognized as part of society, and as a participating member in culture, women occupy an intermediate position between culture and nature. The problem, continues Ortner, is not locating women between culture and nature, "as the fact of marginality per se in relation to the 'centers' of culture.[20] According to Ortner, the problem is that this is a cultural construct, not a problem of nature. She concludes by calling for social and cultural change in which women actively participate in the full range of social and cultural activities and, without negating their relationship with nature, women's participation in culture will be an ongoing dialectic *with* nature.

The collection of peasants' testimonies published by Nuto Revelli in the 1970s is a great source of information on the old generation of women peasants as bearers of the traditional knowledge and relationship with nature. Revelli shares that Giovanna Giavelli was born in 1886 and lived her life in the mountain village of Ferriere, in the region of Piedmont. In the 1970s she moved with her family to the countryside. Here is a short excerpt from the dialogue between Revelli and Giovanna Giavelli,

> Revelli: "What do you think of the mountain?"
>
> Giovanna: "I would like to go back."
>
> Revelli: "But no one is in Ferriere!"
>
> Giovanna: "I would go back to my home. I would be the owner."
>
> Revelli: "What is that you liked so much about Ferriere?"
>
> Giovanna: "To work the field, to be in the open air, the good water. Water was wine; it would cleanse you inside. The air, it was like we had wings. Freedom."[21]

Although permeated with nostalgia, Giovanna's words reflect the feelings of thousands of Italian peasants of the time, but they also echo the historical turn marked by the alliance between partisans and peasants. Giovanna could, in fact, easily be seen in Viganò's novel. Her simplicity can remind us of when Agnese expresses her respect for the Commander. Agnese tells one of the partisans of her group, "[the Commander] knows what we don't. . . That is why he is the Commander."[22] With these simple words Agnese accepts that her world, the one of a peasant woman, and the one of the Commander, a lawyer and a communist, are intellectually separate. Yet, she also acknowledges her role and value in the Resistance, and finally admits that "she found herself suddenly immensely grown, important, 'responsible' for incomprehensible actions and unpredictable decisions."[23] Her backgrounding and presence is necessary and Agnese at the end of the novel fully recognizes it.

The way Giovanna uses the word 'freedom' is connected both to her relationship with the territory, and to the attitude many peasants had when fighting against the Germans and the fascists. Freedom is therefore a sign of Giovanna's intimate relationship with the land. Freedom is not so much as an idea, value, or right, but a natural, realistic, and practical way of living. A way of living that during World War II and other times before, many peasants were denied. Freedom was, for peasants, something concrete to fight for against external and visible enemies. Freedom was the price to pay, in the new postwar Italy of the economic boom, to support the industrialization process. In the middle of pivotal postwar social and economic changes, the price was paid mainly by peasants, women, and the natural environment, that were relegated once again to the role of backgrounding as described by Plumwood.

The protagonist of Viganò's novel is between the "conscious positioning of women with nature" as defined by Plumwood, and the repositioning of women in culture as an ongoing dialectic with nature as proposed by Ortner. Agnese's role and character can be interpreted, in fact, in relation to Plumwood's idea of backgrounding and Ortner's proposal of women's intermediate, or mediate, position between culture and nature. Agnese's character, as representative of women partisans during the Resistance, offers an alternative reading of backgrounding. The backgrounding role of Agnese, however, in contrast to the way Plumwood presents the concept is a supporting yet essential presence. Backgrounding, in the novel and its female protagonist, acknowledges the importance of invisible, silent, and powerful forces of life, like the constant presence of the natural elements, or the discreet and seemingly passive role of Agnese, without whom during the Resistance many missions would have failed. The intermediate and seemingly marginal position of women and peasant communities between culture and nature as defined by Ortner, was a critical role in the partisan movement and in this specific crucial historical moment. Acting in the background as intermediaries, women were able to disguise their partisan actions in the community without creating suspicion or attracting the attention of the Germans and the Fascists. In this way, women succeeded in many important missions during the Resistance, demonstrating that both women and peasants were essential supporting allied presences that allowed the partisans to survive and succeed.

The female character of Agnese mirrors the historical, social, and environmental reality of Italian women in the first half of the twentieth century. Her role in the novel also offers the opportunity to review, reflect on, connect, and reevaluate the testimonies of the women partisans and their role in the Resistance. In Agnese's story there are elements of these daring, rebellious, strong and at the same time humble women, mothers, and young girls. These women, while patiently waiting for their turn to execute their missions—most of partisan women are "staffette"[24]—are ready to make their own decisions, whatever the outcome. Agnese symbolizes the women partisans and the landscape; both are necessary and always present, but do not have primary roles. Like Mother Earth, Agnese is the consistent background that sustains and assists her group, quietly completes her tasks, and doesn't ask anything in return. Her actions are not acts of heroism; she does not lead a group of partisans on specific missions. However, without Agnese, most of the partisan missions portrayed in the novel would not have succeeded.

Backgrounding, in other words, is the primary frame to define the success of the Resistance, not secondary. Although it may sound like a paradox, the success of Viganò's novel lies in making Agnese a supporting character. Agnese's backgrounding position is what makes her essential and the real protagonist of the story. Reading Agnese from an ecofeminist perspective aims therefore to revisit what backgrounding means: transforming it from a negative critique into a positive significance. Backgrounding, as demonstrated in the novel, is a crucial component that takes shape in the form of collaboration, collective action, unity and, as in the case of the partisans, fruitfully coordinated events that create successful outcomes.

L'Agnese va a morire presents a very realistic fictional version of the story of the common people, and more specifically of the women among the common people who, without arms, joined and engaged in the partisan movement. The partisan movement for the first time in Italian history proposed a new form of efficiently organized and localized fighters made of volunteers and common people. Writer Sebastiano Vassalli in his introduction to Viganò's novel stresses that, "Agnese . . . is also the collective image, she is one and many, subject and object of sacrifice, a very real character for many reasons but also superhuman for her greatness."[25] The presence of women, peasants and the natural environment in the novel and stories of and on the Resistance bring to surface key social, cultural, and environmental elements that help better understand the legacy left by the Italian Resistance in the postwar and contemporary social structure of Italy.

Agnese and the Partisans: Between History and the Story

Agnese's story takes place between the end of the summer 1943 and the spring of 1945 and is centered on Agnese's clandestine life with the partisans. The novel covers the period from when her husband Palita is captured by the Germans and dies, until her own death. Agnese is a laundress who lives in the countryside of the northern region of Emilia Romagna. She is a peasant, a middle-aged woman, a wife, a motherly figure and finally, a partisan. Her character embodies several key feminine aspects of the women's participation against the fascists and the Nazis.

From the first page of the novel, the author sets the pace of the book offering valuable details about the protagonist's personality while anticipating the main themes of the story. Agnese is going home, carrying a wheelbarrow full of wet clothes on a dirt road among the fields, when she meets a soldier. It's the day after September 8, 1943. On this historic day during World War II Marshal Pietro Badoglio, head of the Italian government, announced the armistice between Italy and the Allied countries through a series of confusing and contradictory radio messages. Several times during the day, the Italian radio broadcasted the following message, "The Italian military forces will cease every act of hostility against the Anglo-American forces. The latter, however, will react against any possible attack coming from any direction."[26] The lack of direction from Badoglio in his radio message allowed each command post to decide what to do: dismiss their soldiers, abandon their post, join the Germans. General Badoglio's radio announcement of the armistice and the change of alliance also officially marked the beginning of the Resistance movement in Italy. History books refer to this day as the beginning of a new phase of the war in Italy.[27]

On July 25, 1943, Mussolini was deposed and arrested, and king Vittorio Emanuele II named General Badoglio head of the Italian government. The change of alliance declared on the radio by Badoglio in September 1943 created the opportunity for Mussolini to reorganize. On September 18, Mussolini announced the birth of his new movement under the name of RSI, Italian Socialist Republic, and he reinforced his coalition with Hitler. Germany's presence in Italian territory in the following months became stronger, more threatening, and more devastating. Italian former partisan and writer Beppe Fenoglio vividly expresses in *Primavera di bellezza* the experience of the general confusion after Badoglio's radio news from the perspective of the soldier: "They were not even able to give us the correct order. We received a shitload of orders, but one was different from the other, or the opposite. Resist the Germans—do not shoot the Germans—don't let the Germans disarm you—kill the Germans—self disarm—don't give up your weapons."[28] Agnese, however, is unaware of this confusion.

The soldier Agnese meets does not have a name, as if in that moment he exemplifies the condition of many soldiers. "He was a small, young, tattered soldier. He had broken shoes and it was possible to see his dirty and muddy toes," Viganò writes. "Looking at him, Agnese felt tired. She stopped and put down the handles of the heavy wheelbarrow."[29] He is young, as were most of the soldiers during World War II, and he gives the impression of a gaunt figure who has been suffering different kinds of deprivations from the war. The portrayal of the soldier anticipates the state of confusion and abandonment of many soldiers in the days following the armistice, and the choice that many of them made to join the Resistance in the following weeks.[30] The soldier's bare feet and broken shoes are a reminder of the lack of material support during the war, and how soldiers had to rely on their physical strength. His muddy feet, in direct contact with the soil and the land, are the sole support of long walks in wide valleys, hills, and mountains. This description foreshadows forthcoming events. In popular partisans' songs such as "Fischia il vento" "broken shoes"[31] symbolized the iconic partisan, and Viganò's soldier can be similarly interpreted as a typical young partisan.

Historian and politician Gaetano Salvemini reaffirms that the radio news of September 8 marked the beginning of the Italian Resistance and brought to the surface two main features of the movement: the massive presence of young people and the participation of peasants.[32] The initial scene of Agnese and the soldier reflects these aspects of the Resistance. What we learn about Agnese first is her empathy toward the soldier. She feels tired when looking at him, and only after noticing how tired he must be, is she able to sense her own fatigue. She is exhausted from her daily routine and work. Her wheelbarrow is heavy and while she needs to rest, the vision of the soldier mirrors her own condition: a shared condition of poverty and hard work.

"But the soldier had light and happy eyes, and he saluted her. He said:—The war is over. I go home. I've been walking for many days.—Agnese untied the neckerchief under her chin, turned its angles on top of her head, and fanned herself with her hand:—It's still very hot —."[33]

The soldier and Agnese, although both tired and poor, have different attitudes about what the future will bring. Full of enthusiasm, hope, and excitement, the young soldier's behavior is countered by Agnese's movements and comments. The late summer heat of September is humid and suffocating across the flat plains of the Valley of Comacchio in Emilia Romagna, and it doesn't allow her to think or immediately respond. While the third person narrator is revealing Agnese's thoughts about the news on the radio, she looks at the soldier and smiles. Agnese's rough smile discloses her tough personality, unaccustomed to displays of kindness or affection. Agnese's face tanned and toughened by the air reflects her social condition as a laundress, a job performed in constant contact with water and exposed to disparate external temperatures. Like many peasants, working outdoors exposed to the vagaries of weather has molded her body and soul. She is physically strong and more resistant to hardship; and through daily confrontation with the challenges of outdoor life, she is introspective and taciturn, and less prone to share her thoughts and emotions. After taking a short pause fanning herself Agnese continues,

> She added, as if she was remembering:—The war is over. I know. Last night everybody got drunk when the radio gave the news—. She looked at the face of the soldier and smiled, a rough and unexpected smile in her face burned by the air.—I believe that the worst has yet to come,—she suddenly said, with the resigned disbelief of the poor; and the soldier rubbed his hands: he was a very happy young boy.[34]

Only toward the end of the paragraph does Agnese disclose her thoughts, an intuition coming from a specific feminine sensitivity. Contradicting the radio news and the enthusiasm of the soldier, she says, "I believe the worst is yet to come." Like the stillness before a storm, Agnese is anticipating the coming events of the war. As will be revealed in the novel, the war is not over at all; rather the Kingdom of Italy has changed allies. Viganò describes the woman's expression as if she is, in that moment, embodying the prudent detachment of poor peasants. The traditional peasants' mistrust of the State and the government, a mistrust grown out of false promises of land and jobs, emerged during the unification of Italy at the end of the nineteenth century, and was perpetuated during Mussolini's regime. This mistrust is well identified in Agnese's skepticism about the news from the radio. Agnese's encounter with the soldier speaks to a realistic scenario of the days following September 8 and suggests a possible encounter and collaboration between local peasants and military soldiers.

In the aftermath of September 8, the German armies occupied Italian territory without much resistance. In this atmosphere of initial impasse many soldiers deserted, wandering in the Italian countryside thinking they would finally go home. Many others felt lost and without any understanding of what they were supposed to do. Historian Sandro Peli explains the phenomenon of "renitenza," the failure to report to duty, or evasion of military service, as a new phenomenon. One of Mussolini's plans during fascism was to control and define the masses by reshaping their values and way of living. September 8 not only marked the failure of fascism's goal but also revealed elements of fragmentation and discontinuity in Italian national history and identity.

Historians Flores and Franzinelli support the jurist Salvatore Satta's idea that September 8 signaled, in fact, the "death of the nation."[35] This date represented the abyss Italy found itself in after over twenty years of fascism, the alliance with Hitler, the illusion of winning the war, the opportunistic behavior of the monarchy and the military commander, and the inability of the government to guide its people. In the middle of World War II, disobedience, desertion, and refusal to go to war, or to fight, became commonplace among the Italian people and soldiers. After living under a dictatorship that controlled people's lives and opinions through fear, according to Peli, "renitenza" reflected the rediscovery of a new individual and collective morality, the ability to disobey and to accept the risks and consequences that independent choice may bring. For those who joined the partisan movement, "renitenza" also meant the rejection of the current state and a renewed commitment to becoming autonomous from any constituted authority.[36] "Renitenza" therefore, in this moment did not simply mean evading military service, it empowered the disillusioned soldiers to go to war against Fascism and the Italian government, and to join the partisan movement.

The testimonies of women who witnessed and participated in the Resistance offer a tangible and realistic version of the partisan movement. The words of the woman partisan Tersilla Fenoglio demystify the rhetoric of the Resistance. She remembers that most of the partisans were not really volunteering. They were adolescents that hid in the mountains to avoid being enrolled in the RSI (Italian Socialist Republic) army. "Darsi alla macchia," to hide out, describes the action of going to the woods. The Italian term "macchia" literally means "spot," like a spot on a garment. The expression "macchia mediterranea," on the other hand, has an ecological meaning and can be translated as Mediterranean maquis. It indicates a shrubland biota in Mediterranean countries typically consisting of evergreen shrubs or small trees. In the context of the Resistance and Italian geography, "macchia" refers to the inhabited areas of the Italian hills, mountains, valleys, woods, or unfamiliar areas of the countryside. These areas are familiar to the local people, but hard to navigate for foreign soldiers. According to Tersilla, most people who joined the Resistance were deserters. Her analysis explains the regained confidence many civilians felt by joining the Resistance, "this is the first time in history that we rebelled against the war and those who supported the war."[37]

Yet, after September 8 locals did not always take a clear position. In the confusion following the change of alliance, historian Gianfranco Bertolo points out that the reluctance of the rural people to take on specific roles did not mean a lack of participation. If approached, peasants would hide, give food, and guide partisans through the territory; and they built refuges to hide the partisan army. Most of the time, however, they did not actively volunteer to join the Resistance. In October 1943, the partisans who were organized in bands received the first instructions from their commanders on how to engage with the peasants. By then the latter had already spontaneously demonstrated actions of solidarity toward "gli sbandati," the drifters, as they were called. "Gli sbandati" or "renitenti" as explained by Peli, were mostly former foreign prisoners of war who had escaped from the camps, or young soldiers and people who were fleeing from the Germans or fascists.[38] Most of the so-called "sbandati" ended up joining the Resistance along with ex-fascist soldiers and civilians. September 8, therefore, as confirmed by the testimony of Tersilla Fenoglio, represented the first encounter and authentic collaboration between partisans and the rural world.

During the Resistance, peasants and women peasants paid the highest price in terms of violence inflicted by the Germans. Due to the geographical configuration of Emilia Romagna, its abundance of swamps and the diagonal crossing of the Appennines mountains, the internal rural areas of this region were often isolated and when attacked did not receive immediate support from the partisans or the Allies. Peasants in this region were often victims of mass slaughters, and women were subjected to sexual violence. Historian Michela Ponzani in her collection of women testimonies during World War II explains that most of the letters, diaries, interviews, and the collections of notes she retrieved belonged to women living in rural environments.[39] Out of 109 interviews, forty-eight women worked as farmworkers, farmers, sharecroppers, and rice weeders, and only 9 women were factory workers.[40] While there were probably many undocumented women engaged in the Resistance who, like Agnese, were not politically affiliated, most women interviewed by Ponzani were communist. The intolerance expressed toward the Germans and the fascists in rural communities, as in the case of the Cervi family, was expressed by any possible means. The region of Emilia Romagna was, during Mussolini's dictatorship, a strategic geographical area for the spreading of anti-fascist sentiments and the communist ideology. Peasants became fully supportive of the local partisans, many joined the communist party, or directly joined the Resistance.[41]

The relationship between partisans and rural communities therefore is not homogenous, and the stories and experiences shared by the women are not the same. Ponzani explains that women's attitudes and choices often depended on their social, cultural, and economic status. In Emilia Romagna, for example, the daughters of peasants who were politically involved during the 1920s were persecuted and suffered retaliations from the German and RSI soldiers throughout World War II. In contrast, elite educated women could leave the country or take refuge in their holiday homes and live more securely.[42] The autonomy and self-government of the so-called "free zones" and "partisan republics" managed by the partisans was limited to some valleys and mountains of the Alps and Appennines, such as the area around Asti, the valley of Ossola and small areas of Emilia Romagna.

Often peasants saw the partisans' presence and the Resistance movement as an interference. Marisa Sacco was a woman peasant who operated in the division of Giustizia e Libertà, Justice and Freedom, under the command of Giorgio Agosti, in the Piedmont's Langhe Valley. Her memories reveal a sense of isolation and sometimes solitude. "There is a problem that lately is tormenting me: too few women gave their contribution to the Resistance."[43] She refers to the lack of support from some peasants during her missions in the valleys when she was asking the locals if she could spend the night in their home. The understanding, experience, and participation of peasants in the war reflected the class and gender disparity between the rural and urban worlds. Marisa's testimony brings to the surface another important element of the Resistance: the importance of establishing a relationship with the locals in order to receive their support.

Women Peasants and Partisans: Agnese. A Woman and a Partisan

The tension and distrust of Agnese with her neighbors intensifies after Agnese's husband, Palita, is captured by the Germans. Viganò presents another very plausible situation. While Agnese follows Palita's steps and begins to collaborate with the partisans as "staffetta," her neighbors establish friendly relationships with the fascists and the German soldiers, opening their houses to them. If Bertolo claims that peasants did not take a clear position after September 8, Ponzani observes that peasants were forced to take a side, and the Italian rural world was actually the perfect place to investigate the relationship between civilians and partisans.[44]

The episode of Palita's black female cat represents the turning point in Agnese's life. "I recommend the cat,"[45] says Palita when he is captured and is carried by the Germans in the bus. The black cat is the last link between Agnese and her husband. It also connects the protagonist to her home as a domestic, private, and safe space. The black cat, whose name is unknown or that maybe has no name, plays a critical role in Agnese's life and future after Palita's arrest. Historian and writer Piero Bevilacqua points out the general awareness peasants had about the value of domesticated animals in farm production. This implied awareness encourages farmers to care for, protect and value cows, sheep, goats, and chickens by building more stables, fences, and by focusing more on the wellbeing of their domesticated animals.[46] Cats and dogs, however, don't directly contribute to farm production. Nevertheless, they are always present, and they have a double role in their relationship with humans on the farm. They are working animals as well as companions. While dogs work with the shepherd and guard the farm, cats can save entire harvests in barns and stored food in homes by chasing rats, mice, and cockroaches. Cats and dogs are both outdoor and indoor animals and provide company for their caring humans companions. As Viganò writes, "Agnese caressed the cat's shiny and thick fur, feeling the vibration of the whole body as if there was a motor inside. That humming brought peace in the kitchen, the peace that once used to be in the house. But now Palita was dead and outside Minghina and her daughters were still talking to the Germans."[47]

Donna Haraway's perspective on the transformative experience of human encounters with other species is useful to understand how Agnese is affected by her new and transformed relationship with Palita's cat. Haraway argues that "Touch, regard, looking back, becoming with—all these make us responsible in unpredictable ways for which worlds can take shape. In touch and regard, partners willynilly are in the miscegenous mud that infuses our bodies with all that brought that contact into being. Touch and regard have consequences."[48]

The consequences of this new relationship between the black cat and Agnese are, indeed, transformative, and fatal at the same time. We learn about the cat for the first time when Palita is taken by the German soldiers. Agnese's reaction to the presence of this domestic animal is, at first, one of displeasure and disregard. Palita's absence, however, becomes the reason of their strong bond. They both miss him and through each other's presence, and touch, they fill the void of his absence. The cat helps Agnese to reconnect in unexpected ways not only to her husband, but also to herself, as a woman, ex-wife and soon, as a partisan. The relationship Agnese and the cat establish guides the protagonist to get in touch with her emotional intelligence and a renewed inner strength. Touching the cat is not simply bringing back memories of peace, it is also allowing Agnese to live them again. The encounter, presence, and relationship with the cat is the connector to a more profound and unexpected version of Agnese.

The tension between Agnese and the neighbors reaches its climax when la Minghina accuses the black cat of having stolen a sausage. Although we learn soon after that the cat has a mouse in her mouth and not the meat of the neighbor, the cat's fate is marked. The German marshal, who wants to spend some time with one of Minghina's daughters, orders a drunken German soldier, Kurt, to kill the cat. Unaware and inebriated, Kurt's fate is forever changed by killing the cat, as is the destiny of Agnese.

Agnese's response to this sudden and appalling event is at once surprising and revealing. In a state of shock, Agnese grabs the cat's corpse from the ground and spends the rest of the afternoon sitting on the grass under the peach tree in front of her house. The time spent in contact with the soil, the blades of grass, and the coolness provided by the shade of the tree prepare Agnese for the next decisive and fatal move. Kurt is asleep in Agnese's kitchen with his head on the table holding the dark machine gun at his side.

Without second thoughts, as if completing her domestic chores, Agnese acts. "She grabbed the machine-gun, lifted it, and suddenly lowered it on Kurt's head, like when she used to beat the heavy wet sheets on the wash-house."[49] She doesn't know how to use a gun, but her muscles have been trained to perform mechanical and powerful movements, and these movements come naturally. Agnese knows there is no turning back from this action. At the end of the chapter Agnese leaves her house and crosses to the other side of the canal. She looks back at her house in flames. "Then Agnese got up, determined and calm. She followed the path along the canal bank, crossed the fields and arrived at the opposite way of the valley. Walking quickly, she said:—Enjoy the Germans!"[50]

Agnese's final words speak to the values common to Italian women who joined the Resistance. As Bruzzone and Farina indicate, women brought to the Resistance qualities such as spontaneity, modesty, a sense of justice, sacrifice, the ability to read and accept events with an antiheroic attitude giving the movement a new depth. [51] For many women living in the countryside and in the mountains, embracing the anti-fascist movement was the direct consequence of witnessing years of tyranny suffered by their families, first from the fascists and later from the German occupiers.[52] The antiheroic attitude, sense of sacrifice, modesty, and spontaneity the authors refer to are translated into the humble attitude of Agnese's personality.

Only after Palita is captured and dies does Agnese fully commit to the partisan movement. The group of communist partisans, with whom Palita is previously involved, asks Agnese to participate initially as a "staffetta," carrying messages or items on behalf of the partisans between different encampments. "Staffetta" is a term specifically used to address women who volunteered and worked in incognito to help the partisans. According to Anna Bravo, this term is a generalization of the role women took on outside their usual domestic domain.[53] Bravo stresses that it is important to acknowledge the often-essential role of the "staffetta" and the fact that, within the Resistance movement, women's work was considered with respect and admiration.

Tersilla Fenoglio Oppedisano, a peasant from the Langhe, in an interview with Nuto Revelli, recalls her experience as "staffetta" and declares that in her group she was considered part of the family.[54] "In the group I was not a woman but a sister. There were no rude jokes, and no one would touch me. If a man had offended me, he would have been attacked by ten of them. I was surrounded by a familiar environment. I was sleeping among them, shoulder to shoulder, I was the only girl of the faction."[55] Tersilla is appreciated and valued for her work and contribution to the partisan movement and is respected as any other member of her group. Nonetheless, she is the only woman in the group, and she represents the minority, as previously noticed by Marisa Sacco.

These feminine qualities are well represented in Agnese's interaction with the partisans. She is always described through her modest yet dependable and courageous participation; her simple and unpretentious attitude never changes, even when her tasks require higher responsibilities. "If I am good at it. . . —When she was asked to participate on a mission, she always replied like that."[56] Agnese's response signifies that although she has never done anything like this before, she will strive to accomplish her duty. Her practical and realistic attitude is exemplified in this modest yet powerful comment that demonstrates her loyalty to the group. Although her recurring comment might be interpreted as lack of self-confidence, on the contrary, it is a clear sign of humility and simplicity. These human qualities, always in the background, are essential in identifying Agnese's personality and character in the novel. Her practical wisdom reveals an unpretentious honesty that does not allow her to make false claims.

The protagonist displays her pragmatic nature on several occasions, which is often noticed and highlighted by her companions. During the coldest part of the winter, the supplies for the group are almost depleted, and "the Commander" reads a letter aloud ordering the group to dissolve until springtime. Among the general atmosphere of disappointment, the partisans begin complaining and ask Agnese's opinion. Her reply is short and direct, "What do you say, mama Agnese?—I don't understand anything,—she answered, removing the pan from the fire,—but one does what must be done. Agnese was right. 'One does what must be done.' She was used to counting little on others. All her life, more than fifty years, she had managed on her own."[57] Agnese's inner and physical strength, yet quite assertive personality, coupled with a sense of isolation in a century-old rural patriarchal society speaks for the general conditions of peasant women. As the novel progresses, Agnese increasingly acquires psychological independence and inner determination.

Marisa Ombra's insights and testimony about her experience as a partisan woman confirm the plausibility of Agnese's character. She explains, "For the first time in the Resistance we women did not feel like mothers or daughters. Rather people, along with other people, who were doing something that simply had to be done. And this work was considered with a lot of respect."[58] Ombra's personal experience clarifies Viganò's choice of portraying Agnese as a childless woman. This characteristic echoes a common reality among many partisan women without depriving the character of their feminine qualities. The necessity of acting together and uniting under the common interest of fighting against the fascists and expelling the Germans from Italy, displaces the division between genders.

Ombra's acknowledgment of the practical side of women is very much alive in Agnese. She constantly displays it together with her spirit of sacrifice and dedication, qualities often present in peasants that could be considered marginal but that became critical in dire moments during the Resistance. These motherly backgrounding elements presented at the beginning of the novel function therefore as essential links to the physical and moral survival of Agnese's brigade without upsetting traditional social and gender differences.

Agnese's age and physical appearance also contribute to her role as a mother and support her backgrounding role. "Mamma Agnese" as she is often called is, like Mother Earth, a caring, trustworthy, and nurturing point of reference for the partisans. Like Mother Earth, she humbly offers herself until her death at the end of the novel. "She had been with them like their mother, without any rhetorical implication, without saying: I am your mother. This had to be demonstrated through facts, through work. Preparing food, making sure they had everything, washing their things, keep moving to make sure they were well."[59] Partisans lived in the open air and were subjected to the weather: the humidity of the river valley, the cold wind and the snow of the winter. When she is not engaged in specific missions Agnese is knitting socks for the winter; she is finding shoes for the partisans by networking through her local connections; she is cooking for everyone and is the last one to eat.

Involved with a politically engaged partisan group, Agnese slowly and discreetly develops a political awareness, a sense of responsibility for her role, and a conscience about her actions. Agnese is portrayed as a poor woman peasant who "unexpectedly" finds herself part of the partisan fight. Her hatred and resentment of the Germans and the fascists results from the personal abuse she and her husband have suffered. Soon after killing the German soldier Agnese is relieved and filled with pride. She is a woman and a peasant, two subaltern realities within the context of the war and Italian history and culture.[60]

After joining the Resistance, she begins to realize the consequences of her actions and her role in the band. As Ortner stresses, Agnese becomes aware of her active cultural and social contribution to the Resistance. This passive, middle-aged woman develops a new form of compassion paired with an increasing social sensitivity. "Now she understood that her gesture had caused a slaughter, and she was afraid for the pain that submersed her village."[61] At the beginning she does not participate in the group's discussion, and her engagement is marked by her immediate actions. During the winter, as provisions become scarce, Agnese's knowledge of the local territory and community becomes essential to the group. She is now in charge of the "staffette" of the area and in this new acquired role she gains a new political awareness. "She was traveling the same road when she brought the TNT for the bridge, almost a year earlier. Work, fear, and deaths. Back then her body was stronger, and it would take longer to understand; now her mind was faster, but her body was weaker. . . . Like her, also her comrades, the directors, the "responsible":

everyone was paying dearly for their responsibilities. . . Damn the war and those who wanted it, —concluded Agnese, tired of thinking."[62]

Emilio Sereni defines the collaboration between partisans and peasants as a patriotic battle to expel the Germans from Italy.[63] For peasants, this patriotic element is a form of organic patriotism from below and can be identified as well in the character of Agnese. This form of patriotism, as Sereni describes it it, developed without the support of any specific ideological or political structure, and was mainly contingent on practical situations or personal experiences. The main goal for the peasants was the protection of the land, and only secondarily, the country. Former partisan Pina Palma rightly observes that the lack of ideology in Agnese's character is due to the gender divide.[64] Although her remark reflects the Italian century-old historical gender division Agnese's lack of political awareness is mainly due to the peasants' social and political isolation caused by historical oppression and geographical separation.

Many of the testimonies gathered by Revelli disclose an attitude like that of Agnese. The decision on the part of peasants to support the partisans is not dictated by some patriotic idea or national pride, but is driven by "an instinctive choice, more human than political."[65] Tersilla Fenoglio Oppedisano, a woman peasant, stresses the inherent spontaneity and promptness women and peasants expressed in choosing a side, "If [the partisans] told me: "shoot yourself out of a cannon," I would have shot myself out of a cannon. I was sure they were on the right side. I understood little or nothing about politics, I did not know what class struggle was. But I felt a great admiration toward my masters, I never met such men."[66] Oppedisano's dedication and devotion to the partisans comes from a personal and human perspective; she learned about their political orientation by witnessing partisan actions and discussions. She fully trusted, without any condition or reserve, the people she worked with and her partisan group. She was ready to die for them. She was not fighting for any specific ideology while she was risking her life during the Resistance.

Similarly, only toward the end of the novel does Agnese come to understand the spirit behind the actions of "the Commander" and the partisan agenda. Agnese is guided by her hatred of the Germans and the fascists, a hatred conditioned by the death of her husband. After living for months in direct contact with the partisans, Agnese begins to develop a political awareness and class-consciousness. Thinking of the time her husband was meeting with his communist companions, Agnese discloses a new level of understanding. "Now, on the other hand, she could talk with Palita. She knew much more. She understood what in the past she would call "men's business," the party, the love for the party, and that one could get killed to support a beautiful idea, an instinctive power, to solve all the dark mysteries, that begin in childhood and end when old people die."[67] Agnese's political ideology is linked to her partisan experience and the political discourses she hears among the group members. However, her thoughts reveal a sense of class separation. Agnese sees them as "educated people, who understand and love everybody, they don't ask anything for themselves and work for the wellbeing of others while they could do without it, they face death while they could have money, and live peacefully until their old age. . . . This was the party, and it was worth being killed for."[68] Agnese embraces this political ideology because of the trust and loyalty built through her experience living with the brigade, a trust that grew out of her relationship with the Commander and her active involvement in the partisan missions.

The Natural Environment: Water and Marshland

The knowledge and experience of the geographical areas shared by peasants and local communities with the partisans, defined a bioregional perspective that shaped the Resistance and the stories about the Resistance presented in the novel. Surviving in "la macchia" and living the clandestine life as partisans required not only connection with the local population, but also familiarity with the local territory and the climate conditions of the area. The main advantage of the Resistance was to be able to move around and hide in geographical locations not patrolled and unfamiliar to soldiers. Set in the brackish lagoons of the Comacchio Valley of the northern region Emilia Romagna, in the plain of the Po Valley near the Adriatic coast, *L'Agnese va a morire* offers a story of the Resistance of the common people in which natural and human elements coexist as co-protagonists of the events. The interdependence between partisan activity and their natural surroundings is evident in each chapter of the novel and in Viganò's narrative style. Gary Snyder's definition of bioregion is essential for understanding the interconnection between humans and their natural environment. Considering the boundaries of a territory more for its geographical and natural characteristics than its geopolitical implications, Snyder stresses how "our relation to the natural world takes place in a *place,* and it must be grounded in information and experience."[69]

The local inhabitants were connected to these bioregions through a "local sense of place."[70] As landscape architect and scholar Thayer Jr. defines it, "A bioregion is literally and etymologically a "life-place"—a unique region definable by natural (rather than political) boundaries with a geographic, climatic, hydrological, and ecological character capable of supporting unique human communities."[71] Natural environments—be they the coast of the Mediterranean Sea, the vegetation and animals in the mountain woods, or the crops, the fields, or the swamps of the countryside—affect human lives and choices. Agnese represents the critical geographical link with the Comacchio Valley, and on several occasions her familiarity with the natural surroundings helps the brigade survive. In wintertime the icy cold temperatures and humidity of the Comacchio Valley swamps slow down the advancement of the Germans, but they are also terrifying for those who never lived near stagnant waters. With the help of Agnese's knowledge of the area, the partisans of her band found an isolated house to hide in surrounded by a swamp and reachable only by boat. In this remote enclave, the partisans began to lack food and started to become sick. During a conversation with the commander of the band Agnese comments, "They are afraid: everyone is afraid of water."[72] The commander, however, explains that if they were on the ground they would have probably died. "Large water, open water, crossed by flowing canals and wind blowing from the seacoast. . . . Hunger, cold, confinement. Winter sided with Agnese's sentiments."[73] Agnese's reply to the commander is based on her experience of this specific bioregion and her familiarity with the extreme winter and summer climate conditions of the Comacchio Valley.

The book is divided into three parts, and each section is characterized by a season. It begins with the burning heat of the summer in part one, the humidity of the rainy season in the second section, and the brutal cold of the winter caused by the winds and the snow in the last part of the novel. Agnese's relationship with the bioregion is lived and expressed also through natural and spontaneous comments that, although seeming innocent, allude to the ignorant and destructive power of the air force. At the beginning of the novel, after killing Kurt, Agnese reaches the canal.

> Agnese proceeded along a canal and arrived at the riverbank. She struggled to pass through it because it was high and steep. She descended the other side of the riverbank until she reached the trail by the shore. The moon emerged, and the water was white, it looked like a road. 'It must look the same from the sky—Agnese thought—that's why often the British airplanes throw by mistake bombs in the river.[74]

The depiction of Agnese in the wetland offers an example of how natural elements are both dominant and at the same time deceptive for those who are not familiar with the area. The bird's-eye view of the bombers could only have a limited and superficial view and understanding of this semiliquid landscape. The prevalence of water in a swamp region like the Comacchio Valley functioned as a natural border and created physical obstacles for locals as well as outsiders. Blurred and distorted by the moon's light, rivers, swamps, and water intertwined with human interventions like riverbanks, trails, or unpaved roads, and confused the military forces. The pale and surreal nocturnal light deceived the human perception of the surroundings blurring fluid elements with solid man-made entities.

The Po River delta in Emilia Romagna has changed its shape and path over the centuries. Known also as "delta Padano," it was initially mapped by the Romans and remapped during the Middle Ages. Today the Po River reaches the Adriatic Sea in the northern region of Veneto. It is not considered an active delta, but an inactive "fossil" delta characterized by humid areas named valleys. The term valley, however, is not used to refer to the mountain valleys formed by glaciers, but to indicate hollowed wet areas near the sea, shaped by the rivers' flow and filled by salty waters. Like the Comacchio Valley, these valleys are sometimes below sea level.[75]

The land recovery projects implemented in the last two centuries have further contributed to transforming the landscape of the Comacchio Valley. During the Fascist Regime "bonifica," or agrarian land reclamation, was a key word used by Mussolini to generate more productive agricultural land in the Italian territory. According to Marco Armiero, Mussolini's land reclamation did not simply aim to regenerate the land, but also to regenerate Italians. "The agrarian land reclamation implied the so-called human reclamation, namely the Fascist project of "improving" not only the "external" nature, but also the "internal" nature, of people and places at the same time."[76] In the eighteenth century, landlords or small private organizations financed land recovery projects to improve Italian territory and landscape. Under fascism, for the first time, land reclamation projects were sponsored and publicly funded at a national scale by the State.

During the twenty years of the fascist regime, Mussolini focused on developing a more technologically sophisticated country through the mechanization of agriculture, the introduction of chemical fertilizers, and by supporting mass migration of the mountain population to the rural plains, and from the rural plains to the cities. Through its propagandistic plan to transform the rural world to support a new technological expansion, the fascist regime ended up exploiting rural resources in favor of industrial development. While reinforcing old traditions such as the patriarchal social system, fascism supported an authoritarian and male-centered organization of work and society, which continued to leave women invisible and voiceless, and gave more power and control to landowners, keeping peasants and labor in a position of dependence.[77]

In the first half of 1900 Comacchio's economy, the small village located in the island of this valley, was based on eel fishing and salt production. While eel fishing was controlled and managed by the local authorities, a large portion of the local people practiced illegal fishing.[78] Only the locals knew the wetlands well enough to escape local control. In this area poachers were socially accepted criminals and when caught and imprisoned, they were quickly released. In the small community of Comacchio many families were related to each other, and it was common to have in the same family an official working with the local authority and a poacher.[79]

Agnese's familiarity with the bioregion is strengthened by belonging to the local culture and social structure. She is aware of the presence of illegal fishermen and knows where they hide. The readers learn that poachers used reeds to build huts during the summer to fish when the guards were not around. Her knowledge of the local territory assures the survival of the partisans. "In that area of the valley devoid of roads, bridges, and houses, protected by abandoned canals, desolated reed beds, mud, large sluggish ponds. There would not have been attacks, nor battles, nor bombardments, nothing. A wild landscape left behind when the time would have come; here the residents thought to save themselves when their village was invaded."[80] Although unruly, this environment is instrumental to the partisans' survival. In the hot summer the reeds help to hide even if they don't offer any shade. Viganò's description of the summer heat is presented by the sun that burns on the water.[81] We also learn there is no drinking water, a reality common to many areas where the Resistance operated. Agnese therefore has no other choice but to cook using the marsh water, "rather murky and dirty: she removed the foam with steel wool and tossed the pasta."[82]

The climate conditions and the seasons, however, were even more unpredictable and often challenged the emotional and mental strength of the partisans. Agnese, nevertheless, is rarely discouraged by the weather, and despite her age and heaviness, she continues her duty undismayed.

> Agnese grabbed the umbrella, the two full shopping bags, went out in the field and reached the usual place. Since that morning, it was the third time she had gone there. Two women were missing, maybe because of the season. "They might have got sick with this rain,—thought Agnese,—or they may not want to come.' They were not wrong: it was a hard life. . . Her feet were always wet, and now she also had to wear the slippers, the shoes were too tiring for her. The canal was not too far. She closed the umbrella and got more rain on her back. 'A little more, a little less it doesn't matter,—she thought,—now it rains softly.'[83]

Agnese is at ease in her bioregion. It is autumn, and she oversees the provisions for the partisans hiding in the huts. Once again, the dominant presence of water controls human actions and gives more relevance to Agnese's role. The absence of the women is juxtaposed by Agnese's strength and endurance, and she can cover for two women. However, Agnese does not lack compassion or understanding. She knows the sacrifices and dangers everyone is exposed to in supporting the partisans.

Agnese's constant and conscious alliance with the natural environment is paired with her backgrounding position. Her motherly and generous personality, compensated by her resolution to complete her mission, even at the expense of her own health, results in the image of a woman peasant accustomed to living and dealing with natural elements. The soldier at the beginning of the novel had broken shoes and muddy toes. Agnese, in this last part of the novel, is fully involved in the partisan's fight, and her feet are tired and constantly wet. As with the soldier, Agnese's feet represent her roots and connect her to the soil. Like the soldier, and many partisans, Agnese's feet allow her to be operative and efficient. Sacrifice and endurance are part of her and become essential for her survival and the success of her missions.

Agnese Is Not a Fantasy

Soon after the publication of *L'Agnese va a morire,* Viganò wrote an article in the communist party newspaper *L'Unità*, titled "The Story of Agnese Is Not a Fantasy."[84] Like Revelli, Calvino, Fenoglio, Stern, and many intellectuals of the postwar generation, she also was an former partisan and had direct experience with the local people while in the Resistance. The author makes a clear connection between the fictional representation of Agnese and the testimony of rural women partisans whose role was so important in the Resistance. In Viganò's account, the general atmosphere that pervaded the resistance stands out as an "anti-heroic, anti-dramatic, and domestic"[85] climate that pervades the life of everyone, from the peasant to the fugitive, to the citizen, and the intellectual. This climate is reproduced in Viganò's novel and is particularly common in peasant cultural tradition, a culture that soon after the war, in the euphoric economic boom of the 1960s, was once again gradually forgotten.

Viganò offers us an example of this feminine peasant marginalization in *Mondine,* a well-documented short collection of testimonies of rice-weeders published in 1952, a few years after *L'Agnese va a morire.* This publication documents the brutal reality of rural women as a common practice even after the war. "Mondine," or rice-weeders, were women who, from the end of the nineteenth century worked seasonally, from April to June, in the rice fields of the northern regions of Emilia Romagna, Piedmont, Lombardy and Veneto. During these months, thousands of women migrated from all over Italy to work in poor conditions as rice-weeders. The job consisted of standing in water up to the knees and clearing weeds that interfered with the rice seedlings. "A life like animals, a life of injustices and oppressions and abuses; as if the masters had bought for thirty days a herd, and they could throw it here and there, for as long as they wanted, overloading it with work, degrading it with strain, and then giving a handful of calculated money, inspected, coming out with difficulty from their full pockets."[86] As the testimonies included in this valuable document testify, the rice-weeders worked over eleven hours per day and ate only rice and beans, twice a day, for their entire period of employment. Exploited and relegated to Plumwood's backgrounding role as described at the beginning of this chapter, many of them would die while working, due to disease and lack of medical assistance. As Metti Maria of Raffaele shares, many perished simply because of sunstroke, due to the prolonged time spent under the sun.

Women and New Peasantry

Women's role in the Italian contemporary rural world has for the most part continued to be backgrounded. The work of film director and landscape artist Anna Kauber, however, brings to surface a promising, although challenging, reality about new peasantry and how women's participation in culture is an ongoing dialectic with nature. The women shepherds in Anna Kauber's documentary *In questo mondo* (In This World) are a powerful testimony of the increasing presence and added value of the feminine presence in the Italian rural world. Between 2015 and 2017 Kauber traveled over 17,000 kilometers around Italy, from the northern Alps to southern islands and regions of Sicily and Sardinia, to meet and follow the life of over one hundred shepherdesses. When Kauber started her journey and adventure it was not easy to find these shepherdesses. She relied on her connections with local and grassroots organizations such as Legambiente or Slow Food to find these realities.

Traditionally considered a male job, pastoralism is a very physical demanding profession. It is not simply a job but a lifestyle. Shepherds spend most of their time outdoors alone with the animals, four seasons a year, without time off to travel or leave their herds unattended. Agropastoralism is practiced mostly in marginal rural settings. These areas constitute half of the Mediterranean territories with limited access to social, cultural, or institutional services.[87] Despite the physical, cultural and social challenges, and the inadequate financial rewards associated with nomadic life, the protagonists in *In questo mondo* are courageous women who share the conscious choice and joy of choosing this life, their care of the animals, and the freedom acquired from domestic confines.

While watching the documentary we learn about the unique stories and paths that brought these women to choose the life of shepherds. Gabriella, for example, used to live in the city of Pistoia, in Tuscany and worked in a call center. When the call center closed, Gabriella decided to follow her dream of opening a farmstead. The most economic and efficient way to clean the scrubland was to return to the traditional practice of using goats to eat bushes and sheep to mow grass. She soon fell in love with these animals and decided to learn the ancient practice of pastoralism from an old local shepherd. After overcoming the prejudices against a woman practicing a traditional male profession, she slowly created her own herd and added other animals, like a cow, a donkey, and some geese. She built a house for her mother and sister and for several years worked hard to cover her debts. Today she is a full-time shepherdess, she makes her own cheese, she manages a small restaurant, and she offers educational visits for local schools.[88]

From a bioregional perspective, the lives of the shepherdesses are shaped by the places they live, such as the case of Assunta Valente. Assunta lives in the Apennines in the southeastern region of Lazio, the area that belongs to the Abruzzo-Lazio and Molise National Park. This is a particularly depopulated area with a ravaged landscape. Kauber notes that there is a visible difference when compared to the Italian landscape populated by communities and by the presence of shepherds and farmers who take care of the valleys. Assunta doesn't have access to many resources. She purchased a small section of woods and lives in a trailer with no electricity, in extremely uncomfortable and precarious conditions.[89]

Meadows and pastures have an important role in the Italian landscape. The decline of pastureland, according to UNESCO Chair Agricultural Heritage Landscapes Mauro Agnoletti, reflects one of the most severe environmental contradictions of the last decades. Although Italian protected mountain areas seek to curb the loss of biodiversity due to the lack of pastures, little or nothing has been done to change this trend.[90] Wooded pastures continue to disappear at a fast rate due to abandonment and consequent repopulation of arboreal vegetation. In the past, vertical transhumance and the organization of pastures into lower, middle and upper stations, especially in the Alps, created an interdependence between the landscape of the mountains and the landscape of the valleys. Today, Agnoletti stresses, the specialization in agriculture and animal husbandry have changed and transformed the landscape systems. Today, valleys and mountains are independent of one another.[91] The relationship between humans and animal husbandry thereby plays an important role in the preservation of ecosystems and the safeguarding of landscapes. Encouraging biodiversity means supporting autochthon ovine, caprine, and bovine breeds. Today, 10 percent of the ovine population is left in the north and the remaining 90 percent is in the center and southern Italy. Sheep and goats are among the ruminants that forage in low-fertility soils and in residual cultivated soils.[92] From the end of War World II, the mechanization of agriculture and investments in industrial agriculture favored the import of international animals which also brought new diseases.

Recently, farmers have acknowledged that indigenous breeds are more resilient to the specific local environments and, especially in desolated areas, help sustain biodiversity and create a wider variety of products, from cheese to wool and meat. The flavor of the cheese produced by indigenous animals contains the characteristics of the territories and meadows where they pasture. The cheese produced by local breeds reflects the identity of local communities, preserves traditional knowledge, stories, and regenerate marginal land. Consequently, the drop of pastureland also means the loss of the traditional knowledge required to properly manage the territory. Dedicated shepherdesses like Assunta Valente, Gabriella, among others interviewed in *In questo mondo*, including those who do not appear in the documentary, although they may seem like a significant number are not enough. These women occupy the intermediate position between nature and culture as proposed by Ortner, and their backgrounding role is essential. An occupation like shepherding that involves endurance, sacrifice, and the willingness to embrace a nomadic and austere life needs more acknowledgment and a better support from the local communities.

Women shepherding is just one example of how women in the contemporary panorama of new peasantry add critical and needed qualities. Patience, attention to details, care for and empathy with the animals while considered secondary, support the need of a more feminine aspect in the rural world that is based on a more conscious and horizontal relationship with the land, nature, and broadly speaking, Mother Earth tout court.

NOTES

1. Anna Maria Bruzzone and Rachele Farina, *La Resistenza Taciuta*, (Torino: Bollati Boringhieri, 2016) (first edition 1976), 7.
2. Anna Maria Bruzzone and Rachele Farina, *La Resistenza Taciuta.* xiii.
3. Ibid., 6.
4. The Italian term "macchia" can be literally translated into English as "spot," a small black spot that stands out in a uniform color. In Italian the term "macchia" is also commonly used geographically to refer to "macchia mediterranea," the typical bushy vegetation around the coast of the Mediterranean. The expression "darsi alla macchia" —give onself to the "macchia" refers, on the other hand, to the action of hiding in order to not being captured.
5. Marcello Flores and Mimmo Franzinelli, *Storia della Resistenza*, (Bari-Roma: Laternza, 2019), 209.
6. Sandro Peli, *Storia della Resistenza in Italia*, (Torino: Einaudi, 2006), 183.
7. Miriam Mafai, *Pane Nero*, (Milano: BUR Rizzorli, 2022), 16. (The first edition 1987.)
8. Ibid.

9. Ibid., 17.

10. The term Neorealism indicates the literary, cinematic, and artistic production between 1945 and 1955 of artists and intellectuals that in their works approached reality by exposing the hardship of everyday life of the lower classes. It needs to be noted that it cannot be considered an official movement, as there never was an official Neorealist manifesto. While it cannot be considered a movement there are stylistic characteristics and content communalities that allow to use the term neorealism in literature (and cinema) when addressing some authors and film directors. Some elements in common are the use of a simple and direct language and the need to deal realistically with the events of the war and the social problems that emerged afterward.

11. Until today, 2022, *L'Agnese va a morire*, *Agnese goes to die,* has never been translated in English. All the quotes from the novel in this chapter are my translation.

12. "La storia di Agnese non è una fantasia," *L'Unità*, 11-27-1949, included at the end of *L'Agnese va a morire*, (Torino: Einaudi, ed. "I coralli," 1994)

13. Viganò, 245.

14. See *La Resistenza Taciuta*, xii, and *Storia della Resistenza* in Italia 186, "the ideal partisan is the protagonist of *L'Agnese va a morire*, the model novel on the femminine Resistance: shapeless, maternal, with no defined age."

15. Dianella Gagliani (a cura di), *Guerra Resistenza Politica. Storie di donne*, (Reggio Emilia: Aliberti Editore, 2006), 31.

16. Val Plumwood, *Feminism and the Mastery of Nature*, (London: Routledge, 1993), 20.

17. Ibid., 21. The italic of the adverb *consciously* is mine, the italics of the preposition *with* is in the original text.

18. Ibid., 23.

19. Sherry B. Ortner, "Is Female to Male as Nature Is to Culture?" in *Feminist Studies*, vol. 1, no. 2 1972, 12. The italics of the word "with" is the author's. Both Plumwood and Ortner recognize the value, not the opposite, of the connection women have *with* nature.

20. Ibid., 23.

21. Documentary, *Il popolo che manca*, directed by Andrea Fenoglio and Diego Mometti. DVD, 2011. This dialogue was originally audio recorded by Revelli, and it appears in the documentary.

22. *L'Agnese va a morire*, 227.

23. Ibid., 218.

24. The partisan "staffetta," roughly translated as courier in English, were often, but not always, women between sixteeen and eighteen years old as they were less suspicious. The partisan "staffette" would keep the communication between the different brigades, between the partisans and their families, and sometimes they would cover the role of nurses, keeping the contacts between the doctors and the pharmacists. Being a "staffetta" was risky and dangerous because while these women were transporting materials for the partisans they didn't carry any weapons, making impossible to defend themselves if captured. More information can be found in https://www.memorieincammino.it/parole/staffetta-partigiana/.

25. Renata Viganò, *L'Agnese va a morire,* 4.

26. Marcello Flores, Mimmo Franzinelli. *Storia della Resistenza*, (Roma: Laaternza, 2019).

27. *Storia della Resistenza* offers a reconstruction of those messages and how they spurred different and contradictory reactions among the soldiers. Claudio Pavone's important volume *Una Guerra Civile* (1991) is the first historical reconstruction of the Resistance in Italy making a difference between the patriotic war, the civil war, and the class war.

28. Beppe Fenoglio, *Primavera di bellezzza*. (Milano: Garzanti, 1959), 113.

29. *L'Agnese va a morire*, 11.

30. The description of the soldier is reminiscent of Italo Calvino's short article that appeared in *L'Unità* on September 15, 1946, titled "Homer Antimilitarist," quoted by Claudio Pavone in *A Civil War* (first edition is 1991). Calvino revises September 8, 1943, Calvino through a reinterpretation of the Odyssey as the myth of those soldiers brought to fight in unknown territories far from their home and concerned about how to return home after the war.

31. "Fischia il vento," the wind whistles, is one of the most popular songs during the Italian Resistance, together with "Bella Ciao." The melody recalls the old and traditional Russian song "Katyusha," which was first sung after September 8, 1943, and became the anthem of the Brigate Partigiane Garibaldi. After World War II, the song was sung and recorded by several famous Italian singers like Milva, and Italian bands like Modena City Ramblers, Skiantos, Banda Bassotti, and P38Punk, among others.

32. Gaetano Salvemini, *Scritti sul fascismo*, Volume III. (Milano: Feltrinelli Editore, 1974), 426.

33. *L'Agnese va a morire*, 11.

34. Ibid.

35. *Storia della Resistenza*, 36.

36. Ibid., 203–6.

37. *La Resistenza taciuta,* 162.

38. Bertolo Gianfranco, et at. *Operai e contadini nella crisi italiana 1943–1944*. (Milano: Feltrinelli, 1974), 259.

39. Michela Ponzani, *Guerra alle Donne*. (Torino: Einaudi, 2012), 8.

40. *Guerra alle Donne*. This data appears in the note 21 of the introduction to the volume and supports my choice to focus on a rural perspective to better understand the involvement of peasants in the Resistance.

41. The CNL (Comitato di Liberazione Nazionale), the National Liberation Committee, an anti-fascist military and political organization created in Rome the day after September 8, had representative from the main political parties of the time. Each party organized within CNL its own partisan formation.

42. *Guerra alle Donne*, 13.

43. Ibid., 15.

44. Ibid., 86.

45. *L'Agnese va a morire*, 51.

46. Piero Bevilacqua, *Il cibo e la terra: agricoltura, ambiente e salute*. (Roma: Donzelli editore, 2018), Kindle edition, location 990 of 3133.

47. *L'Agnese va a morire*, 51.

48. Donna J. Haraway. *When Species Meet*, (Minneapolis: University of Minnesota Press, 2008), 36.

49. *L'Agnese va a morire*, 54.

50. Ibid.

51. Anna Maria Bruzzone and Rachele Farina, *La Resistenza Taciuta*, 9.

52. Francesco Albanese, *Le campagne italiane e la Resistenza*, (Bologna: Grafis Edizioni, 1995), 164.

53. Anna Bravo, "Resistenza civile" in *Dizionario della Resistenza,* ed. by Enzo Collotti, Renato Sandri and Frediano Sessi, (Torino: Einaudi, 2000), Vol. I of II, 272.

54. Nuto Revelli, *Il mondo dei vinti*, (Torino: Einaudi, 1977), 404.

55. Ibid.

56. *L'Agnese va a morire*, 26. This is the first time we hear Agnese's reply. The novel sets up since the beginning Agnese's personality.

57. *L'Agnese va a morire*, 142.

58. *Contadini e partigiani*, 375.

59. *L'Agnese va a morire*, 92.

60. Ruberto, Laura. "La contadina si ribella: Gendered Resistance in *L'Agnese va morire*." *Romance Languages Annual* 9 (1997). Ruberto writes, "Agnese's story upsets the dominant Resistance literature and brings to light the complicated position of women and peasants in Italian culture," 328.

61. *L'Agnese va a morire*, 70.

62. Ibid., 123–24.

63. Albanese, Francesco, et al. *Le campagne italiane e la resistenza*, 194.

64. Pina Palma, Food in War: *L'Agnese va a morire* in *NEMLA Italian Studies*, vol. 25–26, 2001, 65.

65. Revelli, Nuto. *Il mondo dei vinti*, cxvii.

66. *Il mondo dei vinti*, 405.

67. *L'Agnese va a morire*, 166.

68. Ibid.

69. Gary Snyder, *The Practice of the Wild*, (San Francisco: North Point Press, 1980), 39. The italics is from the author.

70. Tom Lynch, Cheryll Glotfelty, and Karla Armbruster. *The Bioregional Imagination. Literature, Ecology and Place.* Athens: University of Georgia Press, 2012, 2.

71. Thayer, Robert L. *LifePlace: Bioregional Thought and Practice*, (Berkeley: University of California Press, 2003), 3.

72. *L'Agnese va a morire*, 173.

73. Ibid., 175.

74. Ibid., 55.

75. https://www.treccani.it/vocabolario/valle/.

76. Marco Armiero, Roberta Biasillo, Wilko Graf von Hardengerb. *La natura del duce. Una storia ambientale del fascismo*, (Torino: Einaudi, 2022), x.

77. Luigi Ganapini, "Con la vanga e col moschetto: ruralità, ruralismo e vita quotidiana nella RSI," records of the conference titled *Agricoltura e vita quotidiana nella RSI,* Salo' 19–20 Nov. 2004 (Venezia: Marsilio, 2006), 173.

78. "Dall'acqua ai campi. Dai campi al silenzio." https://www.youtube.com/watch?v=Zb0rRv4tAKM Last viewed on October 23, 2022.
79. Ibid. (4:43).
80. *L'Agnese va a morire*, 65.
81. Ibid., 63.
82. Ibid., 66.
83. Ibid., 144.
84. The article "La storia di Agnese non è una fantasia," published by *L'Unità*," the newspaper founded by Gramsci, on November 17, 1949, is included at the end of *L'Agnese va a morire* in the 1994 Einaudi edition.
85. *L'Agnese va a morire*, 245.
86. Renata Vigano, *Mondine* (Modena: Tipografia modenese, 1952), 30.
87. Michele Nori and Farinella Domenica. "Mobility and Migration in Mediterranean Europe: The Case of Agropastoralism," in *Migration, Agriculture, and Rural Development*, (IMISCOE Research Series, Cham: Springer, 2020), https://doi.org/10.1007/978-3-030-42863-1_6.
88. Cristina Giannetti. "Pastore italiane: sostantivo femminile, rurale," RRN Magazine, n.13 April 2021, p. 67-69. Pdf.
89. Ilaria Tabusso Marcyan. "An Example of Circular Collaboration. A Conversation with Anna Kauber on the Making of *In Questo Mondo*," *The Italianist*, 2021.
90. Mauro Agnoletti. *Italian Historical Rural Landscapes: Cultural Values for the Environment and Rural Development*, (London: Springer Science+Business Media, 2013) Kindle edition, 52.
91. Ibid.
92. Agnoletti, 57.

Chapter Four

Ecological and Cultural Landscapes in Ermanno Olmi's Documentaries

ERMANNO OLMI THROUGH THE LENSES OF ECOCINEMA

On May 7, 2018, Italy lost one of its most prominent film directors and artists, Ermanno Olmi. A poet of cinema, known also as "il Maestro," Olmi's films and documentaries have made a significant contribution to the history of Italian cinema over the last seventy years. Some of his films have gained international fame and recognition. *The Job* (1961) won the Italian Film Critics' Awards at the Venice Film Festival; *The Tree of the Wooden Clog* (1978) received the Palme d'Or at the Cannes Film Festival; and *The Legend of the Holy Drinker* (1988) captured the Golden Lion at the Venice Film Festival; these are just a few of his many awards. As Olmi himself admits in several interviews and written testimonies, his cinematic training and background had two major influences: Roberto Rossellini's 1945 film, *Rome Open City,* and the American film documentarist Robert Flaherty. The first time Olmi saw *Rome Open City* he noticed that the film "did not divide the screen from the street, but [that it] presented a continuity through an ideal mediator that is, or should be, the poet."[1] The second influence in Olmi's cinema, Robert Flaherty, deeply affected the Italian artist's cinematographic style and approach to film. After seeing Flaherty's documentaries Olmi was inspired to conceptualize cinema not simply as an artistic means to dream and escape from the daily routine, but also as an instrument to learn something more about life.

Although there are traces and reminiscences of Italian neorealism, Olmi's cinema does not fit any specific genre or style of Italian cinema. Author and cinematic critic Bert Cardullo describes Olmi's cinema as "the best exemplar after neorealism of the *neorealist style.*"[2] As in neorealism, most of his films and documentaries offer a slice of life, presenting ordinary people engaged in their everyday life and work. Olmi's films feature nonprofessional actors, they are shot in real locations, and they depict undefined or inconclusive endings. His films, however, go beyond the characteristics of neorealism, and his documentaries, like Flaherty's, present an opportunity to reflect on the dangers of the indiscriminate actions of humans, as well as a hope for liberation from it through a more conscious relationship with the natural environment.

Olmi's first short films and the documentaries of his late career provide meaningful visual testimonials and stories about the relationship between Italian peasant culture, tradition, and landscape. His early filmic production offers visual evidence of an Italian society and economy in full transformation. These films document the disappearing peasant world chronicled by Nuto Revelli. Olmi's last documentaries, on the other hand, depict the survival of peasant communities, while exhibiting the cultural and intellectual seeds passed on to new generations striving to resist the pressures of contemporary corporate, industrial agriculture. His last film documentaries are a testimony to the intellectual tools necessary to regenerate not only the land, but also the knowledge and practices needed to create a more sustainable and resilient rural culture. In the final phase of his career, Olmi, with his unique and gentle style, celebrates examples of a new peasantry and an emerging rural resistance, which reconnects the Italian peasant past with the contemporary grassroots movements of food justice including Slow Food and Terra Madre.

Olmi's early documentaries, for example, reveal the artist's attention to the interrelationship between the Italian landscape and the so-called "ordinary people" who inhabit it. Olmi's first short films of the 1950s laid the groundwork for his conceptualization of the link between Italian peasant culture and the rural landscape. Later, by presenting the international gathering of farmers at the Terra Madre event in Turin and by documenting the ancient work, and art, of stone walling in the Italian Alpine valley of Valtellina, his film documentaries *Terra Madre* and *Rupi del Vino* released in 2009 focus on what has persisted in the Italian rural tradition and society of the twenty-first century. His last documentary, *Our Host Planet*, released in 2015 for the inauguration of Milano Expo, sidesteps celebrity advertising, and instead presents a personal and artistic testament in support of a more environmentally and ecologically conscious relationship among all living beings and the planet that hosts us.

Olmi's documentaries can be situated among an array of films in recent years, both in Italy and abroad, that have devoted increased attention to the environment and environmental issues. Ecocinema, a recent branch of critical scholarship in film studies that investigates the intersection of cinema with environmental understanding, has become more complex since Scott Macdonald first coined this term in 2004. Initially ecocinema was mainly an extension of ecocriticism, focused on positive ecological messaging. In the last decade ecocinema has expanded to include other forms of media such as photography, comics, television and new media along with film,[3] which move beyond ecological issues to present "needed perspectives on the relations between the human and nonhuman."[4] This wider perspective repositions the role of humans in relation to the environment and invites viewers to consider the relationship between humans and nonhumans in a more horizontal way.[5]

Paula Willoquet-Maricondi distinguishes between environmentalist films and ecocinema explaining that the latter includes "consciousness-raising and activist intentions" and purposely aims "to heighten awareness about the contemporary issues and practices affecting planetary health."[6] As noted by environmental humanities scholar Kiu-wai Chu, the anthologies on ecocinema over the last decade have probed the perception of nature in different ways, exploring the intersections, relationships, "and blurred boundaries between nature and culture."[7]

Film scholar Scott MacDonald in his essay "The Ecocinema Experience" looks at popular films and digital videos about the natural world as instances of ecocinema because, he explains, "each [film] offers a depiction of the natural world within a cinematic experience that models patience and mindfulness—qualities of consciousness crucial for a deep appreciation of and an ongoing commitment to the natural environment."[8] Contrasting these movies to the style and approach of commercial media and advertising, which condense the maximum number of images in the least amount of time in order to mimic the consumer experience and constantly stimulate the audience, MacDonald stresses that "the job of eco-cinema is to provide *new kinds of film experiences* that demonstrate an alternative to conventional media spectatorship and help to nurture a more environmentally progressive mindset."[9]

Ecocinema encourages a more progressive mindset, to use MacDonald's words, by raising awareness about other characteristics of cinema. Italian literary and cultural studies scholar Pasquale Verdicchio points out that ecocinema reconsiders two intrinsic features of cinema—temporality and impermanence—more mindfully. Temporality, Verdicchio notes, points to "actual sustained time that environments are given presence in a film," while impermanence refers to the representation of "impermanent elements (growth, reproduction, biological and biochemical processes, etc.)."[10] From this perspective, Verdicchio observes, some film documentaries play out an ethical relationship with the land through a slow rhythm suggesting that cinema can participate in the "ever-changing economy of impermanence, in other words, awareness, patience, and renewal."[11]

Italian cinema scholar and ecocritic Elena Past offers a groundbreaking eco-cinematic reading of a selection of Italian films on location, paying attention to what happens "before the film makes it to the screen."[12] Past focuses on the nonhuman presence and agency in the process of the filmmaking and her interviews and conversations with crewmembers acknowledge how inevitably the nonhuman presence, be it the landscape or living beings, animals, plants or natural elements in general, "are actors in the natural cultural life on set."[13] Most importantly, Past eloquently demonstrates how their presence, like the camera angle, sound, photography or editing, "can shift our understanding of what, and how, the world signifies."[14]

Through the lens of ecocinema, Olmi's documentaries engage the power of cinematic images to shape viewers' ideas and imagination, compelling viewers to think critically about human impact on the natural environment in light of our contemporary ecological and environmental crisis. Temporality and impermanence, as Verdicchio observes, are crucial elements to consider in ecocinema and can be seen in the relationship between the humans and the natural settings chronicled in the early short film documentaries by Olmi. On the other hand, in his last film documentaries *Rupi del Vino* and *Terra Madre,* the film director shifted to more civil and social engagement, offering the necessary visual understanding of the role and value of peasant culture and tradition. Olmi challenged the viewer to consider the relationship between humans and nonhumans through traditional farming practices and cultures showing how rural communities can more mindfully reconnect humans to the land.

Ermanno Olmi, who, surprisingly, has received only limited scholarly attention, is one of the most environmentally conscious Italian artists of the past seventy years.[15] A self-taught filmmaker, Olmi began experimenting with films in the 1950s with short documentaries for the Italian energy company Edisonvolta. These years marked the beginning of his filmic career and gave him the opportunity to develop his talent, filmic style, and his lifelong passion for short documentaries. Olmi's first short documentaries reveal a geographical and social image of Italy in full metamorphosis. These are the years of the so-called Italian economic boom during which Italy witnessed waves of migration from the rural areas to what would soon be the industrialized north. The protagonists of Olmi's Edisonvolta documentaries are the new laboring classes, most of whom belong to the Italian cultural and social recent past—the peasant world. Their physical features and movements carry the signs of hard outdoor work and a familiarity and deep connection to the land and the landscape surrounding them.

Olmi's peasant roots have, indirectly at first and more explicitly in his mature career, influenced his personal and artistic environmental sensitivity. The biological bond between humans and the land is always present in his films, and when, or if, this bond is not explicitly represented, there is still a reference, a reminiscence, or a memory, that serves as reminders that the lack of this connection creates, and has created, new and dangerous issues in the Italian natural environment and contemporary society. This collection of Olmi's first short film documentaries, such as *La Pattuglia del Passo San Giacomo* (1954), *Il Racconto della Stura* (1955), and the last film documentaries of his career, *Terra Madre* (2009), *Rupi del Vino* (2009) and *Our Host Planet* (2015) inevitably invite the viewer to understand and embrace a more ecological and environmental conception of the cultural, social, geographical, technological, and ecological transformations of the Italian landscape.

Shifting the gaze to a more environmental and ecological reading of these documentaries clarifies Olmi's poetic yet dispassionate talent in representing the Italian geo-social landscape. His film documentaries are not nostalgic and do not present threatening or apocalyptic images and messages. The images and stories presented discreetly invite viewers to reflect on their inherited biological connection to the natural world. In line with writer, poet, and filmmaker Pier Paolo Pasolini, Olmi believes in the importance of poetic editing. According to Olmi, a documentary serves "not just to inform specific reality through a series of frames. Sometimes it is the poetic editing, performed by the author, of images of reality and, in this case, the documentary is not simply information anymore, but becomes an authentic form of communication."[16] This precise vision of how a documentary should be understood, and what it should communicate, explains Olmi's poetic and ecological vision as reflected in his filmic career.

Olmi's documentaries also add one more piece to the larger mosaic of the environmental humanities. Advocating for a more interdisciplinary approach to environmental change, Robert S. Emmet and David E. Nye argue, "the global environmental crisis demands new ways of thinking and new communities that produce environmental solutions as a form of civic knowledge."[17] Serenella Iovino, Enrico Cesaretti and Elena Past's introduction to *Italy and The Environmental Humanities,* points out in fact, that no single discipline has the answer for complex environmental problems. They claim, "To really know what 'environment' means and what 'ecological crisis' implies, we must . . . move beyond unilateral approaches and engage in cooperative conversations that boost our imagination of reality."[18] While Olmi's thoughts about cinema and life never claim to produce environmental solutions, his films nevertheless do inspire more conscious ways of thinking and, above all, more thoughtful ways of perceiving, understanding, and experiencing the Italian landscape and its people. *Terra Madre* and *Rupi del Vino,* Olmi's last long film documentaries, focus on what Slow Food calls food communities and disclose the film director's position on the role of the new peasantry in contemporary society. According to Olmi, the contemporary economic (and ecological) crisis is, above all, "a crisis of human civilization."[19] The visual component of the films allows the viewer to have a glimpse of the peasants' universe in Italy and around the world, showcasing the innate film director's sensitivity toward "the humble people," a humanity too often undervalued and dismissed but that, according to Slow Food's founder Carlo Petrini, "holds in their hands the keys of our future."[20]

Landscape as Source of Energy. *La Pattuglia del Passo San Giacomo* and *Il racconto della Stura*

Born in 1931 in Bergamo, a small town in the northern region of Lombardy, Ermanno Olmi was the son of peasants on his mother's side and railway workers on his father's. These two social backgrounds, the rural and the urban, influence and shape the artist's cinematic style as well as his personal vision. Olmi's father was an engine driver for Edison and died when Olmi was just thirteen. At his father's death, Edison employed his mother, who up to that point was a housewife. In 1947, the electric company also hired the son, Ermanno Olmi. After a few years working as an employee for Edisonvolta, Olmi was promoted to director of the cinema section and began to film the first documentaries for Edisonvolta. Between 1954 and 1961, Olmi shot over forty short documentaries for the Italian electric company. These documentaries, ten to twelve minutes long, were screened in movie theaters before the main feature and served as advertisements for the company's electric energy service and production across the country.

The documentaries Olmi created for Edisonvolta correspond with the so-called economic boom or economic miracle that transformed Italy after the war, ushering in a new phase of industrialization, economic growth, and social transformation. Reflecting the mainstream values of the period, these early documentaries mirror the trust and enthusiasm for technological and industrial progress Italy experienced during the postwar years. The films of this period pay attention to this new phase through what is commonly identified as anthropological and industrial cinema.[21] Cinema historian Marco Bertozzi recognizes in these two genres a sort of dichotomy that nonetheless "forces us into a reflection of our recent [Italian] history."[22] While industrial films are directed toward the future and what is new, anthropological films investigate "buried humankinds,"[23] such as the remarkable testimonies recorded in the 1950s in Vittorio De Seta's documentary shorts about the rural villages of Sardinia, Sicily, and the southern region of Calabria.

Olmi's short films, however, are a fluid hybrid that harmoniously and poetically bridge the two categories of industrial and anthropological films. His documentaries look toward the future like industrial films, and yet their protagonists are people from the past who don't yet belong to the industrial world. The bodies and faces of Edisonvolta workers presented in the films, the marks on their faces due to long hours of physical outdoor work and exposure to the weather, harken back to Italian cultural and social roots, forcing viewers to confront the common contemporary lack of familiarity with the Italian recent past.

Olmi's filmic eye focuses on the places and the modest people who work and live in these places. He doesn't offer mere publicity for Edisonvolta, rather he shoots real short films. Each documentary follows a similar pattern and includes a storyline with three elements—location, people, and the company. Unlike the anthropological testimonies in Vittorio De Seta's documentaries of the 1950s and 1960s, where the camera and the director discreetly record what happens with the least amount of interference and manipulation, Olmi's documentaries are carefully edited in postproduction, and primary attention is given to sound. Voice-over, dialogue, music, and sounds of nature stress the artist's attention to the human element immersed in the surrounding natural environment.

The 1954 short documentary *La pattuglia del Passo S. Giacomo* is an example of Olmi's first, and perhaps unconscious, step toward what in the following years would become a fully developed environmental and ecological perspective, both in his documentaries and in his life. In 1954 the short documentary won the first prize at the Trento Film Festival in the category "The Industrial Problems of Mountains." In a very neutral style, the film narrates and shows how the employees of Edisonvolta efficiently intervene to fix a broken electric cable in a mountain valley. This eleven-minute short film brings to light a common thread in Olmi's first and last documentaries of his career: human labor operates in and with the natural environment, sometimes working in its favor and other times against it. In both cases, human intervention always and inevitably modifies the original natural landscape. Olmi's sensitivity and attention to the Italian landscape and its people, his attention to the human and more-than-human relationship in his art, invites the viewer to reconnect and rethink the role of humans in their natural environment.

La Pattuglia del Passo San Giacomo opens with a series of still shots, postcard style, of a small mountain village of the Piedmont Alps. It begins with the silence of the first image where we see a few houses covered with snow, followed by a series of shots of the surrounding landscape accompanied by a vibrant and energized soundscape: bells ringing from the village bell tower, a dog barking and running in the snow, a rooster crowing among hens. Finally, the first scene continues with the voice-over and image of a couple of young boys having a conversation about homework while skiing on the way to school. The scene resumes, showing images of small children playing outside, while in the background we hear the rhythmic sound of wood chopped by men in a courtyard. In this picturesque panorama of the Italian Alps, the viewer is introduced to the simple and peaceful daily routine of mountain people. Olmi consciously alternates images of humans with domesticated animals to communicate that in these altitudes human labor and life cannot be performed and sustained without the support of nonhumans.

The village shown early in the film is Riale, situated at the bottom of Val Formazza, a valley in the extreme northern region of Piedmont, bordering with Switzerland on the west and the region of Lombardy on the east. Characteristic of Piedmont's less-frequented mountain valleys, the houses of Riale awaken a sense of familiarity, recalling similar landscapes, homes, and mountain villages. Indeed, Riale appears, to the eye of the contemporary Italian viewer as a symbol or representation of the typical Alpine village, or of similar inland and isolated rural settings that today barely survive and that are in condition of semi-abandonment.[24] From Riale, following a trail in the mountains, it is possible to arrive at the S. Giacomo pass, an Alpine pass connecting Italy and Switzerland, located over 7,500 feet above the sea level. The rhythmic sound of the ax in the first scene creates a bridge to the second scene, in which a lumberjack uses an ax to cut a tree in the woods. The trunk of the tree accidentally falls on a cable line nearby, breaking the electric cable. The viewer then learns that Edisonvolta's electric cable is located near the S. Giacomo pass. The camera follows two Edisonvolta employees leaving a house and skiing down the white snowy valley while the voice-over comments, "this is an everyday story with everyday heroes."

In Olmi's eyes everyday people are indeed the true heroes. But who are the everyday heroes? They are common people who assure the success of the company. They are technicians, manual workers, miners, guardians of dams, and the company's personnel. In other words, Olmi's protagonists are not the brains of the company, such as engineers or executives. This is a narrative and strategy used even today by many construction or energy companies to address the work involved in realizing great projects. Olmi's protagonists hold, however, historical and cultural relevance. They are the bodies and hands of modest people who, until recently, worked in the fields. The same hands that used to plow the land now use that strength and ability to pull cables, connect villages and cities through electricity, and dig mountains to build new mines. In *La pattuglia del passo S. Giacomo,* Olmi shows close shots of the calloused hands and lined faces of the Edisonvolta crew members to draw attention to their hard manual outdoor labor. Their faces and hands have the same features as those villagers' faces and hands, as well as that of the lumberjack who accidentally breaks the cable at the beginning of the documentary. The Edisonvolta technicians, the mountain people, and the lumberjack all have similar social backgrounds and in the 1950s those roots were linked to their peasant origins.

Film critic Sergio Toffetti notices that Olmi's first documentaries were shot during a unique period when agriculture and industry coexisted. These two worlds meet in Olmi's early films and their encounter, Toffetti claims, "produces not an annihilation, but a comparison between two lifestyles."[25]

Olmi's representation of this moment of equilibrium between agriculture and industry—farmer and worker—contrasts with that of Nuto Revelli. Revelli focused on the annihilation of the peasant world and culture, lamenting the lack of effort to preserve the balance between rural and industrial society. After the war, many farmers became part-time farmers, supplementing their life in the fields with work in the factories. Performing two jobs, they split their time working in the factory during the week and in the fields on weekends. For Revelli, this transition from agriculture to industrial work, farm to factory, brought on by industrialization initiated the process of rural decline. As farmers began to work second and third factory shifts during the week, they ended up being too tired to perform their work in the field on the weekends.[26]

Olmi's short documentaries present an alternative view, more open and confident about the promises of these new technological and industrial times. His early films, like Revelli's testimonies, chronicle the transition from agriculture to industrial society. They document a specific historical moment of ecological transformation in which land workers—the farmers—and machine workers—the laborers—were often the same people who were connected to the land in similar ways. Edisonvolta workers had rural origins, they were linked through family ties to the countryside, their bodies carried the signs of this physical relationship with living matter: soil, plants, trees, and animals. In Olmi's view, the "everyday story with everyday people" includes specific settings and contexts. Olmi's optimistic representation of the laboring class who had peasant roots and was now helping to make a new industrially advanced Italy, reflects his enthusiasm and young identification with the postwar resurgence of the Italian economy.

Olmi's scenes add another important layer in displaying the human relationship with the surrounding natural and built environment. The lumberjack who cuts the tree at the beginning of the documentary, and the Edisonvolta technicians who fix the broken cable, express the same attitude of human power over the natural and technical elements. Within the first two minutes of the short film the viewer sees a silhouetted scene with a lumberjack chopping the trunk of a large mountain tree. Soon after the camera, in a reverse shot, pictures clear details of the large spruce and the lumberjack using an ax to cut its trunk. In this frame, the size of the tree is visibly much larger than the man, yet its size does not intimidate the lumberjack.[27] The lumberjack expertly keeps chopping the trunk with the strength and confidence of an experienced mountain dweller, suggesting a century-old established relationship of dominance and control of natural elements physically bigger than humans. The majestic tree trunk, displayed now in a wider shot that includes the whole mountain valley covered in snow, passively surrenders to the progressive skillful cuts of the lumberjack who, a small figure in between the two big tree branches of this old tree, knows how to cut it down. The knowledge, technique, and strength of the lumberjack triumph over the firm, mighty, and robust presence of the tree. Nevertheless, the lumberjack makes a serious mistake, and the tree falls near an electric pole and tears apart a cable line, causing a blackout in the nearby village of Riale. Despite his skills, he lacks knowledge of the new era of energy power, introducing the need for new skills and abilities.

Regardless of the power of the lumberjack and the technician over nature, the majestic backdrop of the Alps, with their peaks and glaciers, valleys, slopes, grasslands, meadows, trees, woods, rivers, and streams, play an important role in this film. As the news of the broken cable reaches the headquarters of the electric company, a new scene shows two men exiting a mountain house and skiing down the snow-covered mountain valley to assess the damage. The voice-over explains that this story happened in the spring in the valley of Val Formazza, in the Piedmont region. "An everyday story with everyday heroes. A story that could have as a background, all Alpine valleys, wherever men have extended through high poles the electric cables that bring electricity to cities, homes, and factories." In a celebration of human progress and technology, the voice-over admits that these strong cables can be broken by natural events such as an avalanche or, in this case, a human mistake. The technicians, who are also mountain experts, use their skills and knowledge to bridge the local mountain community with the power of urban electricity.

The electric company sends a crew with a sleigh pulled by donkeys to fix the cable. They carry the equipment and material necessary for the repair on their shoulders to the last tract of the mountain. Close shots of the crew members' faces, their foreheads, and cheeks, show, once again, the details of people accustomed to extreme weather. While walking and climbing the snow-covered trail to reach the broken cable, they stop to drink from a thin rivulet of water surfacing from the rocks. A close-up focuses on their faces approaching the rocks and their hands forming small cups to drink showcasing the cuts on their hands and the wrinkles around their eyes and necks. These faces can easily represent those of the lumberjack and of peasants. The people who live in these areas know how to move and engage with the natural environment and are aware that a wrong or hazardous move could compromise the operation and be fatal to the worker.

When the crew is ascending the trellis to install the new cable, the voice-over compares their action to "a test of electric mountaineering" where the "expert" foot quickly finds the right spot to reach the top. The viewer sees the crew members climbing the trellis to reach its top with the same agility as if they are hiking the peak of a mountain. "There won't be any flowers from the Alps to gather at the top," the voice-over comments, "only a job to perform." The panorama of mountain peaks now includes non-natural elements that not only disrupt the view, but also divert the role of humans in these areas. The technicians are, in fact, specialized people and, while familiar with these environments, they also present the first signs of disconnection from their natural environment.

Surrounded by the immense white mountain peaks, which the camera deceptively presents as soft and enveloping, the technicians pull and lift cables, climb and carry weights, sit in small chairs, and climb the electric towers carrying large heavy cables without protection; a large steep valley provides the backdrop to their labor. A camera shot from the top of the electric tower looking down shows how the physical hard work of these men is coupled with extreme agility and courage. The familiarity in holding and using the ropes and grabbing the metallic structure of the trellis display qualities developed from the hardships of working in the countryside and mountains. In the 1950s, the Edisonvolta technicians were, as both Toffetti and Revelli pointed out, simultaneously urban and rural people, familiar with both worlds.

La pattuglia del Passo S. Giacomo, in line with times of progress and innocent trust in the future, ends in praise of technology. Electricity is finally restored to cities and towns, lighting up windows and buildings, street signs, and theaters. The documentary ends with the camera following a young boy in the small mountain village of Rialto. The voice-over makes a final comment that now the boy will be able to dream again, with his eyes brightened in joy while watching the illuminated window of a store displaying chocolate candies. Olmi's poetic vision of the future was, as he admitted later in his life, naively hopeful, trusting the potential of industry and economic growth. His confidence in the future is also directed at younger generations who, in the eyes of the young film director, had the potential to better serve this new technological and industrial age.

A young artist in the 1950s, Olmi fully believed the promises offered by the Italian socioeconomic and political panorama. In contrast to Revelli, he was a boy during World War II, and did not fight as a soldier or participate in the Resistance. He still recognized the role of the Resistance and deeply respected its immense value in breaking with fascism and shaping the modern Italian democratic republic, as documented in *Nascita di una formazione partigiana* (1973), in which he retraces the first months of Resistance in the valleys of Cuneo and the birth of the partisan brigade Justice and Freedom. Like Revelli, however, he has a deep respect for and connection to the rural world through his mother's family and grandmother, of whom was very fond. Olmi believed that when a child discovers the outside world he goes through a second birth. His first childhood memories relate to his grandmother's rural house, the spacious kitchen with the fireplace where she cooked, the porch by the farmstead, and his first tricycle.[28] These first experiences remained imprinted in his memory and marked a permanent link with his peasant roots, which helped to shape his understanding and interpretation of the rural world. It is his peasant roots and the memories connected to his second birth, as he called it, that in the following decades help him realize, like Revelli, the dangers of so-called progress and the threats of the disappearance of the peasant world. Olmi's resistance to a subtler form of hegemony, the one that arrived after World War II in the guise of industrialization, progress, and technology, begins to surface in his last film documentaries. In his late documentaries the artist readdresses the great value and role of the rural world by pointing out the immense value of rural knowledge and genuine connection with the land.

Although Olmi's first documentaries present a continued bond between humans and their natural environment, they also display human manipulation and exploitation of nature for the sake of progress and industrialization. Commissioned by Edisonvolta, *Il racconto della Stura* (1955) tells the story of the construction of the hydroelectric power station and the pro-industry attitude is evident from the first scene. This short documentary, which runs nine minutes, begins with a vertical pan of the side of a rocky mountain. The voice-over comments, "The river is born from this bare mountainside. The river, bent by human will, is the main character of our story." The river Stura, situated in the Stura Valley of Demonte, in the southwest of the Piedmont region, in the province of Cuneo, near the French border, is the protagonist of this short film. The landscape of the Stura Valley is introduced as a typical, idyllic Alpine valley, rocky at the top, ringed by coniferous forestland, which is softened at the bottom of the valley by green meadows.

The story of this river is narrated as the story of the struggle and victory of humans over nature. The signs of the recent passage of World War II, visible in the images of a ruined village in the valley, prompt the narrator to vaguely invoke the war. While the camera shows the ruins, the voice-over intones, "It seems impossible that a conflict took place in such a quiet landscape." The fight of humans against humans is beyond grasp, however, the human domination of nature is justified and supported. The narrator continues, "The only comprehensible struggle, a struggle that fills us with revered astonishment, is that of humans who carved up a beautiful but greedy nature into small pieces of land to make a small field." Nature is presented as lavish, abundant, and peaceful, yet is perceived as selfish. It must be controlled and subjugated, only in this way can progress ensue and humans benefit. The 1950s mark the beginning of a mode of production that justifies the exploitation of natural resources and the intensive management of the natural world as a human right. While the voice-over reiterates these concepts, the camera follows a woman farmer leading a donkey toward some farmers working in the fields. The camera then cuts to the Stura river, and the voice-over continues:

A river is much more than water: it is alive, it has a movement and a voice. It can be good and bad, calm and threatening, slow and whirling. There is an unmistakable humanity in each river, even if it is as ordinary as our Stura. Soon its clear and garrulous water, properly curbed through a series of human endeavors will create wells, waterfalls, and mysterious liquid veins in the mountain's viscera and, finally, will produce electric energy.

This anthropomorphic interpretation of the river confirms the anthropocentric experience of nature typical of western cultures, which is characterized by a hierarchical relationship in which the natural elements are conceived as unlimited resources to fulfill human needs and fuel unending growth. In the Italian panorama, this vision reflects the euphoria of the economic boom of the 1950s and 1960s and reaffirms a century-old, highly anthropized landscape, a landscape where it is almost impossible to find a clear separation between wild nature and one molded by humans.

Environmental historian Marco Armiero describes Italian natural landscape as a socially constructed space. He writes, "several generations have shaped [the landscape] with their work, their life and their stories, but the social aspect, when it blends with nature, inserts itself in an extremely material environmental substratum."[29] Armiero points to hybrid Italian landscapes, resulting from being controlled and modeled by humans and for human purposes. From this perspective, landscapes become new materially constructed spaces where the social and the natural blend to create new hybrid relationships, like the mountains that have been shaped by bombs, or damns, as well as the stories and memories of the inhabitants. In the years following War World II, new factories in the valleys, dams in the mountains, and electric poles and wires strung across the peninsula transformed the landscape. As Armiero states, and Italian landscapes confirm, Italy's lands are intimately connected with human stories, and the boundary between nature and culture is constantly blurred like a porous puzzle making it difficult to distinguish between the two. The result is "a hybrid landscape"[30] with a multilayered and multifaceted narrative in which nature, human action, and history all contribute to the contemporary Italian landscape.

Il racconto della Stura depicts this hybrid landscape. The film presents a technical description of how Edisonvolta will control and reroute the flow of the river. The concluding images and voice-over show workers busy building the future dam and the hydroelectric center, in a final glorification not of nature's abundance but of human ingenuity that through labor, technology, and engineering bring water and electricity to cities and villages across the nation. With one eye toward landscape and one eye toward technological progress, the young film director's spirit and attitude resembles the characters of his first documentaries. Olmi had an innate appreciation and poetical sensitivity for the natural surroundings, however, he was also fully invested in the promises of technology and industrial development. This tension between natural personal inclinations and reverence toward nature, combined with the social and cultural ambitions of the times are visible in the majestic and at times poetic images of the natural landscape, the comments of the voice-over, the choice of the music, and the postproduction editing. At times, a tension results from the seemingly contradictory messages presented in the film. For the trusting young artist, however, the final choice and duty was to celebrate the successful work of Edisonvolta, as it offered in his eyes a solution and a future for the younger generations, including his promising future cinematic career.

A Return to Peasant Traditions Through Food Communities. *Terra Madre* and *Rupi del Vino*

Olmi's career grew exponentially after his beginnings with Edisonvolta and his rich film production reached international recognition after winning the Palme d'Or at the Cannes Film Festival with *L'albero degli zoccoli* (*The Tree of Wooden Clogs*) in 1978. After a number of other films focused on disparate themes, from novels and fairy tales, like *The Legend of the Holy Drinker* (1988) and *The Secret of the Old Woods* (1993), to more historically centered stories, like *The Profession of Arms* (2001), Olmi returned to document the rural world at the end of his career. In 2009 Olmi shot two documentaries, *Terra Madre* and *Rupi del Vino*. While the former follows, with an undeniable artistic touch, Carlo Petrini's grassroots international gathering "Terra Madre," the latter is set in Valtellina, in the mountains of the region of Lombardy, and records a century-old, ingenious but also physically strenuous, tradition: the technique of cultivating vineyards in the mountains. Olmi's focus on traditional farming cultures not only presents a way to look back at his own rural roots, but might also be seen as an attempt to redeem humans for their indiscriminate environmental and economic actions. Farmers, Olmi believed, could show us the way toward a more sustainable relationship with nature. "I remember my teachers," Olmi says, "those who gave me directions when I was not able on my own to see or understand something. These teachers did it with their example, with their behavior, through their way of being. My peasant grandmother was my first true teacher."[31] Olmi's memories reveal the film director's recognition of the connection of practical knowledge with good practices, and of the peasant tradition as a leading example to follow for a revival of these good practices.

In this last phase of his career, Olmi developed a deeper and clearer awareness of the contemporary cultural and environmental crisis. With his gentle, poetic, and yet sober style "the maestro" used the filmic genre that opened the doors to his artistic career, documentary, to return to his peasant roots and to document the bio-cultural value of rural traditions. Coming full circle through *Terra Madre* and *Rupi del Vino*, Olmi addresses the role of the peasant tradition on a global and national scale, and shows how the new peasantry, which even in the 21st century continues to be underrepresented, embodies the new organic intellectuals who can re-connect humans to their natural roots.

In 2006, Carlo Petrini, founder of the International Slow Food Movement, invited Ermanno Olmi to document the stories and people of Terra Madre, a network of sustainable food communities, born out of the Slow Food Movement in 2004. Terra Madre embodied the next level in the emergence of Slow Food, designed to revive and recognize local food communities across the globe.[32] As Petrini claims, "Terra Madre is a concrete way of putting into practice what has been defined as 'glocalism': a set of actions carried out on a local scale to generate major repercussions on a global scale."[33] Terra Madre was conceived as a network of rural communities, including farmers, shepherds, fishermen, as well as cooks, chefs, and bakers, among many others, who through their work and consumer choices, seek to support local communities and sustain the natural environment. While there is a gathering every two years in the Italian city of Turin, where delegates from all over the world meet and share their knowledge and practices, the networking promoted by Terra Madre expands far beyond the time and space of the city to encompass a global web that slowly and constantly works to promote cultural change and ecological awareness in support of the deep interconnection between soil, food, ecology, and the environment.

Starting with food, a concrete and material human need, as well as a source of nourishment and pleasure, the Slow Food Movement proposes a new intellectual perspective and material culture: a political, social, economic and more importantly, ecological paradigm shift coming from below, from the margins, from the global South, as a form of liberation from poverty, hunger, inequality, and ecological and human exploitation.[34] In common with Terra Madre's attention to farm cultures and a renewed ecological and environmental paradigm, these ideas echoed Olmi's attention to the work and role of peasants and farmers. Consequently, Olmi accepted Petrini's invitation, and he used his art, talent, and experience in narrating peasant stories, to create a faithful documentation of the first gatherings of Terra Madre in the city of Turin, Italy, in 2004. In addition, the images, sounds, and narrative, offer a very personal and ecologically mindful interpretation of the deep connection between humans and planet Earth. The film director gracefully recalled, "That rural world, poor and yet as enchanted as my childhood memories, entered my life like a chorus enters an opera: always shifting scenes with the flow of seasons. The breath rich with fragrances that, like light, make you discover the beauty present on this Earth."[35] This rural ideal is artistically conveyed through the documentary as it surveys a range of disparate farming cultures in familiar and remote areas around the world.

The fecund first scene of *Terra Madre* builds on the evocative images of apples. The viewer sees a detail of three apples on a wooden table: "Musetto" apple—medium size, "Gran Alessandro" or "Prussiana" apple—large size, and a wild apple—very small in size. Olmi's opening shot is an extreme close-up of these apples, set on a rustic table by the wrinkled hands of an old farmer. Small cuts on his hand display visible traces of dirt and serve as testament to the physical work performed by peasants. This simple gesture of the farmer's hands, the handmade wooden table, and the three different kinds of apples, two of which represent centuries of human interaction with nature, reveal the depth of connection, dependence, and the intricate alliance between humans and the natural world. The aged hands suggest the wisdom and knowledge gained by long, direct experience of humans in the fields, and introduce the sequences that follow. Music bridges the following scene, where images of nature and the rural countryside are accompanied by a voice-over narrating a few verses from Virgil's *The Georgics*, which recounts the original pact between humans and nature, memorializing the farmer's work in the fields as the basis for human civilization. Olmi's poetic images of the countryside, and the contemporaneity of Virgil's lines describing the farmer's struggle in nature, contain the seed of the documentary and anticipate the main message of the Terra Madre movement.

The film repeatedly confronts the viewer with the contradictions and paradoxes of our current social and economic system. Through the lens of the director, the film provides an important record of the interventions of thousands of world delegates in Turin and constantly confronts the viewer with the contradictions and paradoxes of the current societal and economic system. While the titles are still scrolling, a little screen on the left shows a few images of the first 2004 Terra Madre meeting. Extreme long shots reveal a crowded conference hall with people of different ethnicities as Carlo Petrini's voice-over announces, "There are 1,022 communities here in Turin, with a total of 4,888 delegates." Against medium-long shots of the delegates parading into the hall, mimicking the opening ceremonies of the Olympic games, we hear Petrini's voice saying "129 countries are represented" and listing all present. Even before the film fully unfolds, in these first introductory minutes, the viewer feels the impact of the presence of farmers in the industrialized city of Turin.

Next the viewer hears excerpts from an interview with environmental activist Vandana Shiva, conducted at the first Terra Madre meeting in 2004. Her words resonate as a wake-up call, making visible what is often ignored: "How many lies can they tell when they starve the African child and create a skeleton body, yet they malnourish the American child and keep creating an obese body? The obese body of the American and the skeleton in Africa are products of the same exploitative food system and both are avoidable."[36] Olmi, by showing Shiva's comment during the first minutes of the documentary while the opening titles are still running, is endorsing her environmental activism and work with Slow Food. As with the entire film, Shiva's provocative words cry out for new possibilities and underscore the potential and responsibility for different behavior. In the opening of the documentary, Olmi sets up the tone of denunciation of the paradoxes of the global food system and, at the same time, features the grassroots work of Slow Food and the farming communities that support bio-cultural diversity around the world.

The documentary proceeds with Carlo Petrini's opening statement from the second Terra Madre meeting in 2006. Petrini exclaims, "What are the seeds we should sow? I thought about it, and I believe that Terra Madre's strongest seed is the use of local economy, to shorten the distance between producer and consumer. The local economy is in perfect harmony with nature. Communities are first and foremost a place. A place and people. People from a place." Different images accompany Petrini's words, encouraging an emotional and sensory connection with his message. Illustrating the words "to shorten the distance between the producer and consumer," the viewer sees a long shot of a farmer spreading seeds in a plowed field. A studied choice of images, edited to the rhythm of Petrini's discourse, gives the viewer a better sense of the interdependence between humans and the fruits of the land. In a medium close-up, a farmer in a field lets go of a few grains from one hand, while in the other he holds a sickle. Due to necessity, human intellect has, through centuries, designed and produced technological devices to help deal with nature and find ways to work with nature. With these images, Olmi guides us through this technological journey, and when the farmer drops the last of grains in the soil, a sharp cut shows a close-up of hands mixing flour with water on a wooden table. The movement of the hands toward the right of the screen connects to the next shot, a close-up of the two arms pulling out, from right to left, a loaf of bread from a wood-fired oven. This last image concludes the sequence and accompanies Petrini's last words: "the local economy is in perfect harmony with nature." By stressing the fact that the local economy is in harmony with nature, Olmi is directly highlighting our responsibility and daily practices when it comes to food choices.

Olmi gives life to Petrini's words through the image of hands. Hands, those of the farmer showing the apples in the opening shot, the hands plowing the wheat in the fields, and finally the hands of the baker molding the bread dough, are the ones who feed humans. Olmi, who was fascinated by the faces and the hands of the Edisonvolta technicians in the 1950s, returns to the hands in this film, the hands of farmers and food producers. For the attentive viewer, the hands, the lines, and the wrinkles, are the same and produced by the same hard work and climate. The hands represent labor and the time required to produce the final product. Their work is locally based, and as Petrini points out, is in harmony with nature and produces a mutually beneficial outcome both for humans and nature.

Olmi's *Terra Madre* is also an important visual testimony to the active engagement of the unrepresented farming communities that inhabit the planet. Especially in the South of the world, these communities are often the majority of the entire population and are those who feed the world.[37] A close-up of an indigenous farmer from Latin America speaking to Terra Madre's large audience perfectly identifies the attitude and values behind Terra Madre's project, and the political impact that this meeting has, at both the national and international level. An Indigenous farmer from Latin America is dressed in his traditional costume and, standing behind the podium, pronounces these words to a crowded hall, "I would first like to thank the President of Italian Republic, for welcoming all these indigenous peoples, the Quechuas, Aymaras, Guaranìs, Atzecs and children of the Incas. . . . We are humble custodians, guardians of agrobiodiversity. We want to defend the right to healthy food for the whole world, and we continue to fight for this food, and for the sovereign right to food, to share with all the peoples from the world." The biannual events of Terra Madre continue to be organized in the city of Turin, where Slow Food and Petrini have, over the years, created a civil and political coalition with the local institutions.

The director's personal artistic and poetic interpretation and understanding of peasant culture becomes fully visible when Olmi brings us to three hectares of land at the margins of the small city of Roncade, in the region of Lombardy, in northern Italy. Images of wild woods whose soil is covered by autumn fallen leaves are contrasted with details of the nearby dry and cracked agricultural land. Two very opposite ecosystems and habitats, one uncontaminated and the other manipulated by humans, are separated by a double row of wood stacks supported by poles and covered by dried grass. This is the wall Ernesto, the inhabitant of the three hectares of land, built to shield his land from the curious eyes of passersby. While the camera shows these images, we hear Vandana Shiva and other people discussing the condition of the two soils, life flourishing with the humus and humid soil in the wild woods, and the hard and lifeless soil in the plowed and re-plowed land across the street.

While filming the documentary, Olmi surprised Petrini and other experts by inviting them to visit the small farm of Ernesto. His story of voluntary isolation and solitude, of a man who separated himself from the rest of the world, lived for forty years on this land and died a few years back, is portrayed through Olmi's images, accompanied by clips of the speeches at Terra Madre and the soothing voice-over of the narrator. The voice-over is the same narrator who reads Virgilio's lines at the beginning of the film and, while describing Ernesto's life, takes us back to ancient times, as if Ernesto was a character from the *Georgics*. While showing us details of the woods and the small farm covered by grape vines, the voice-over continues, "His land's genetic heritage has remained intact for fifty years. His humble cultivations are a monument to knowledge and survival. He ate corn, potatoes, plums, cabbage—just what's essential, with no waste. Poor, yet rich. He knew how to get a lot from a little, the necessity to live in health and dignity." Resisting any contact with the external world and any modern technology, Ernesto was able to build any tool for his needs from scratch using the wood of the forest. He used no electricity, had no car, and used no technical devices to communicate with the external world. He only grew food that was easy to produce and preserve, did not use any pesticides, nor did he accept any kind of help from his family. We learn eventually that Ernesto died in the winter of 2004 in his house, alone, after a summer of drought that ruined most of his small crops and prevented him from gathering enough supplies for the winter.

Olmi does not want the viewer to feel pity for the farmer, nor does he want the viewer to judge Ernesto. In the film, the experts invited by Olmi wander around Ernesto's property left untouched after his death and discuss the value of his story. The film director takes the viewer inside the house where dishes are piled in the sink, a pan on the stove, and a panama hat on the table. Small objects and furniture are displayed as if someone suddenly left the house. The accumulated dust over the years is the sign that in this place time stopped after Ernesto's death. Yet, even in Ernesto's absence, his presence is strong and palpable. "Some scientists begin to see his wealth, hidden in poverty," continues the voice-over, confirming that specialists from the most diverse fields—economics, biology, history, agriculture, and politics recognize, in Ernesto's life, a powerful message.

Olmi presents Ernesto's story as an example of resistance against the indiscriminate and accelerated process of industrialization and development, and as a confirmation of the interconnection of social and ecological issues. Ernesto's life is an example of the socially and economically isolated Italian peasant world. He was fully committed in establishing a fruitful and beneficial relationship with his land and knew every single species of vegetable and tree that could be cultivated to satisfy his basic needs. Ernesto's choice of relying on the fruits of his land by creating a small food forest is also an invitation to reflect on humans' contemporary relationship to the land. His life bridges two historical and cultural moments of Italian peasantry: the isolated and forgotten one of the past century, and the new peasantry, which has become more socially and environmentally engaged. Ernesto's story is therefore a reminder that a respectful coexistence of humans with the natural surroundings, in these times, is crucial and essential for the survival of both society and the planet.

Olmi's other film of 2009, *Rupi del vino,* filmed in Valtellina, in the northern region of Lombardy, delivers a similar message. In the Alps, Olmi pays homage to Italian viticulture: to the vineyards planted on man-made terraces carved into the mountain slopes bordering Switzerland, and to the skillful workers and the ancient tradition of dry wall construction that reshaped this landscape. *Rupi del vino* also pays homage to the art of homemade wine. In this documentary, more than any other, Olmi lingers on the intimate interconnection between the local inhabitants and their land. In an interview released to a local TV station from Valtellina, Olmi confessed to being particularly attached to this valley, where he traveled for the first time in 1949. He recalled how, at that time, it was still possible to grasp "the [local] identity that was the fruit of a relationship between the human and nature."[38] It is exactly this feeling and memory that Olmi brings back to life in this documentary.

While Virgil's *Georgics* is the muse and sets the tone in *Terra Madre,* Olmi's inspiration in *Rupi del Vino* is Mario Soldati's *L'Avventura in Valtellina.* After a lyric and oneiric opening of a piano transported by a helicopter to a green area on the peak of a mountain, the following scene continues with a passage from *L'Avventura in Valtellina.* From the window of a train passing near Lake Como, a fixed camera offers the perspective of the author's view along his journey. With the shining lake in the background, the afternoon sun peers through the leaves of the trees, and a series of images faithfully give life to a passage from Soldati's account.

> For those arriving from Lake Como, six in the afternoon, from June to September, is Valtellina's triumphant hour! If I turned round, I saw from the rear window that the sun was almost setting. It still seemed to be high, as it slipped into the Adda canyon. It shone down in the terraced vines, on the walls, on the rocks, on the plateaus and woods, on the peaks of the Rhaetian Alps to my left. It touched with gold the corn fields, the mountain spurs, the peaks of the Orobian Alps on my right.[39]

These images of Valtellina reveal a nature creatively and ingeniously shaped through centuries of human labor and sacrifice and invite the viewer to enjoy the beautiful Italian landscape while pondering the relationship of interdependence between humans and their natural environment.

Essayist and critic Goffredo Fofi observes that *Rupi del Vino* tells a relatively unknown story about this Italian mountain valley where only extreme "human strain could make it that beautiful, making culture out of nature, and nature out of culture."[40] As scholar Monica Seger remarks, "I truly believe that nature and culture in Italy are and have always been engaged in conversation."[41] Olmi's documentaries are, indeed, a perfect visual testimony of this dynamic human and nonhuman relationship. The terraced vineyards of this valley are the largest of Europe, and the patient result of human skill, endurance, and physical labor. The dry walls are made of rocks brought by the river to the valley and manually carried and cut by locals.

In 2018, almost ten years after Olmi's documentary and paradoxically the year of his death, UNESCO recognized the "Art of dry walling, knowledge and techniques" on the representative list of the Intangible Cultural Heritage of Humanity, acknowledging this incredible bond between human labor and natural resources manifested in the knowledge and practice of dry wall construction. This practice, based on traditions dating back to prehistorical time, has helped preserve and protect the surrounding landscape by preventing landslides and avalanches in the mountains while also guarding against erosion and desertification. The rural communities that implement the use of dry walls, like the Valtellina area, have been able to enhance biodiversity by creating "microclimatic conditions for agriculture."[42] Dry walls embody a positive visible example of human beings living in harmony with their natural surroundings in a mutual and beneficial relationship. As a story about wine, *Rupi del vino*, also celebrates this beneficial relationship by dramatizing the fruit of the accord between seasons, soil, plants, and human labor. Because of the local cultivation practices embraced by winegrowers in the region, Olmi renamed the wines of this valley "wines of rock" to stress how this production is "more heroic, onerous, and demanding than any other wine production."[43] In this comment it is possible to recall Edisonvolta technicians in the short film *La pattuglia del passo San Giacomo*, when they climbed the electric power tower with the ability of a mountaineer, embedding in their strength and agility the peasant rock climbers. In the same way, the winegrowers, Olmi seems to tell us, have the same endurance, physical and mental strength that materialize in the perseverance necessary to continue to build and maintain the dry walls of Valtellina. The "wine of rock" is the unique fruitful result of this local collaboration between humans and landscape, and proof of the delicate and yet fragile balance between nature and culture.

A Testament for the Future: *Our Host Planet*

In 2015, Italy hosted the Milan World Expo, a food-focused six-month international event, from May to October, whose main theme was "Feeding the Planet, Energy for Life," with the aim of encompassing culture, innovation, tradition, creativity, and technology in relation to food. The planning of the exposition included years of preparation with the realization that the Expo would have to address increasing concerns about food security, the right to food and health, food and agriculture, and food quality, just to name a few issues. The Expo site was in the suburbs of Milan, between the small cities of Rho and Pero, and covered an area of 2.9 square kilometers. A total of 145 countries, several civil society organizations, and a number of nongovernmental organizations participated in the six-month event. Most of the countries had self-constructed pavilions which competed, somehow, in architectural creativity and innovation.

Ermanno Olmi was asked by the organization of the Milan Expo 2015 to make a short film for the inauguration of the event that would represent the main idea of the Expo. *Our Host Planet* is Olmi's artistic, philosophical, and ecological testament, and his last environmental short documentary before his death. In eleven minutes, the film director covers the entire Italian landscape, from the sparkling springs of Monte Bianco in the northern Alps, to the fatal and simultaneously redeeming Mediterranean waters of Lampedusa in the south. Olmi worked free of charge for three years to gather the visual material, considering his work a sort of introduction and manifesto for the 2015 Expo. Eleven minutes, Olmi said during the press conference, to "narrate the planet that hosts us and the debt that humans have toward nature." The aim of this universal event, the artist continued, "is first of all the commitment the rich countries have to guarantee food, water and dignity to every human being, according to a principle of justice that dictates the coexistence among people on Earth. In the same way, equally to food, the peoples who conquered the privilege of freedom through the sacrifice of their martyrs, should be an example of democracy and civil coexistence."[44] The short inaugural film received the admiration and compliments of the Expo organization who recognized Olmi's scenes as pure poetry.

Our Host Planet fills the void left by the six-month-long event and, despite the consumerist and commercial turn of the Expo, invites the spectator to reflect on the true meaning of the topic chosen for the event. The film begins with the impactful image of a drifting boat in the middle of the Mediterranean Sea. This powerful image immediately recalls the sad and unresolved issue of migration from north Africa to Europe and the uncountable number of people who have died while crossing the waters of Mediterranean. The image of the empty boat is reminiscent of the short film *Asmat*, "Names" (2013), by Ethiopian-born Italian filmmaker Dagmawi Yimer.[45] His film was dedicated to all the sea victims, and in memory of the boat that sunk near the coast of the island of Lampedusa in October 2013 resulting in thousands of deaths. In Yimer's film the victims are remembered through a voice-over that gives a long list of names in Arabic and offers their translation in Italian. Literary scholar Pasquale Verdicchio notes that Yimer "requires us to shift over a different sort of epistemology, based on the acknowledgment and initiation of an unconventional relationship with the invisible."[46] The invisible that Verdicchio refers to is both the identity of the victims as well as the depth of the sea. Olmi, by showing the empty boat, talks about humans by pointing out their absence, as if phagocytized by the Mediterranean Sea. Interestingly, Olmi decides to open *Our Host Planet* by showing the remains of what could be a tragic human story. The empty boat offers testimony to the untold stories of human suffering, of stories we'll never know. To the inauguration of the World Expo, Olmi chose not to begin the film with a scene celebrating nature, or its fruits, or an example of harmonious relationship between human labor and the natural environment, as in his past film documentaries. Rather, he chose to begin with a pregnant image: an homage to disaster and a metaphor for the ship of state. Through his gentle style Olmi, in this last short film, takes a last provocative position of condemnation to convey a serious warning.

The title, *Our Host Planet*, is also a reminder of our limited time on in this planet. There is no narration or spoken dialogue throughout the film. Rather, Olmi pairs music tuned to the rhythm of a heartbeat with the visual imagery for the duration of the short film. All that is required is an attentive eye and an open mind to see the natural wonders of the planet we inhabit and the consequences of human actions. Music and sounds from nature tap the emotions and inspire personal feelings, immersing the viewer in a journey through the Italian landscape. For eight minutes (the last three minutes contain the end credits), the viewer witnesses a breathtaking succession of images shot in different seasons of the year: winter, spring, summer, and autumn. Mountain peaks, rivers, lakes, seacoast, sea horizon and deep sea, valleys, woods, wildlife, domesticated animals, agricultural fields, bread dough rising, refugees in Lampedusa, and construction workers building and preparing the space for the World Expo are shot during different seasons and climatic conditions. Olmi returned to the same locations and presented them in the heat of the summer, covered by soft white snow, or immersed in rainy storms. Natural elements are interwoven with artificial objects, human artifacts, and technology. Together these images shape and present the complex texture of Italy. A multifaceted fabric made of natural wonders, Olmi stresses, in which human presence is represented only by refugees, workers, and the arms of a baker. He presents these people as deserving of the same dignity as global corporations and wealthy consumers. In this short film Olmi is not engaging with the impressive and celebratory preparations of the Milan Expo 2015. As with his first short films for Edisonvolta, the "everyday people" are for Olmi the true protagonists. This time, however, while the director accepts the commission to make the short, he refuses to be paid, freeing himself from any commitment to the organizers and participants. The protagonists are, Olmi seems to tell us, those who take part in dangerous journeys, who build, and who feed us, those are the people to whom we should pay homage in the inauguration of this World Expo.

Food, the center point of the Expo, on the other hand, is represented only through images of blades of wheat, bread dough, and bread. Grain and bread form the basis for the Neolithic Agricultural Revolution which paved the way for settled human civilization. Bread is linked to civilization and to revolution. Bread, symbol of poverty and humility, metaphor for life in many religions and ancient cultures, is the basic, essential, and most representative Italian staple food, and stands alone in front of the abundance of produce and dishes that will flow from all over the world like a flooding river during the six months of the Milan World Expo. By focusing only on bread, Olmi is implicitly criticizing the Expo. Bread, and grain are the real source of abundance, the natural resources that guarantee our life on Earth such as air, water, and soil. By not succumbing to the visual attractions of trendy food products and showing the natural wonders of the Italian geography and landscape, the film seems to ask the organizers of the World Expo to keep in mind where the food comes from and who is producing it. What food do we produce, how much, and how are we using the natural resources of this planet? These could be some of the questions the viewer may ask while watching the short film.

Our Host Planet ends with a tribute to one of Olmi's artistic mentors and one of the most famous postwar Italian film directors, Vittorio De Sica. The film director represents the famous sequence in *Miracle in Milan* of the orphan boy found in a cabbage patch by the old lady, a recollection of the popular saying that children are born under cabbages. In the twenty-first century, watching this scene in black and white from this fantasy film while hearing the lyrics from Alessandro Cicognini's old song "Miracolo a Milano" can be perceived as an anachronistic attempt to connect with the naïve and simple dreams and reality of the 1950s. By replaying De Sica's scene Olmi offers a playful ending to push the viewer, once again, to ponder what really matters, "the commitment of the rich to guarantee food, water and dignity to each human being, according to the principle of justice that should rule the coexistence among peoples on Earth,"[47] as he declared during the press release for the film.

Eight years after the Milan World Expo, very little trace has been left in the space that hosted World Expo, no mention of that promising and captivating motto "Feeding the Planet, Energy for Life." Most of the architectural structures of the Expo, including the decumanus inspired by Roman cities, have been dismantled and the new project is to become the new Silicon Valley of Italy. The Italian operations of AstraZeneca have already moved there, and next will be the University of Milan.[48] Technology, innovation, and education will be filling the space that in 2015 hosted around 22 million visitors with a promise bigger than could be kept in and beyond the space of the Expo. It would be proper to ask, if possible, what Olmi would think about the legacy left by the Expo 2015. The event remains alive in the distracted memory of those who visited it. Olmi's short film, however, serves as a reminder of the original promise of the Expo and as an epilogue of his artistic career; it offers his final environmental and ecological testament, a look back to his early short films, and last documentaries, to remind future generations not to forget that we are guests on this planet that is hosting us, and it is our duty to treat it accordingly.

Olmi's early short films in the 1950s are the visual testimony of the Italian new and young society that carried the physical and cultural marks of its peasant past. In *Rupi del Vino* and *Terra Madre* Olmi focuses on the new peasantry as the solution to the contemporary global environmental and cultural crisis. Through his artistic talent and love for peasant culture, Olmi shows in these films who the real organic intellectuals are and offers continuity from the preservation and visibility of peasant culture as presented by Cervi, Revelli, Viganò, and the postwar intellectuals to an ideal of new peasantry that continues through the mission of Slow Food. Olmi's dedication to peasant culture and connection to Slow Food is confirmed by film director Giuseppe Bertolucci's comment on the documentary *Terra Madre*: "Ermanno Olmi and Carlin Petrini, seemingly distant (because of their competences and practices), are in reality very close, due to their cultural sensibility and human passion. Their common interest in the peasant universe ties their destiny together."[49]

NOTES

1. Ermanno Olmi, "Olmi su Olmi," in *I volti e le mani*, edited by Benedetta Tobagi. Milano: Feltrinelli, 2008, p. 27. This volume is included in. the DVD "Ermanno Olmi. Gli anni della Edison. Documentari e Cotromegraggi 1954–1958."

2. Bert Cardullo, *Worlds Directors in Dialogue: Conversations on Cinema*, (Lanham, Maryland: The Scarecrow Press, 2011), 21.

3. Stephen Rust, Salma Monani, and Sean Cubitt, editors. *Ecomedia: Key Issues*. (New York and London: Routledge), 2015.

4. Paula Willoquet-Maricondi, editor, *Framing the World. Exploration in Ecocriticism and Film*, (Charlottesville: University of Virginia Press, 2010), 3.

5. This entry offers an introduction to the most influential film anthologies that have contributed to introduce and frame ecocinema https://www.oxfordbibliographies.com/display/document/obo-9780199791286/obo-9780199791286-0252.xml#obo-9780199791286-0252-bibItem-0005 Last accessed on 02/05/2023.

6. Paula Willoquet-Maricondi, editor, *Framing the World. Exploration in Ecocriticism and Film*, (Charlottesville: University of Virginia Press, 2010), 45.

7. https://www.oxfordbibliographies.com/display/document/obo-9780199791286/obo-9780199791286-0252.xml#obo-9780199791286-0252-bibItem-0005 Last accessed on 02/05/2023.

8. Scott McDonald, "The Ecocinema Experience" in *Ecocinema Theory and Practice*, edited by Stephen Rust, Salma Monani, and Sean Cubitt, (New York: Routledge, 2014), 19.

9. Scott McDonald, "The Ecocinema Experience," 20. The italics in the quote are from the author.

10. Pasquale Verdicchio, "Ecocinema: The Practice of Impermanence." Paper presented at the PAMLA Conference at Western Washington University, Bellingham, WA, 2018.

11. Ibid. Verdicchio presented at the conference some films from Italian film director Manuele Cennonello. His filmography includes *Olga e il tempo*, 2007; *Sentire l'aria*, 2010; *Sorgenti del burro*, 2017.

12. Elena Past, *Italian Ecocinema. Beyond the Human*, (Bloomington: Indiana University Press, 2019), 12.

13. Ibid.

14. Ibid., 13.

15. Ian Pettigrew, in his recent monograph *The Cinema of Ermanno Olmi* (2020), considers his demanding style as the reason of the lack of literature, and national and international attention to Olmi's films when compared to other Italian filmmakers such as Roberto Rossellini, Vittorio De Sica, Federico Fellini, Luchino Visconti, Pier Paolo Pasolini, or Bernardo Bertolucci. While I support Pettigrew's interpretation, I also attribute this lack of attention since his films and style cannot be easily categorized into a genre and require a more active role from who's watching them and interpreting his style. It is sad to admit though, as Pettigrew underlines, that most of his filmic production is not commercially accessible.

16. Olmi, *I volti e le mani,* 20.

17. Robert S. Emmett and Davaid E. Nye, eds. *The Environmental Humanities: A Critical Introduction*, (Cambridge: MIT Press, 2017), 7.

18. Serenella Iovino, Cesaretti Enrico, and Elena Past, eds. *Italy and the Environmental Humanities: Landscapes, Natures, Ecologies*, (Charlottesville: University of Virginia Press, 2018), 3.

19. Alessandro Bignami, *Ortolani di civiltà*. Milano: Feltrinelli, 2010, 20. This book is included in the DVD of the documentary *Terra Madre*.

20. Ibid., 11.

21. Italian Industrial cinema, or Italian industrial film documentary is the film production dedicated to document the activity of an industry and destined to be circulated mostly within the industry. For a broad understanding of what is considered Industrial film production https://www.treccani.it/enciclopedia/film-industriale_%28Enciclopedia-del-Cinema%29/.

22. Marco Bertozzi, *Storia del documentario italiano. Immagini e culture dell'altro cinema*, (Venezia: Marsilio, 2008), 129.

23. Ibid.

24. Historian Antonella Tarpino, anthropologist Vito Teti, archaeologist and art historian Salvatore Settis, point out how the contemporary degradation of Italian landscape is connected to the abandonment of marginal areas.

25. Toffetti, *I volti e le mani,* 10.

26. Nuto Revelli, *Il mondo dei vinti*, xxiv.

27. *La pattuglia del Passo San Giacomo* is available in the DVD *Gli Anni Edison. Documentari e cortometraggi 1954–1958*. Milano: Feltrinelli editore, 2010. The DVD includes the book *I volti e le mani* edited by Benedetta Tobagi. Many short films, including this one, are also available on YouTube and have been posted by the Edison Channel, and the Archivio Nazionale Cinema Impresa.

28. Ermanno Olmi, *L'apocalisse è un lieto fine*, (Milano: Bur ed, 2012), 13.

29. Marco Armiero, *Le montagne della patria*, (Torino: Einaudi, 2011), xv.

30. Ibid.

31. Ermanno Olmi, with Marco Manzoni. *Il primo sguardo*, (Milano: Bompiani, 2015), 17.

32. A detailed discussion on Slow Food and Terra Madre is in my last chapter of this book, and in my article "Slow Food and Terra Madre: A Conversation with Carlo Petrini on Ecology, Rural Traditions, and New Food Cultures" included in the volume *Italy and the Environmental Humanities*, edited by Serenella Iovino, Enrico Cesaretti, and Elena Past, (Charlottesville: University of Virginia Press, 2018).

33. Carlo Petrini, *Terra Madre: Forging a New Global Network of Sustainable Food Communities*. Trans. By John Irving, (White River Junction, VT: Chelsea Green Publishing, 2010), 1.

34. Carlo Petrini, *Cibo e Libertà*, (Milano: Giunti, 2013), 7.

35. Ermanno Olmi, *L'apocalisse è un lieto fine. Storie della mia vita e del nostro futuro*. Milano: Rizzoli, 2012. Ebook version ("La pianta di pomodori"). The English translation is mine.

36. A reality, that despite the passage of fifteen years, has not shown signs of improvements, as is visible in the recent documentary *The Ants and the Grasshopper* (2022) directed by environmental activist and scholar Raj Patel.

37. One of the most representative international grassroots organizations that protect and defend the rights of peasants in the South of the world is La Via Campesina. For an update report on their work https://viacampesina.org/en/ offers also free downloads of their latest reports and publications.

38. Teleunica, youtube "Morto Ermanno Olmi, in valle nacque Rupi del vino." https://www.youtube.com/watch?v=45tUo22cmxg.

39. The text used in this article is from the English subtitles of the documentary. The original voice-over in Italian recites the pages from the book *L'Avventura in Valtellina* by Mario Soldati.

40. The DVD Rupi del Vino includes a book with essays on the film and Ermanno Olmi. The article by Goffredo Fofi is titled "Ermanno Olmi in Valtellina."

41. Monica Seger, *Landscapes in Between*. (Toronto: University of Toronto Press, 2015), 7.

42. https://ich.unesco.org/en/RL/art-of-dry-stone-walling-knowledge-and-techniques-01393 last accessed on 12/10/2022.

43. *Rupi del vino*, book included in the DVD, 10.

44. https://www.ansa.it/canale_expo2015/notizie/news/2015/04/29/olmi-racconta-il-pianeta-che-ci-ospita_c82c65ff-d1bc-4fe8-8fa8-10e93dfc6ab2.html last accessed on 02/09/23.

45. Dagmawi Yimer, *Asmat*, 2014. The film is available in Youtube https://www.youtube.com/watch?v=ruqNO38DhQk.

46. Pasquale Verdicchio, "The Nostrum That Is Neither Sea nor Remedy: Mediterranean Re-visions," in *Italy and the Environmental Humanities,* 203.

47. https://www.filmforlife.org/2015/05/ermanno-olmi-per-expo-2015/ Last accessed on 12/11/2022.

48. https://archinect.com/news/article/150296199/milan-s-former-expo-2015-site-is-being-remade-into-a-tech-centric-innovation-district; https://www.bie-paris.org/site/en/blog/entry/5-things-you-might-not-know-about-expo-2015-milan; last accessed on 12/11/2022.

49. Bernardo Bertolucci, "I due padri di Terra Madre," in *Ortolani di civiltà*, 13. Bertolucci, by calling Petrini with his nickname "Carlin," is indicating his personal and affectionate relationship of friendship with the international food activist.

Conclusion

Slow Food

ITS BEGINNINGS

Founded in 1986, the Slow Food Movement surfaced the same year the largest MacDonald's in the world to date opened its doors across from the Spanish Steps in Rome. As a corrective to the spread of American fast-food chains like McDonald's, Wendy's, and Burger King, many Italians began to support the social, cultural, and ecological aspects of eating. The first version of the Slow Food Manifesto was released in 1987, but as Carlo Petrini, founder of the Slow Food Movement, remembers, it was a bad meal in 1982 that caused him to rethink the nature of food.[1] A passionate wine lover, Petrini was a member of Associazione degli Amici del Barolo (Association of the Friends of Barolo), connected to Arci Langhe.[2] On a weekend wine-tasting trip to the small village of Montalcino, located amid the beautiful hills of Tuscany, Carlo Petrini and his friends stopped at the local Arci branch for lunch. Unexpectedly, they found themselves in a large, crowded hall eating "cold pasta, inedible ribollita,[3] and dirty salad; they were unable to eat the dessert because a second group was waiting at the door."[4] A lunch meant to be enjoyed with company in a relaxed atmosphere, ended up being served in a rush resulting in a mediocre experience. This bad meal provoked this young group to form Arcigola, the precursor to what would become the Slow Food movement.

Carlo Petrini was born in 1949, 55 kilometers from Turin in Bra, a small town in the province of Cuneo in the region of Piedmont. The Slow Food founder has never cut ties with the territory of his origins. Today, in fact, the National and International Slow Food headquarters are still located in Bra, and the international University of Gastronomic Sciences of Pollenzo is less than 5 kilometers away. Petrini's charismatic personality and rich social, cultural, political, and gastronomic engagements prior to the foundation of

Slow Food foregrounded his destiny. Son of a family of simple origins in which both parents worked, his mother taught kindergarten and his father was an artisan. His mother's Catholic faith and his father's socialism added to his working-class origins. The political and cultural tumult of the late 1960s influenced Petrini's social and political beliefs. Working with friends in the 1970s, he established a number of local cultural and social activities in Bra, such as Circolo Leonardo Cocito, named after a local protagonist of the Resistance, which presented theatrical performances, and a private radio station, Radio Bra Onderosse. In the beginning of the 1980s Petrini also helped found a few restaurants in Bra focused on traditional local food. During these years he also met influential artists and intellectuals of the Italian panorama, such as playwrights, actors and theater directors Dario Fo and Franca Rame, songwriter Francesco Guccini, and ex-partisan and writer Nuto Revelli, just to name a few. These encounters and friendships helped him shape the mission and direction of the future Slow Food movement.[5]

Petrini is a lifetime gourmand and wine expert. His comments in an article published in the 1980s in the historic Italian food and wine magazine *Gambero Rosso* and reprinted in *Slow Food Revolution,* contain the early seeds of the Slow Food movement and the many organizations born from it in the following years:

> I have the great luck of having been born and now living in an extraordinary part of southern Piedmont, the Langhe, which borders on the end of the Ligurian Apennine foothills and is surrounded by the slow and sinuous course of the Tanaro River. In this sub-alpine part of our beautiful country, we grow up having conversations and discussions about good wine, the typical dishes of our tradition, and about food as a redemption from our ancient misery. Fenoglio, Pavese, Lajolo, and Nuto Revelli are our literary legends; in their works we can read our story, our way of being, and also the extraordinary development of the local wine industry, once poor and dispossessed.[6]

In this passage, food is presented in a new dignified form, as the element that redeems the land and its people. A sense of pride in belonging to the Langhe blooms into a sense of belonging to the local, a very important aspect of the Slow Food philosophy. Petrini, in fact, recognizes his cultural origins in the intellectual fervor of the postwar era, and the literary legends he is referring to are the ex-partisans and authors of the so-called literature of the Resistance.

By the mid-1980s Petrini was poised to take action. The opening of McDonald's near the Spanish steps in the historic center of Rome attracted a lot of attention and instigated a number of controversies,[7] including protests and strong reactions among Italian intellectuals and artistic circles. This chain of events galvanized Petrini and the members of Arcigola to come out with a new name and a sharper and more determined message.[8] On November 3, 1987, the prestigious Italian food and wine magazine *Gambero Rosso* published the unabridged version of the manifesto of Arcigola, precursor to the Slow Food manifesto, condemning the basic principles of industrialization and supporting instead ideals of enjoyment and slow ways of living. The manifesto was a powerful condemnation of fast life, looking toward the future, but clearly opposed to the industrial culture glorified by Filippo Tommaso Marinetti's infamous Futurist Manifesto. The new manifesto begins with a condemnation of the artificiality imposed by the fast rhythms of contemporary society, stressing how this devotion to speed and efficiency leads to self-destruction. This preliminary document helped sow the seeds for the Slow Food Movement pointing to the importance of personal, elementary, and fundamental human needs such as the right to pleasure and cheerfulness, in opposition to the modern obsession with speed in the name of productivity where mechanization is the model for all life.

> This then is the proposition for a progressive and progressionist recovery of the human being, both as an individual and as a species while he awaits a restoration of environmental balance, in order to make life livable again from the standpoint of his basic desires. This implies eating slowly . . . setting aside time for its highest purpose, namely, pleasure (and not intensive production, as the owners of machines and the proponents of things fast would have us believe). The alternative, hyper-efficient lifestyle, is just stupid and sad one need only observe it to see that.

The manifesto elucidates the connection between humans and their natural environment by advocating for the recovery of basic human qualities, such as the right to pleasure, namely the pleasure of eating. The manifesto critiques the impersonal and standardized practices of fast food, calling them "stupid and sad," while pointing out the need for people to take the time to enjoy their meals without external pressures or demands.

> Besides, thousands of years of experience have taught us that fast-footed Achilles never reaches the turtle, who in fact wins the race: it's an important lesson, both mathematical and ethical. That sums up: we are on the side of the turtle, or rather, on the side of the common snail, which we have chosen to be the emblem of this project. Under the sign of the snail, we will welcome lovers of food culture and those who still love the enjoyment of easygoing, slow pleasures. The snail *is* slow.[9]

The manifesto uses the term *slow* for the first time: a forward-thinking term adopted by the movement two years later and reaffirmed in the 1989 Slow Food Manifesto. The term *slow* today has become a popular keyword used by different movements and intellectuals to counteract systems that standardize experiences, obliterate human histories and human time, and push for efficient, superficial solutions.[10]

Paradoxically, the opening of McDonald's in Rome prompted a reconsideration and revaluation of core Italian traditions such as eating together. Historian Massimo Montanari notes that eating together is typical of (though not exclusive to) the human species. In *Dispute Conviviali*, Montanari notes that Plutarco talks to one of his characters and says, "We don't invite each other to simply eat and drink, but to eat and drink together."[11] A social and convivial act, eating together is also an intimate moment of shared life and memories, a moment in which people engage with each other while performing the vital act of eating. The English adjective convivial, in fact, means a festive atmosphere or event. Both "convivial," and the Italian noun "convivio" stem from the Latin adjective "convivialis" and noun "convivium," "con-vivere," living together. Both terms associate the practice of living and dining together. A synonym of the Italian noun "convivio" is, in fact, banquet.

Although the term banquet evokes lush feasts for a company of wealthy guests, Montanari reminds us that food and cooking do not have high origins, do not come from luxury or rich people, but originate often out of necessity and poverty.[12] As he observes, we cannot be deceived by the noble origins of the word, as the tradition of eating together actually has very rural origins. In the Middle Ages, "even the peasant family defined its own identity at the table. 'To live on one bread and one wine,' that is, to share food, is in medieval language an almost technical way of signifying that one belongs to the same family."[13] The act of eating together is not relegated to a particular social class. For the poor and the peasant, it also implies a moment of connection and recognition between one another.

To give the new movement an international scope, the first Slow Food manifesto was announced and presented in Paris on December 10, 1989, at the Opéra Comique. Over four hundred members from eighteen different countries participated, and the manifesto was translated in several languages and released in front of a press review representing the five continents.[14] Some points presented in the 1986 document were narrowed down. This new version offered a clearer opposition to fast foods.

> Our defense should begin at the table with Slow Food. Let us rediscover the flavors and savors of regional cooking and banish the degrading effects of Fast Food. In the name of productivity, Fast Life has changed our way of being and threatens our environments and our landscapes. So Slow Food is now the only truly progressive answer. That is what real culture is all about: developing taste rather than demeaning it. And what better way to set about this than an international exchange of experiences, knowledge, projects?[15]

Carlo Petrini and the new Slow Food movement was bringing the historical and social roots and reality of postwar Italy to the world. Coming from the hills of Piedmont, Petrini and his group inherited the history and ideals of the Resistance grounded in the region. This cultural and historical legacy was also passed on by former partisan Nuto Revelli's documentation of the rural world. Slow Food's focus, however, was not interested in collecting memories or testimonials of this disappearing world. This new international gastronomic movement wanted to "interact with [peasants]"—to revitalize peasant traditions, to regenerate the land, and to reinvigorate the ideals of the Resistance.[16] They understood that the value of peasants was in their relationship to the land, in the food cultivated and presented on their tables, in their local knowledge of the territory, in their traditional practices. Their knowledge was their strength, and it was powerful enough to counteract the push of the global food system and industry. They, the new peasantry, emerge as the new organic intellectuals. Slow Food and Petrini understood that this reality, despite its distinct Italian roots, extended beyond national boundaries. The international movement of Slow Food, while still mainly focused on the gourmet nature of food and cooking, was inviting the world to share the common roots of peasant knowledge and tradition in the kitchen.

The Slow Food Manifesto advocates quality, taste, flavors, local food traditions, knowledge, experiences, cultures, and landscapes, and rejects the fast life that damages the environment, undermines ecological systems, and threatens biodiversity across our planet. During its thirty-plus years of work, this has become the main objective of the global Slow Food Movement. Slow Food, and its founder, Carlo Petrini, are engaged in intellectual and political discourses around food and food politics, not only in Italy, but also in Europe, the United States, Latin America, Africa, India, and China. Indian ecofeminist and environmental activist Vandana Shiva embodies the global impact of slow food. From 2008 to 2012 she served as Slow Food International vice president. Her collaboration with Petrini and the International Slow Food Movement illustrates how the political culture of Slow Food in Italy transitioned to a global movement. In the preface to the first Italian edition to *Slow Food Revolution*, she explains:

> Carlo Petrini started from the culture of food, I started from the ecology of food production; but it was inevitable that the celebration of taste would lead Carlo to biodiversity and to the small producers, and that the defense of biodiversity and sustainable agriculture would take me to celebrate quality and taste. The convergence of the two movements connected to food—one originated from the land, by principles of ecology and sustainability, the other from the pleasure of the table, food quality, the variety and uniqueness of food cultures—has liberated new forces, new possibilities, and a new creativity.[17]

Food sovereignty advocate Vandana Shiva has been actively engaged in the last thirty-five years as an environmental activist and intellectual both in India and around the world supporting biodiversity, seed freedom, local farmers and opposing GMOs. One of Shiva's main goals has been to demonstrate that multinational agribusiness corporations pose serious ecological problems and that what they call "efficiency and productivity"[18] is, in reality, a "theft from nature,"[19] and paradoxically a threat to human beings as well. Her organization Navdanya, which in Sanskrit means "nine seeds," supports local farmers, crops and plants that are at risk of extinction. Navdanya International is headquartered in Florence, Italy. Shiva's work represents just one of the global alliances forged by the Slow Food Movement. The grassroots international organization has developed numerous projects and its snail symbol has become a guarantee for both those who produce and who consume food around the world.

The ideal of *slow* has branched out in several themes and networks and has encompassed and further developed the vision of Slow Food. [20] Today Slow Food is the largest and most instrumental grassroots nonprofit organization in Italy. It constantly monitors Italian and European legislation counteracting and counterbalancing the politics of food in Italy and it has significantly contributed to the revival of traditional food products and practices around the world. In Italy, its presence and actions in the political and social landscape have opened the door for other organizations and small-scale agriculture realities to develop and rise.

The terms "good," "clean," and "fair," have become the motto and representative philosophy of the movement.[21] "Good" refers to taste and knowledge, personal and cultural spheres of experience, but also to the natural integrity of the product, as well as the sensorial pleasure of eating. "Clean" relates to the ecological impact of the food product, from farm to table. "Fair" implies the practice of social justice toward those who produce the food, making sure farmers and workers around the world are respected for their experience and knowledge and fairly compensated for their work.[22] Petrini understood the need to shift toward a more just and concrete way to value those who produce food. By acknowledging those who produce food, the idea of "fair" restores the right value to food as a product of human labor while holding responsible those who buy and consume food. Petrini stresses that, "Should anyone be tempted to ignore the complexity of the world and consume their food irresponsibly and unfairly, indifferent to social justice, I say that the fair has become indispensable. The human elite must be made up of those who produce food, not by those who consume it by consuming the land."[23]

The ideas expressed in the Slow Food motto have cultural roots in the Italian peasant tradition as seen in Alcide Cervi's memoir and documentation of his work to improve the land for the sake of food quality, in Revelli's peasant testimonies describing their connection to the land, in Agnese's and the women shepherds' knowledge of the territory and care for animals, and in Olmi's documentaries and the faces and movements of his protagonists. The 2021 Slow Food position paper on biodiversity, however, adds to the cultural aspect the role of biodiversity in agriculture and food production as implied in the three key concepts presented for the first time as part of the title in the publication *Slow Food Nation*: *Why Your Food Should be Good, Clean, and Fair*. The document states, "To ensure good, clean and fair food for all we need to start from biodiversity and invert a production model that continues to generate environmental and social disasters, undermining the foundations of food security for present and future generations."[24] In the twenty-first century, good, fair, and clean emphasize the organization's stronger commitment in light of climate change, social justice, political ecology, and food politics.

According to Petrini, however, diversity doesn't refer only to biodiversity and traditions, "but also to anything new, anything good, clean, and fair that comes into being when cultural exchange becomes a way to rethink one's local area and create something that was not there before. After all, only the naïve and the incompetent believe that tradition, just like identity, is fixed and immobile, . . . Everything is in motion, what is important is that it goes in the right direction."[25] Petrini and Slow Food have been constantly paying attention to what is happening in Italy and the world. They have been expanding and readjusting their positions supporting any cause that enhances their philosophy and revitalizes food cultures and food traditions. That is, indeed, the root of the idea of Terra Madre.

Slow Food and Terra Madre

From the beginning, Petrini understood the crucial role played by local food traditions and rural cultures. Only at the local level is it possible to "render fertile both the biodiversity of nature and the cultural diversity that results from it. For food culture—and not only food culture—has to be formed in connection with context, with the resources available in local areas, with ecosystems, and with one's relationship with one's neighbors."[26] As a slow, careful process of bringing knowledge, awareness, pleasure, and quality to the table, food diversity is conceived by Petrini as a source of richness and an opportunity to recover and rediscover humans' bio-cultural roots. With local as a key concept, today there are 643 Slow Food communities called "presidia" in 79 countries around the world, working to save native biodiversity that help sustain quality food production and revitalize traditional local food cultures, native breeds, and local native plants, as well as preserve those plants and food products facing extinction.[27] In 2022, the small red snail symbol on a food product cultivated and produced by a Slow Food Presidia is a guarantee of quality both for those who produce and consume the food.

Terra Madre completes the mission of Slow Food by focusing on those who produce food instead of the food product itself. Born under the umbrella of the Slow Food Movement, Terra Madre is a network of small-scale farmers, shepherds, fishermen, breeders, and food artisans who protect their local environments and communities. Terra Madre is also a gathering of these food communities in the city of Turin, in Italy, every two years. Terra Madre is therefore a concrete expression of food justice, food communities, and a successful example of an alternative food and economic system. During this five-day event, Terra Madre abounds with conferences, workshops, presentations, representatives of the Slow Food presidia, and an ark of traditional food products at risk of extinction. Terra Madre displays, discusses, and shares ideas on what works, what can be improved, and how to empower local food communities. These five-day events bring back the deserved dignity to the invisible realities of small-scale food producers in a convivial and joyful atmosphere filled with food events such as food tastings, dinners, and product presentations.

With the goal of celebrating and honoring food producers and food products, Terra Madre Salone del Gusto are events open to the public. Over the years Terra Madre has accomplished a double function, it has become an important recurrent event for the territory of the region of Piedmont and the hosting city of Turin, and it has strengthened the network and connection among many small-scale food producers and custodians of land(s) around the globe. For those attending Terra Madre who are not food producers, the result is transformative. Here the new peasantry is fully taking ownership of its role as organic intellectuals, inspiring those who attend to follow their example whatever their role in society and regardless of the region or country they live. It is a deep and humbling experience to witness the joy, the care, and the knowledge presented, and to connect directly with farmers and indigenous land custodians from around the world. As Olmi showed in his film documentaries *Rupi del Vino* and *Terra Madre*, this is a labor of love growing out of the resurgence of the new peasantry and deserves our deepest respect and public recognition.

Small-scale farmers and herders play a strategic part in supporting local economies and in building resilience in the community. In December 2018 the General Assembly of the United Nations adopted the Declaration of Rights of Peasants and Other People Working in Rural Areas. The declaration is the result of over five years of negotiations under the Human Rights Council open-ended intergovernmental working group (OEIGWG) and other people working in rural areas.[28] The need to create such a declaration emerged from the realization by international organizations of the United Nation such as FAO (Food and Agriculture Organization), and IFAD (International Fund for Agricultural Development), of the need to create international juridical instruments to acknowledge and protect those who constitute half of the world population and who still live in poor conditions and food insecurity.[29] In 2018, when the declaration was released, it was estimated that 80 percent of 821 million people suffering hunger in the world live in rural areas, and it was recognized that, "on average, small food producers contribute 70 percent of the world's food, with this figure rising to more than 80 percent in so-called developing countries."[30] If 70 percent of the world's food comes from small food producers, why do multinational food industries and global corporations continue to control the food markets?

The data presented by the United Nations declaration of the rights of peasants demonstrates that industrial agriculture has been failing on multiple levels: ecologically, politically, socially, and ultimately economically. Ninety percent of the world's 1.5 billion hectares of agricultural land is under the control of industrial agriculture.[31] Not only does industrial agriculture depend on external inputs such as artificial fertilizers and pesticides, but it also is more vulnerable to diseases. Corporate industrial monocultures are one of the most highly polluting human activities on the planet. Furthermore, wherever industrial agriculture has been implemented, there has been a loss of biodiversity. Since the mid-1960s, industrial agriculture has been guided and funded by the Green Revolution with the goal of ending world hunger. Despite these policies, hunger in the world has not been reduced; on the contrary, research demonstrates that hunger is "less related to production and more to poverty and inequality."[32]

Resisting industrial agriculture and global food systems by protecting the cultivation and promoting the consumption of local food products is also the commitment of the Slow Food alliance of chefs. "Fagiolo poverello," poor little bean, is today a Slow Food Presidia from the Italian southern area of Lucania, in the region of Basilicata. The chef Flavia De Marco uses it in her dishes as an opportunity to reconnect with the local territory. It is a small revolution. She explains, "to choose your food is a political act. When we choose what to bring to the table, we are also choosing which economy we want to support, what impact we want to leave for the environment, if and how we want to defend workers' rights."[33] As a chef who is committed to offering quality food in line with Slow Food principles, Flavia is also inviting those who eat to follow the same guidelines and become more aware of what choices they make and their consequences.

Being part of Terra Madre, as producers or coproducers, as Slow Food calls those who we would simply consider as consumers, is an opportunity to experience and understand the meaning of glocalism from a first-hand perspective. As Petrini states, glocalism is "a concrete way of putting into practice . . . a set of actions carried out on a local scale to generate major repercussions on a global scale."[34] The term "global," according to Petrini, can be understood using a more holistic approach and, as Shiva claims, instead of a global system ruled by corporations and industry, global can refer to "our universal values as humans. . . . It can refer to humans as one species among many, which both differentiates us from and connects us with other species. We can experience the global belonging to the earth family."[35] During the Resistance, the partisans realized they couldn't solely rely on their own resources to fight fascism and the Germans, and they needed the support of the locals through their knowledge of the territory and and their community network. From this perspective, the term global stresses the deep interconnection and interdependence between humans and their surroundings, be it with other living beings, as well as physical matter, such as the atmosphere. This connection doesn't refer simply to human proximity to their local surroundings but extends throughout the planet like single strings in a chain.

An Example of Slow Food and Terra Madre in Action: Agroecology

When Petrini met agronomist, entomologist, and professor of agroecology Miguel Altieri in 2005, agroecology was not yet popular. After Altieri attended Terra Madre several times, in 2015 Slow Food officially endorsed the practices of agroecology.[36] A discipline developed in the 1970s, agroecology combines ecological theory with indigenous knowledge to study and manage agricultural systems. Nowadays agroecological practices are recognized by the FAO,[37] supported by the Committee on World Food Security (CFS) as well as The Farm to Fork Strategy.[38] Through a transdisciplinary approach, agroecology recognizes that agriculture must be considered together with environmental, social, cultural, and economic issues. The work of agroecology centers on linking farmers' knowledge, social science, and rural social movements. The three keywords identifiable with Slow Food philosophy and practice, "good, clean and fair," fit with the practices of agroecology. Both seek to reclaim justice not only for food "per se," but also, and especially, for the land, the ecosystems, those who work the land or, as indigenous people call themselves "the custodians of the land, and all those who are food insecure."

Like agroecology, Slow Food has been supporting food communities working on a local scale. Petrini believes that food culture "has to be formed in connection with context, with the resources available in the local area, with ecosystems, with one's relations with one's neighbors."[39] Fostering ecosystems means safeguarding diversity in all its forms, from natural to cultural diversity, and the territories where these cultures manifest and develop. While it is critical to consider local areas from the perspective of bioregions, it is the collaboration between diverse cultures and identities that foregrounds the blossoming of communities and knowledges.

Altieri's approach is based on his work experience with indigenous cultures in Latin America and is influenced by traditional farming practices and knowledges. According to Altieri, traditional farming knowledge needs to be recognized as a science, given the same dignity as other sciences, and integrated by finding a synthesis between the two approaches.[40] This is the core principle of agroecology, not the techniques used, as the latter may change and depending on the bioregion. Agroecology bases its practices on the local traditional knowledge and can be applied both to small and large agricultural fields.

> Appropriate technologies should be based on indigenous knowledge and rationale; be economically viable, accessible, and based on local resources; be environmentally sound and socially, culturally and gender sensitive; be risk-adverse and adapted to heterogeneous circumstances; and enhance total farm productivity and stability. There should no longer be a top-down approach with farmers as passive recipients of information, but farmers should exchange information within farmer networks, supported by organizations ready to commit to the agenda of farmers.[41]

Agroecology is an inclusive holistic and scientific method that pays attention to all the different components necessary to regenerate the soil, restoring agricultural practices without depleting the environment while simultaneously empowering local communities. The term "indigenous" comes from the Latin word "indigēna" and is composed by the verb "gìgnere" (to generate) and the prefix "indu" (inside). Indigenous knowledge is specific to the people who are born and live in a region; it is place-based knowledge that grows out of the experience of working in a specific territory or area, as Alcide Cervi testifies in his memoir. Like the collection of testimonies gathered in the 1970s by Revelli, agroecology makes clear that this bottom-up practice supports and gives back the dignity and respect to farmers, peasant cultures, and local rural communities.

Agroecology is an integrated approach that recognizes that agriculture cannot be considered separately from environmental, social, cultural, and economic issues. Its transdisciplinary approach offers the theoretical and practical tools to implement sustainable and just food systems at a local and global scale. Broadly defined, agroecology is "a holistic approach that incorporates ecological, health, social, and economic considerations into agricultural and food systems designs and implementations."[42] For agroecology to be successful, it is necessary that there be a shift of consciousness in society where richness and prosperity are not based in or synonymous with economic profit. A revitalized cultural and economic landscape challenges the dominant capitalistic paradigm and ideas and practices of degrowth and post-growth can function as a guide for society to thrive within ecological limits. Slow Food continues to endorse and support agroecological principles. As the new president of Slow Food International recently stated, "The Slow Food movement knows that the only way we can overturn the injustice of a food system based on the plundering of natural resources is a transition to agroecology."[43]

Slow Food and Agroecology Together toward a More Just Food System

In 2016, The United Nations, the European Union, and the Paris Agreement produced a set of goals to adapt to the impacts of climate change. Europe's goal is to be a climate-resilient society by 2050.[44] The Paris Agreement acknowledges "the fundamental priority of safeguarding food security and ending hunger, and the particular vulnerabilities of food production systems to the adverse impact of climate change," and notes "the importance of ensuring the integrity of all ecosystems, including oceans, and the protection of biodiversity, recognized by some cultures Mother Earth."[45] The 2022 United Nations Sustainable Development Goals Report lists "zero hunger" as their second most important goal, second only to the goal of "no poverty."[46] To become reality, these claims require a commitment among all countries in the world to implement policies and practices that do not harm the local ecology and environments, that support local communities, and that help restore the damage made in the last century through intensive industrial farming and monocultures. Slow Food, by opposing the invasion of fast-food chains first, and consequently by promoting food cultures and communities, has demonstrated that it is possible to resist the pressures of the globalized industrial food system by giving intellectual support and space, in theory and practice, to the new peasantry.

Food security, hunger, and food systems are directly related to and depend on healthy ecosystems. Preserving and promoting biodiversity is the key to mitigate and possibly reduce climate change and the environmental effects caused by industrial agriculture. Therefore, if industrial food production results in the disruption of ecosystems, then small-scale farming and ecologically oriented practices grounded in local food traditions and knowledge can help restore local ecosystems. There are innumerable successful examples that support this approach, both in Italy and around the world. The principles of agroecology and the practices of regenerative agriculture make clear that small-scale agriculture is the solution to avoid further loss of biodiversity, alleviate the effects of climate change, create happier and healthier communities, and support the development of socially and economically just food systems in opposition to the global capitalist food system that puts profit over people.

During the COVID-19 pandemic, food insecurity and malnutrition increased all over the world, including in the so-called North of the world. The experience of the last three years confirms the crucial role of creating a more resilient food system at the local and regional level by supporting local small-scale producers and local economies. The FAO report on the state of food security 2021 projected that between 720 and 811 million people in the world faced hunger in 2020, and stated that new projections confirm that hunger will not be eradicated by 2030 "unless bold actions are taken to accelerate progress, especially actions to address inequality in access to food."[47] The call for bold action is an opportunity to review and honestly admit what has failed in the agricultural and food system promoted by the Green Revolution at the end of World War II. On the other hand, this is the time to implement initiatives that support local resiliency, traditional knowledge, cultures, and apply sustainable agricultural and food practices such as agroecology that have the instruments to counteract climate change and support biodiversity.

Slow Food and agroecological practices offer practical and successful solutions to the concerns stated by the FAO and the goals set in the Paris Agreement, and give back the power and dignity to the local communities. Like never before, COVID-19 has shown the vulnerability of the industrial global food supply system. The decline of trucking and air traffic during the global pandemic, for example, limited the capacity of moving fresh produce long distances and this increased food insecurity. By focusing on diversity and resilience while delivering reasonable yields, agroecology offers the best agricultural system to cope with future environmental challenges and the climate crisis.[48] The industrial agricultural system has used technology and science to increase efficiency in agricultural production generating, as a result, ecological and environmental imbalance. Miguel Altieri recognizes that COVID-19 accentuated the need for a transformation of the agricultural system from a "market economy to a solidarity economy."[49] He envisions that this new phase will be led by social movements actively involved in developing local alternatives to establish sustainable and healthy agrolandscapes.[50] The European Green Deal prioritizes fresh air, clean water, healthy soils, biodiversity, healthy and affordable food.[51] While the proposals are all imperative and the EU goals are clear and well presented, they remain on paper, and the path to achieve these goals cannot be a competitive race among nations. It is crucial to collaborate and act fast.

Terra Madre and its protagonists, the food producers, the producers of "heroic culture" as Olmi defines the men and women who build the dry walls for the terraces containing the grape vines in Valtellina,[52] the "intellectuals of the land" as Petrini calls them,[53] the new organic intellectuals as I call them, tirelessly continue to work and act in supporting what Altieri calls healthy agrolandscapes. In 2016 Terra Madre went through some crucial changes. The two separate events happening every two years, Salone del Gusto, which promotes quality and diversity of food, and Terra Madre, which supports the producers of food, became a single event under the name "Terra Madre Salone del Gusto" and opened their doors to the whole city of Turin. The purpose of unifying the two events was to make clear that "there cannot be pleasure without responsibility and sustainability."[54] The event took place in the streets throughout the city, in the historical park of Valentino, and in some of the most prestigious and historical buildings of the city. Thousands of farmers and food producers from all over the world met and mingled with the city residents. Petrini's hope was to make "visitors and foreigners even more aware of the need to preserve our common heritage."[55] The common heritage is not only the local region of Piedmont, with its vineyard landscapes, hills and mountains, history, and culture, but it is also our host planet, from the rivers to the oceans, woods, valleys, plains, deserts, mountains, and all its nonhuman inhabitants.

As with the rest of the world, in 2020 Terra Madre Salone del Gusto dealt with the consequences of the pandemic. The event offered two platforms: in person and online. The first week in October, Terra Madre was held in person in the city of Turin, and from October 2020 to April 2021, Terra Madre Salone del Gusto organized a series of events online, many of which were open to the public for free. The central theme was "Our Food, Our Planet, Our Future," which addressed the direct link between the food we eat and produce, the planet that hosts us, and how our actions will affect the future. The graphic of the title on the website delivered a clear message. The possessive adjective "our," was written in capital letters in a large font in the first line, the three key words "food, planet, future" written one below the other, and placed next to the word "our," communicated a sense of belonging common to all. The graphic also implied responsibility and accountability toward ourselves as humans, our home and all beings in it, and the responsibility humans have toward the future generations. In six months, Terra Madre Salone del Gusto hosted 625 exhibitors and 1,113 events divided in different formats such as conferences, food talks, forums, cooking classes, and more.[56]

The 2022 Terra Madre marked another significant turning point. After the pandemic restrictions, the event was held in person in Parco Dora, a park located in the peripheral area of Turin and "characterized by its industrial past and spatially defined by the river Dora, by main traffic arteries and relatively new residential quarters."[57] The strategic location choice gave residents the opportunity to attend the event while drawing attention to a marginal area of the city. During Terra Madre, Slow Food also announced its new president and the passing of the baton from Carlo Petrini, founder of Slow Food who had led the movement since 1986, to Edward Mukiibi, a millennial African farmer and social entrepreneur.[58] The location and the new leadership were in perfect tune with the message of the 2022 gathering, "Regener-Action," a regenerative action to "develop a fresh outlook and new enthusiasm for the future of our food." "Our," once again, was the focal point as pointed out in 2015 by Ermanno Olmi's short film *Our Host Planet*; "our" as stressed in the 2020 online Terra Madre main theme; "our" as in belonging as a global community living in this planet. Terra Madre in 2022 demonstrated through the attendance of international guests and farmers, the workshops, forums, conferences, food talks, and food taste events, that a better future is possible, and that we all have an active role to play in it.

Asor Rosa's concept of "populismo" and Gramsci's elaboration of the organic intellectual, as argued in the previous chapters, have demonstrated that post–World War II Italian intellectual strata realized the need to be more socially engaged. The experience of the Resistance and the partisans, fight against the Nazi and the fascists made them understand that real transformation would have not come from a culture of the elite. Former partisans who directly and personally came in contact with the Italian peasant world were not only intellectually transformed but also realized that a great part of Italian culture lies in peasant knowledge and tradition. Carlo Petrini and Slow Food activism carry this cultural legacy and value the essential role of what I call new organic intellectuals. In the twenty-first century, Slow Food knows that the new peasantry honors peasant traditions and safeguard rural landscapes. Drawing from the recent Italian history of the Resistance, Slow Food has created a global movement that empowers a new cadre of organic intellectuals that champion local traditions linked to distinct ecosystems.

Chef Sean Sherman, an Oglala Lakota Sioux chef and food activist, participated in 2022 at the Terra Madre food talk on Indigenous people, and his words speak to many traditional small-scale food communities around the world.

> We are in a different world. We can't go back in time and just be in a different time period. We lost a lot of Indigenous knowledge in the United States because of the way Indigenous people were treated. Some tribes retained a lot of their knowledge and some tribes lost everything, including language. It's really hard, but I feel there are a lot of pieces we can rebuild. For me it's about being on the path to try to understand as much of that knowledge and education as possible and applying it in the world we live in today. . . . It's a chance to evolve into something different. We have all the technology, and we can share all the knowledge so quickly across the world. It is important to utilize that, but it is also important to understand the amazing knowledge our ancestors had and try to move forward into a better direction. As Indigenous people we can process the two worlds we live in and walk through that line to evolve and change into something else. And that's what we have to do."

New organic intellectuals such as Chef Sherman, the chefs and farmers living in the Italian national park of Pollino, and all the small-scale farmers, farms, food communities and food activists throughout the world are the promoters and custodians of knowledge and practices in harmony with local ecologies. Hearing and learning from their stories and, with their permission, sharing their stories, eating their food products as the result of good, clean, and fair food practices is not simply a way to support their work. It is, most importantly, the way to truly take care of ourselves and all beings—both humans and nonhumans—we encounter on our life journey. While I am reaching the end of my book journey, I can only admit that I am at the beginning of this journey. Unveiling what is behind the food we bring to our table every day, the work, and the ethics behind the products we consume is essential in regenerating and grounding humans' bio-cultural roots and repositioning our role in, using Olmi's words, the planet that hosts us.

NOTES

1. Carlo Petrini, *Slow Food Revolution*, 17.
2. Ibid., 14. Barolo is one of the most prestigious and typical wines of the region Piedmont. Arci (Associazione ricreativa culturale italiana) was created in 1957. In the 1980s Arci works with Case del Popolo and organizes many social and cultural activities. Case del Popolo, established at the end of the nineteenth century, literally means House of the people and were recreational places owned and managed by the people. Arci activism in the 1980s is evident through the creation of different branches, from ARCI RAGAZZI, ARCI DONNA, ARCI GAY, ARCI CACCIA, to ARCI GOLA (later Arcigola), the organization from which Slow Food was born. For more information on the history of Arci see https://arcitoscana.it/storia-arci/.
3. Typical Tuscan soup.
4. *Slow Food Revolution*, 17.
5. To read a more detailed background of Carlo Petrini, refer to the latest edition and chapter "Le radici: 1949–1982" in *Carlo Petrini in conversazione con Gigi Padovani. Slow Food: Storia di un' Utopia Possibile*. Firenze: Giunti, Bra: Slow Food editore, 2017. A previous English similar publication, *Carlo Petrini in Conversation with Gigi Padovani: Slow Food Revolution*, (2005) contains also this chapter, "The Roots: 1949–1982."
6. *Carlo Petrini in Conversation with Gigi Padovani: Slow Food Revolution.* (New York: Rizzoli International, 2005), 55.
7. The first McDonald's in Italy opened on October 15, 1985, in the northern city of Bolzano. The first McDonald's in Rome was inaugurated on March 20, 1986, and it was the largest McDonald's in the world with seating for 450 people. Located in the historical center of Rome, near the Spanish Steps, the inauguration of this McDonald's attracted many people. https://www.upi.com/Archives/1986/03/20/Romes-first-McDonalds-opens-near-Spanish-Steps/6194511678800/.

   To have an idea of the controversy that the opening created among the Roman and Italian intellectual strata read the article "Romans Protest McDonald's" published by the *New York Times* in 1986 https://www.nytimes.com/1986/05/05/style/romans-protest-mcdonald-s.html.
8. Arci Gola changed into Arcigola in 1986 and transformed the historical Italian association, "Arci," into a prefix meaning "super" or "very." In this way, to the idea of "gola" (throat) intended as gourmet and food connoisseur is added, as Petrini

remembers, a gluttonous character. A more detailed story of the beginnings of the international movement is available in "L'idea: 1986–1989," *Slow Food Revolution.*

9. Carlo Petrini in conversation with Gigi Padovani, *Slow Food: A New Culture of Eating and Living.* Trans. By Francesca Santovetti, (New York: Rizzoli, 2006), 72. The italics are in the original text. Gambero Rosso International offers a slightly different English translation available online https://www.gamberorossointernational.com/news/30-years-ago-gambero-rosso-published-the-slow-food-manifesto-here-is-the-complete-copy/ The Italian text of the manifesto is in *Slow Revolution,* (93–94), and its updated edition, *Slow Food. Storia di un'utopia possible*, Firenze, Giunti Editore, 2017: 109–11. The authors of the 1986 manifesto are, in the order they appeared, Folco Portinari, Carlo Petrini, Stefano Bonilli, Valentino Parlato, Gerardo Chiaromonte, Dario Fo, Francesco Guccini, Gina Logorio, Enrico Menduni, Antonio Porta, Ermete Realacci, Gianni Sassi, and Sergio Staino.

10. Some examples are slow cinema, Rob Nixon's concept of slow violence, and the slow science movement.

11. Massimo Montanari, *Il cibo come cultura*, (Roma: Laterza Editors, 2004), 129.

12. Massimo Montanari, *Food is Culture*, (New York: Columbia University Press, 2004), 17.

13. *Food is Culture*, 94.

14. *Slow Food Revolution*, 97. Many Italian intellectuals and artists like Folco Portinari, Dario Fo, Francesco Guccini, Ermete Realacci, Sergio Staino, and Antonio Porta signed the 1989 Manifesto.

15. *Slow Food Revolution: A New Culture of Eating and Living,* 76.

16. *Carlo Petrini in conversazione con Gigi Padovani: Slow Food: Storia di un' Utopia Possibile,* p. 50.

17. Carlo Petrini in conversation with Gigi Padovani, *Slow Food Revolution* (Milano: Rizzoli, 2005), 9. The English translation is mine. Although the book has been translated into English, Vandana Shiva's preface in the Italian edition is not present.

18. Vandana Shiva, *Stolen Harvest*, (Cambridge, MA: South End Press, 2000), 17.

19. Ibid.

20. Slow fish, slow meat, slow cheese, slow wine, Slow Food Chefs Alliance, Ark of Taste, Slow Food Presidia, and also slow cities, slow travel, or slow Europe are some projects that Slow Food focuses on together with the different networks like Slow Food Youth Network, University of Gastronomic Science, Terra Madre Network, and Indigenous Terra Madre Network. For a complete list of the different themes, network, latest projects, and events supported and followed by Slow Food, visit https://www.slowfood.com/ ; https://slowfoodusa.org/ ; https://www.slowfood.it/.

21. Carlo Petrini. *Buono Pulito e Giusto* (Bra: Slow Food Editore, 2005); *Slow Food Nation: Why Our Food Should be Good, Clean, and Fair* (New York: Rizzoli, 2007), trans. By Clara Furlan and Jonathan Hunt.

22. Carlo Petrini, *Slow Food Nation,* 96–143.

23. Ibid., 143.

24. Slow Food, "If Biodiversity Is Alive, so Is the Planet." Position paper synthesis, 2021, pdf.

25. Petrini, *Food and Freedom*, location 1181 of 3111.

26. Carlo Petrini. *Food and Freedom: How the Slow Food Movement Is Changing the World through Gastronomy*. Trans. By John Irving, (New York: Rizzoli, 2015). Kindle ed., 91.

27. The numbers presented are updated to February 2023. For a more updated total of Slow Food Presidia in the world visit https://www.fondazioneslowfood.com/en/what-we-do/slow-food-presidia/.

28. The Declaration was adopted on December 17, 2018, and distributed to the general public on January 21, 2019. https://documents-dds-ny.un.org/doc/UNDOC/GEN/N18/448/99/PDF/N1844899.pdf?OpenElement.

29. The latest report published by FAO on *The State of Food Security and Nutrition in the World 2021* can be found at http://www.fao.org/publications/card/en/c/CB4474EN.

30. La Via Campesina, "Press Release: Peasants' Rights Declaration Presented Before the UN General Assembly," 26 October 2018. https://viacampesina.org/en/press-release-peasants-rights-declaration-presented-before-the-un-general-assembly/.

31. SOCLA, pdf, 1.

32. Ibid., 3.

33. https://www.fondazioneslowfood.com/it/avanguardia-legumi-la-cucina-semplice-e-gustosa-della-tradizione-lucana/ Last accessed on 18/12/2022.

34. Carlo Petrini. *Terra Madre: Forging a New Global Network of Sustainable Food Communities*. Trans. By John Irving (White River Junction, VT: Chelsea Green Publishing, 2010), 1.

35. Vandana Shiva. *Earth Democracy: Justice, Sustainability, and Peace*, (Cambridge (MA): South End Press, 2005), 82.

36. Slow Food, "Documento di posizione sull'agroecologia," https://www.slowfood.com/wp-content/uploads/2020/12/ITA_agroecologia-1.pdf.

37. http://www.fao.org/agroecology/home/en/.

38. https://ec.europa.eu/food/horizontal-topics/farm-fork-strategy_en.

39. Carlo Petrini, *Food and Freedom: How the Slow Food Movement Is Changing the World through Gastronomy.* Trans. By John Irving, ebook, Kindle edition (Firenze: Giunti editore, 2015). Location 1172 of 3111.

40. Carlo Petrini. *Voler bene alla terra. Dialoghi sul future del pianeta* (Italian edition), ebook, Kindle edition, location 423 of 2646.

41. *Agroecology: Key Concepts, Principles and Practices*. Third World Network and SOCLA, 2015. Pdf p. 8–9.

42. Rachel Bezner Kerr, Sidney Madsen, Moritz Stüber, et al, "Can agroecology improve food security and nutrition? A review." *Global Food Security* 29 (2021), https://doi.org/10.1016/j.gfs.2021.100540, available online 23 April, 2021.

43. "Slow Food: Agroecology is the best way to celebrate Earth Day." https://www.slowfood.com/press-release/slow-food-agroecology-is-the-best-way-to-celebrate-earth-day/ Last accessed on 25/05/2023.

44. https://ec.europa.eu/clima/policies/eu-climate-action_en.

45. "Paris agreement" pdf, 1–2.

46. https://www.un.org/sustainabledevelopment/progress-report/ Last accessed on 15/12/2022. The pdf document of the 2022 Sustainable Development Report is available for download and the chapter on "Zero Hunger" is on 28.

47. http://www.fao.org/publications/sofi/2021/en/.

48. Miguel Altieri and Clara Ines Nicholls. "Agroecology and the Emergence of a Post COVID-19 Agriculture," *Agriculture and Human Values* 37 (September 2020), p. 525–526, published May 12,2020. https://doi.org/10.1007/s10460-020-10043-7.

49. Miguel Altieri and Clara Ines Nicholls. *Agroecology and the Emergence of a Post COVID-19 Agriculture,* pdf.

50. Ibid.

51. "A European Green Deal. Striving to be the first neutral-climate continent," https://ec.europa.eu/info/strategy/priorities-2019-2024/european-green-deal_en#documents.

52. Ermanno Olmi, "La Valtellina eroica" in the booklet *Rupi del Vino* edited by Paola Cristalli and Alessandro Cavazza, included in the DVD *Rupi del Vino*.

53. Carlo Petrini writes this in the introduction to *Ortolani di Civiltà*, book included with the DVD *Terra Madre*.

54. "Terra Madre Salone del Gusto 2016 Steps Outside," https://www.slowfood.com/terra-madre-salone-del-gusto-2016-steps-outside/.

55. Ibid.

56. For a complete list of events and more information on the format of the 2020 Terra Madre edition visit https://terramadresalonedelgusto.com/en/. Many of the events were recorded and are still available on YouTube.

57. https://www.latzundpartner.de/en/projekte/postindustrielle-landschaften/parco-dora-turin-it/ last accessed on 12/18/2022.

58. https://www.slowfood.com/press-release/the-8th-slow-food-international-congress-opens-a-new-era-for-the-organization/ last accessed on 12/18/2022.

Bibliography

Agnoletti, Mauro. *Italian Historical Rural Landscapes: Cultural Values for the Environment and Rural Development.* London: Springer Science+Business Media, 2013.

Agroecology: Key Concepts, Principles and Practices. Malaysia: Third World Network, and Berkeley (CA): SOCLA, 2015. Pdf.

Akcaalan Reyhan, Ricard Davesa-Garriga, Andrea Dietrich, Martin Steinhaus, Andreas Dunkel, Veronika Mall, Maura Manganelli, et al. "Water taste and odor (T&O): Challenges, gaps and solutions from a perspective of the WaterTOP network" in *Chemical Engineering Journal Advances*. 12, 11/15/2022 https://doi.org/10.1016/j.ceja.2022.100409.

Albanese, Francesco. *Le campagne italiane e la Resistenza*. Bologna: Grafis Edizioni, 1995.

Altieri Miguel, and Clara Ines Nicholls. "Agroecology and the Emergence of a Post COVID-19 Agriculture," *Agriculture and Human Values* 37, September 2020. https://doi.org/10.1007/s10460-020-10043-7.

ANSA. "Olmi racconta 'Il pianeta che ci ospita." https://www.ansa.it/canale_expo2015/notizie/news/2015/04/29/olmi-racconta-il-pianeta-che-ci-ospita_c82c65ff-d1bc-4fe8-8fa8-10e93dfc6ab2.html.

———. "Enpa, i lupi in Italia sono solo 3.400, non c'è emergenza." 11/23/2022. https://www.ansa.it/canale_ambiente/notizie/animali/2022/11/23/enpa-i-lupi-in-italia-sono-solo-3.400-non-ce-emergenza_4e76cfc0-c921-4672-81de-11ab3b1fbc65.html#:~:text=La%20popolazione%20di%20lupi%20che,presente%20(Alpi%20e%20Appennini.

Armiero, Marco. *Le montagne della patria*. Torino: Einaudi, 2011.

———. *A Rugged Nation. Mountains and the Making of the Modern Italy.* Cambridge, UK: The White Horse Press, 2011.

Armiero Marco, Roberta Biasillo, and Wilko Graf von Hardenberg. *La Natura del Duce. Una storia ambientale del fasciemo.* Torino: Einaudi, 2022.

Asor Rosa, Alberto. *Scrittori e popolo. Il populismo nella letteratura italiana contemporanea*. Roma: Savelli, 1976.

Benjamin, Walter. *Illuminations*. New York: Schocken Books, 1968.

Bertolo, Gianfranco. *Operai e contadini nella crisi italiana 1943–1944*. Milano: Feltrinelli, 1974.

Bertolucci, Bernardo. "I due padri di Terra Madre," in *Ortolani di civiltà*, edited by Bignami Alessandro. Milano: Feltrinelli, 2010.

Bertozzi, Marco. *Storia del documentario italiano. Immagini e culture dell'altro cinema.* Venezia: Marsilio, 2008.

Bevilacqua Piero. *Storia dell'Agricoltura Italiana in Età Contemporanea*, Vol. I. Venezia: Marsilio, 1989.

———. *Il cibo e la terra: agricoltura, ambiente e salute.* Roma: Donzelli editore, 2018.

Bezner Kerr Rachel, Sidney Madsen, Moritz Stüber, Jeffrey Liebert, Stephanie Enole, Noélie Borghino, Phoebe Parros, Daniel Munyao Mutyambai, Marie Prudhon, and Alexander Wezel. "Can Agroecology Improve Food Security and Nutrition? A Review." *Global Food Security* 29 (June 2021), https://doi.org/10.1016/j.gfs.2021.100540.

Bignami, Alessandro, ed. *Ortolani di civiltà*. Milano: Feltrinelli, 2010.

Bo, Oddino. "Considerazioni sulla politica agraria del post-fascismo." in https://www.israt.it/editoria/asti-contemporanea/8-asti-contemporanea-n-4/11-la-lotta-al-femminile-4.html.

Bochicchio, Davide, Sujen Santini, and Marcello Volanti. "Il pascolo." With the collaboration of FederBio, https://feder.bio/wp-content/uploads/2017/07/PASCOLO-Final-Web.pdf.

Bravo, Anna. "I partigiani e la popolazione contadina nell'astigiano," in *Contadini e Partigiani*, record of the conference in Asti-Nizza and Monferrato, December 1984. Alessandria: Edizioni dell'Orso, 1984.

———. "Resistenza civile" in *Dizionario della Resistenza,* ed. Enzo Collotti, Renato Sandri and Frediano Sessi. Torino: Einaudi, 2000, Vol. I of II.

Bruzzone, Anna Maria, and Rachele Farina. *La Resistenza Taciuta.* Bollati Boringhieri: Torino, 2016.

Buell, Lawrence. *The Future of Environmental Criticism. Environmental Crisis and Literary Imagination*. Malden, MA: Blackwell Publishing, 2005.

Calvino, Italo. "Nei sette volti consapevoli la nostra faticosa rinascita," *Patria Indipendente,* January 1953.

———. *The Path to the Spiders' Nests,* tran. Archibald Colquhoun. London: Jonathan Cape, 1998.

———. *Il sentiero dei nidi di ragno.* 6th ed. Cles: Oscar Mondadori, 2012.

Cardullo, Bert. *Worlds Directors in Dialogue: Conversations on Cinema.* Lanham, Maryland: The Scarecrow Press, 2011.

Cervi, Alcide. *I miei sette figli*, edited by Renato Nicolai. Torino: Einaudi, 2010.

"Cicloturista partigiano." https://www.facebook.com/cicloturistapartigiano/.

"Cicloturista partigiano. Di bici e di storie." 05/18/2015. https://www.festivalitaca.net/2015/05/cicloturistapartigiano-di-bici-e-di-storie/?fbclid=IwAR0Otv7EYpabTXPOORAuzLiAfHj9EGbi9deKcokZO5f3AODdsxaM5uko6wQ.

Dall'acqua ai campi. Dai campi al silenzio. Documentary. https://www.youtube.com/watch?v=Zb0rRv4tAKM.

Dipartimento delle Finanze. "1868–1884 Tassa sul macinato." https://www.finanze.gov.it/it/il-dipartimento/fisco-e-storia/i-tributi-nella-storia-ditalia/1868-1884-tassa-sul-macinato/.

Emmett Robert S., and David E. Nye, eds. *The Environmental Humanities: A Critical Introduction*. Cambridge, MA: Massachusetts Institute of Technology, 2017.

European Commission. "Farm to Fork Strategy." https://food.ec.europa.eu/horizontal-topics/farm-fork-strategy_en.

———. "European Deal." https://climate.ec.europa.eu/eu-action/european-green-deal_en.

———. "A European Green Deal. Striving to be the first neutral-climate continent." https://commission.europa.eu/strategy-and-policy/priorities-2019-2024/european-green-deal_en#documents.

FAO, Food and Agriculture Organization of the United Nations. "The State of Food Security and Nutrition in the World," pdf. Available https://www.fao.org/publications/card/en/c/CB4474EN; https://www.fao.org/publications/home/fao-flagship-publications/the-state-of-food-security-and-nutrition-in-the-world/2021/en.

———. "Agroecology Knowledge Hub." https://www.fao.org/agroecology/home/en/

Fenoglio, Andrea, Diego Mometti. *Il Popolo che manca*, DVD, 2009.

Fenoglio, Beppe. *Primavera di bellezzza*. Milano: Garzanti ed, 1959.

Flores Marcello, Mimmo Franzinelli. *Storia della Resistenza*. Laterza Editors: Bari-Roma, 2019.

Fofi, Goffredo. "Ermanno Olmi in Valtellina," in *I volti e le mani.* Milano: Feltrinelli, 2010.

Fondazione Nuto Revelli. "Chi siamo. Coltivatori di memoria." https://nutorevelli.org/chi-siamo/

Gagliani, Dianella ed. *Guerra Resistenza Politica. Storie di donne*. Aliberti Editore: Reggio Emilia, 2006.

Ganapini, Luigi. "Con la vanga e col moschetto: ruralità, ruralismo e vita quotidiana nella RSI," records of the conference *Agricoltura e vita quotidiana nella RSI,* Salo' 19–20 Nov. 2004. Venezia: Marsilio, 2006.

Genoeffa Cocconi. Donna, Madre, Contadina. In Quaderni del Museo Cervi, Number 2, November 2004. Reggio Emilia: Tecnograph, 2004.

Giannetti Cristina. "Pastore italiane: sostantivo femminile, rurale," RRN Magazine, n.13 April 2021. Pdf.

Goodbody, Axel, and Kate Rigby. *Ecocritical Theory: New European Approaches*. Charlottesville: University of Virginia Press, 2011.

Gramsci, Antonio. *The Southern Question,* trans. Pasquale Verdicchio. West Lafayette: Bordighera Inc., 1995.

———. "The Formation of the Intellectuals" in *Selections from Prison Notebooks,* edit. and trans. Quintin Hoare and Geoffrey Nowell Smith. New York: International Publishers, 1971.

———. *Selections from the Prison Notebooks*. New York: International Publishers, 1977.

Guerra Giulia, Isabella. "Macinato e le rivolte del 1868," *Massime dal Passato* (blog). https://massimedalpassato.it/la-tassa-sul-macinato-e-le-rivolte-del-1868/.

Hamid A., Bhat S.U., and Jehangir A. "Local Determinants Influencing Stream Water Quality." 12/03/2019 https://doi.org/10.1007/s13201-019-1043-4.

Haraway, Donna J. *When Species Meet*. Minneapolis: University of Minnesota Press, 2008.

Iovino, Serenella, Cesaretti Enrico, and Elena Past, ed. *Italy and the Environmental Humanities. Landscapes, Natures, Ecologies*. Charlottesville: University of Virginia Press, 2018.

Istituto Alcide Cervi. *Le campagne italiane e la Resistenza*. Bologna: Grafis Edizioni, 1995.

Italia Libera. *Storia di una formazione partigiana*. RaiPlay, documentary film, 2019. https://www.raiplay.it/video/2019/04/La-Grande-Storia-Anniversari-La-Liberazione-ad255a77-3d34-4829-94dd-7dd5d2663c27.html.

Kauber, Anna. *In Questo Mondo*. Documentary directed by Anna Kauber. Parma: Solares Fondazione delle Arti, AKI Film. DVD.

Lajolo, Laurana. "L'interprete del mondo contadino" in *Nuto Revelli, Percorsi di memoria*. Michele Calandri and Mario Cordero ed. *Il Presente e la Storia,* n. 55, 1st semester, June 1999.

Lucenti, Eva. *I fratelli Cervi nascita di un mito*. Istituto Alcide Cervi, Annali 27–28, 2005–2006. Reggio Emilia: Tecnograf S.p.A.

Luperini, Romano. *Il Novecento: apparati ideologici, ceto intellettuale, sistemi formali nella letteratura italiana contemporanea*. Torino: Loescher, 1981.

Lynch, Tom, Cheryll Glotfelty, and Karla Armbruster. *The Bioregional Imagination: Literature, Ecology, and Place*. Athens: University of Georgia Press, 2012.

Mafai, Miriam. *Pane Nero*. Milano: BUR Rizzoli, 1987.

McDonald, Scott. "The Ecocinema Experience" in *Ecocinema Theory and Practice*. Ed. Stephen Rust, Salma Monani, Sean Cubitt. New York: Routledge, 2014.

Montanari, Massimo. *Il cibo come cultura*. Roma: Laterza Editors, 2004.

———. *Food is Culture*. New York: Columbia University Press, 2004.

"Morto Ermanno Olmi, in valle nacque Rupi del vino." https://www.youtube.com/watch?v=45tUo22cmxg.

Museo Cervi and Bibioteca Archivio Emilio Sereni. "Le donne dei Cervi." https://www.istitutocervi.it/2014/09/29/le-donne-dei-cervi/.

———. *Genoeffa Cocconi. Donna, Madre, Contadina.* Quaderni del Museo Cervi, n. 2, November 2004. Reggio Emilia: Tecnograph, 2004.

———. *Raccolta di scritti e poesie sui fratelli Cervi*.

Nori, Michele, and Farinella Domenica. "Mobility and Migration in Mediterranean Europe: The Case of Agropastoralism," in *Migration, Agriculture, and Rural Development.* IMISCOE Research Series. Springer: 2020 https://doi.org/10.1007/978-3-030-42863-1_6.

Olmi, Ermanno. "Olmi su Olmi." In *I volti e le mani*, Benedetta Tobagi, ed. Milano: Feltrinelli, 2008.

———. *Terra Madre*. Documentary directed by Ermanno Olmi. DVD. Milano: Feltrinelli, 2009.

———. *Rupi del Vino*. Documentary directed by Ermanno Olmi. DVD. Bologna: Cineteca di Bologna and Slow Food Italia, 2009.

———. *L'apocalisse è un lieto fine. Storie della mia vita e del nostro futuro.* Milano: Bur, 2012.

———. with Marco Manzoni. *Il primo sguardo*. Milano: Bompiani, 2015.

———. *Gli Anni della Edison. Documentari e Cortometraggi 1954–1958*. Directed by Ermanno Olmi (1954–1958). Milano: Feltrinelli, 2010. DVD.

Ortner, Shery B. Is Female to Male as Nature Is to Culture?" in *Feminist Studies,* vol. 1, n. 2, 1972.

Parri, Ferruccio. "Una dichiarazione di Ferruccio Parri. La Resistenza fu anche contadina" published in the weekly magazine *Lavoro*, Rome, n.21, 22–28 May 1949.

Past, Elena. *Italian Ecocinema. Beyond the Human*. Bloomington: Indiana University Press, 2019.

Pavone, Claudio. *Una Guerra civile. Saggio storico sulla moralità della Resistenza.* Torino: Bollati Boringhieri, 2006 (third edition).

Pazzagli, Rossano. "Il paesaggio della mezzadria," in *Quaderni* n.8 "La Costruzione del Paesaggio Agrario nell'Età Moderna." Summer School Emilio Sereni, III ed. Gattatico RE: Istituto Alcide Cervi, 2012.

Peli, Sandro. *Storia della Resistenza in Italia*. Einaudi: Torino, 2006.

Petrini, Carlo, Gigi Padovani. *Slow Food Revolution. Da Arcigola a Terra Madre. Una nuova cultura del cibo e della vita.* Milano: Rizzoli, 2005.

———. *Buono Pulito e Giusto*. Bra: Slow Food Editore, 2005.

———. *Carlo Petrini in Conversation with Gigi Padovani: Slow Food Revolution.* New York: Rizzoli International, 2006.

———. *Slow Food Nation: Why Our Food Should be Good, Clean, and Fair*. Trans. by Clara Furlan and Jonathan Hunt. New York: Rizzoli Ex Libris, 2007.

———. *Terra Madre: Forging a New Global Network of Sustainable Food Communities*. Trans. John Irving. White River Junction, VT: Chelsea Green Publishing, 2010.

———. *Cibo e Libertà*. Firenze: Giunti, Slow Food, 2013.

———. *Voler bene alla terra. Dialoghi sul future del pianeta.* Firenze: Giunti, 2014. Kindle ed.

———. *Food and Freedom: How the Slow Food Movement Is Changing the World through Gastronomy*. Trans. by John Irving. New York: Rizzoli, 2015. Kindle ed.

———. Gigi Padovani. *Carlo Petrini in conversazione con Gigi Padovani: Slow Food: Storia di un' Utopia Possibile*. Firenze: Giunti, Bra: Slow Food ed., 2017.

Plumwood, Val. *Feminism and the Mastery of Nature*. Routledge: London, 1993.

Ponzani, Michela. *Guerra alle Donne*. Torino: Einaudi, 2012.

Pradános, Luis I. *A Companion to Spanish Cultural Studies*. Woodbridge: Tamesis, 2023.

"Press Release: Peasants' Rights Declaration presented before the UN General Assembly." La Via Campesina. https://viacampesina.org/en/press-release-peasants-rights-declaration-presented-before-the-un-general-assembly/.

Ragionieri, Ernesto. "Dall'unità ad oggi. La storia politica e sociale," in *Storia d'Italia*, vol. IV. Torino: Einaudi, 1976.

Renzi, Renzo, ed. *La Terra dei Cervi prima dei Cervi. L'Agricoltura a Campeggine dal Settecento al Fascismo.* Reggio Emilia: Amministrazione provinciale di Reggio Emilia, 1982.

Revelli, Marco. "Non solo un padre." In *Nuto Revelli. Uno storico tra le montagne*. Torino: Accademia delle Scienze di Torino, 2015.

Revelli, Nuto. *Il mondo dei vinti*. Torino: Einaudi, 1977.

———. L'anello forte. Torino: Einaudi, 1985.

———. *Le due guerre. Guerra fascista e guerra partigiana*. Torino: Einaudi, 2003.

Ruberto, Laura. "La contadina si ribella. Gendered Resistance iin L'Agnese va a morire." *Romance Languages Annual* 9, 1997.

Rust, Stephen, Salma Monani, and Sean Cubitt. *Ecomedia: Key Issues*. New York and London: Routledge, 2015.

Sale, Kirkpatrick. *The Dwellers in the Land: The Bioregional Vision*. San Francisco: Sierra Club Books, 1985.

Seger, Monica. *Landscapes in Between*. Toronto: University of Toronto Press, 2015.

Sereni, Emilio. *Il capitalismo nelle campagne (1860–1900).* Torino: Einaudi, 1947.

Shiva, Vandana. *Stolen Harvest*. Cambridge, MA: South End Press, 2000.

———. *Earth Democracy. Justice, Sustainability and Peace*. Cambridge (MA): South End Press, 2005.

Signorile, Lisa. "Uno, Nessuno e Centomila: quanti lupi ci sono in Italia?" In *National Geographic Italia,* 10/26/2015. http://www.nationalgeographic.it/natura/animali/2015/10/25/news/uno_nessuno_centomila_quanti_lupi_ci_sono_in_italia_-2817615/.

Slow Food. "Documento di posizione sull'agroecologia." https://www.slowfood.com/wp-content/uploads/2020/12/ITA_agroecologia-1.pdf.

———. "Terra Madre Salone del Gusto 2016 Steps Outside!" https://www.slowfood.com/terra-madre-salone-del-gusto-2016-steps-outside/.

———. "Avanguardia legumi, la cucina semplice e gustosa della cucina lucana." https://www.fondazioneslowfood.com/it/avanguardia-legumi-la-cucina-semplice-e-gustosa-della-tradizione-lucana/.

———. "The 8th Slow Food International Congress opens a new era for the organization." https://www.slowfood.com/press-release/the-8th-slow-food-international-congress-opens-a-new-era-for-the-organization/.

Snyder, Gary. *The Practice of the Wild*. San Francisco: North Point Press, 1990.

Sorcinelli, Paolo. *Identikit del Novecento. Conflitti, Trasformazioni Sociali, Stili di Vita*. Roma: Donzelli editore, 2004.

Spaggiari, Fabrizio. "Dalla Restaurazione all'Unità d'Italia fra Campeggine e Santa Vittoria," in *La Terra dei Cervi prima dei Cervi. L'agricoltura a Campeggine dal Settecento al fascismo*, edited by Renzo Renzi. Reggio Emilia: Amministrazione Provinciale di Reggio Emilia, 1982.

Tabusso Marcyan, Ilaria. "An Example of Circular Collaboration. A Conversation with Anna Kauber on the Making of *In Questo Mondo*," *The Italianist,* 41:2. 2021, 202–11. https://doi.org/10.1080/02614340.2021.1933321.

Tarpino, Antonella. *Spaesati*. Torino: Einaudi, 2013.

Thayer, Robert. *LifePlace: Bioregional Thought and Practice*. Berkeley: University of California Press, 2003.

The Wolf in the Italian Alps. https://www.lifewolfalps.eu/en/the-wolf-in-the-alps/the-wolf-in-the-italian-alps/.

UNESCO Intangible Cultural Heritage. "Art of dry stone walling, knowledge and techniques." https://ich.unesco.org/en/RL/art-of-dry-stone-walling-knowledge-and-techniques-01393.

United Nations. *United Nation Declaration on the Rights of Peasants and Other People Working in Rural Areas.* Resolution adopted by the Human Rights Council on 09/28/2018. Pdf downloadable at chrome-extension://efaidnbmnnnibpcajpcglclefindmkaj/https://documents-dds-ny.un.org/doc/UNDOC/GEN/N18/448/99/PDF/N1844899.pdf?OpenElement.

———. "Sustainable Development Goals Report." https://www.un.org/sustainabledevelopment/progress-report/#.

Verdicchio, Pasquale. "Ecocinema: The Practice of Impermanence." Paper presented at the PAMLA Conference at Western Washington University, Bellingham, WA, 2018.

———. "The Nostrum That Is Neither Sea nor Remedy: Mediterranean Re-visions," in *Italy and the Environmental Humanities,* 203.

Verri, Beatrice, and Lucio Moncao. *Resistenze, quelli di Paraloup*. Torino: Gruppo Abele, 2013.

Verrini, Benedetta. "Le donne 'resistenti' in Fa' la cosa giusta." https://www.iodonna.it/attualita/costume-e-societa/2016/03/16/le-donne-resistenti-di-fa-la-cosa-giusta/.

Viganó, Renata. *L'Agnese va a morire*. Torino: Einaudi, ed, "I coralli," 1994.

Vittorini, Elio. "Una nuova cultura," *Il Politecnico* n.1, 1945, in *Il Novecento* by Romano Luperini.

Willoquet-Maricondi, Paula, ed. *Framing the World: Exploration in Ecocriticism and Film*. Charlottesville: University of Virginia Press, 2010.

Yimer, Dagmawi. *Asmat.* Film. 2014. https://www.youtube.com/watch?v=ruqNO38DhQk.

Index

About the Author

Ilaria Tabusso Marcyan is a teaching assistant professor at Arizona State University, Tempe, Arizona, where she teaches courses in Italian language and literature, courses in English with experiential learning components on the environmental impact of food activism and farming, and online courses in English on the Mediterranean lifestyle.

Her research focuses on environmental cultural studies and environmental humanities in relation to food cultures, contemporary farming, and landscape. She has published several articles on farming and food cultures, including an article on Slow Food and Terra Madre containing a conversation with Slow Food founder Carlo Petrini. She is one of the coeditors of the volume *Contesting Extinctions. Decolonial and Regenerative Futures* (Lexington Books, 2021).

www.ingramcontent.com/pod-product-compliance
Ingram Content Group UK Ltd.
Pitfield, Milton Keynes, MK11 3LW, UK
UKHW041839031026
15587UKWH00002B/873

9 781793 639493